JEANNE BETANCOURT

Pflaum Publishing
Dayton, Ohio

"Anne Marie, the younger daughter, spent her childhood on a chair. She was taught to be bored, to sit up straight, to sew. She was gifted: the family thought it distinguished to leave her gifts undeveloped; she was radiant: they hid the fact from her. Those proud, modest bourgeois were of the opinion that beauty was beyond their means or below their station; it was alright for a marquise or a whore. Louise's pride was utterly barren: for fear of making a fool of herself, she refused to recognize the most obvious qualities of her children, her husband or herself. Fifty years later, when turning the pages of a family album, Anne Marie realized that she had been beautiful."

—Jean-Paul Sartre.
The Words. A Fawcett Premier Book. 1964. Page 8.

Library of Congress Catalog Card Number 74-78728
© 1974 by Jeanne Betancourt
Paperback ISBN 0-8278-0260-9
Cloth cover ISBN 0-8278-0261-7
Book Design by Joseph Loverti

Introduction
V

The Films Index
An alphabetical list with page numbers.
XIII

The Filmmakers
An alphabetical list with page numbers.
XVII

The Films
Annotated, in alphabetical order by title.
1

Thematic Index
159

Program Possibilities
163

Bibliography
Compiled and annotated by Madeline Warren.
Note: The annotation for each film is followed by
"suggested feminist reading" related to that film.
167

Distributors of the films
183

To Jeff and Nicole
with love

Thank you
Ken Axthelm, Beatrice Granger, Jack Heher,
Ted Perry and Madeline Warren
for your help and encouragement in preparing
these pages.
I also thank my students
and other friends
who have sat with me through screenings
and willingly shared their ideas
about the films we saw.

introduction

Introduction

I hope *Women in Focus* can serve many people. By reading about and seeing films that present real women, those who have been oblivious to the stereotypes of women in film may begin to recognize them by the contrast offered in the films I suggest. Filmmakers, present and future, can be inspired. Librarians have here a guide for new purchases—where and how to use them. College and high school personnel have a manual that helps them determine how to use their audiovisual funds without spending the hours to search out films as I have.

When I started to teach in an all-women high school three years ago, I had just begun a graduate program in cinema studies at New York University and was investigating my own experiences as an American woman. My students' teen years in the inner city differed greatly from my youth in Vermont. The books that occupied me then (*The Life of St. Maria Goretti, Silas Marner,* and *The Scarlet Letter*) had little to do with their lives, with mine anymore, or with the times. I turned to film, particularly the short film, and found that, though many films dealt with the times and were interesting, they had little to do with me and my students as women. I had come to decide that what I lacked most as a young woman were guidance in understanding and relating to my own sexuality, realistic and positive models, and an awareness of the sexism in our culture. I wanted films that could help give the young women in my class that guidance. Though we differ in race and culture, our sex binds my students and me together and our common concerns need to be explored.

As I investigated available films, it became increasingly important to me that the films I showed my students be nonsexist. I also knew that I wanted a fair share of them to be films made by women. Starting with a few films by New York filmmakers, I went on to discover that some of the most significant films in the history of cinema have the double blessing of being made by women and having a nonsexist attitude (*The Smiling Madame Beudet* by Germaine Dulac; *Maedchen in Uniform* by Leontine Sagan; *Something Different* by Vera Chytilova; *Meshes of the Afternoon* by Maya Deren). I also found that a choice few masterpieces, though done by men, were refreshingly sympathetic to women (*Menilmontant* by Dmitri Kirsanov; *Bed and Sofa* by Abram Room; *Salt of the Earth* by Herbert Biberman).

While I was discovering these older works, new films were being made that documented women's concerns about their bodies (*It Happens to Us* by Amalie Rothschild and *How About You?* by Bonnie Friedman, Deborah Shaffer, and Marilyn Lubois); about famous women (*Gertrude Stein: When This You See, Remember Me* by Perry Miller Adato; *Virginia Woolf—The Moment Whole* by Janet Sternberg; *Madalyn*, a portrait of Madalyn O'Hare, by Bob Elkins); and about women whose hidden sufferings are creating the demands of the women's movement (*Janie's Janie* by Geri Ashur; *I Am Somebody* by Madeline Anderson). Some of these films are understandably angry, but many are refreshingly humorous (*What I Want* by Sharon Hennessey; *Dream Life* by Mireille Dansereau).

I found that a new group of filmmakers with a feminist consciousness are making movies. Their films, most of them short documentaries, are united only by the shared consciousness of the women who made them. They take as their themes the qualities of life that concern women, the oppressions that women share with all oppressed groups, or the problems women have particularly as women. The most successful of these efforts have combined a deep conviction and sincerity with a growing mastery of film forms. What I notice in many of these works is that the exploration and development of a filmic vocabulary are motivated by a stirring and excitement of the will to communicate at particularly deep, personal levels.

A few of these filmmakers—Julia Reichert, James Klein, Amalie Rothschild, Joyce Chopra, Liane Brandon, and Claudia Weill—have organized their own distribution cooperative for films about women. They feel that "the sharing of ideas via distribution is an integral part of the process of producing films. Our films are our contribution to what we see as progressive forces in society." (New Day Films flier, 1973.) Thus, in distribution each filmmaker keeps close control over her/his film. Though they produce films independently, they share ideas, resources, and energy because they believe in 'the importance of cooperative action in bringing social change."

I didn't discover, as I screened and discussed these films with my students and older friends, that there is a feminist aesthetic, or that women are better or worse filmmakers than men. What I did come to realize more and more is that women, over the years, have had limited opportunities in the film industry, that concerns specific to a woman's sexuality have received little or no exposition in film, and that most narrative films reflect the sexist views on women that are accepted by our culture. Don't assume, either, that because a filmmaker is included in these pages I am saying that all of her/his works are nonsexist or feminist. My endorsement is for the specific works reviewed on these pages.

You will notice that my approach to some films is more in terms of their content and feminist aspects, while for others it is more in terms of their filmic qualities. In a fleeting desire for uniformity and order I considered adjusting the reviews so that they all did one or the other, or, magically, both. As I reflected on how I wrote the reviews, however, I realized that each was an entity in itself, a reaction to an individual work. I can't place these films, as diverse as they are, into a critical mold or format. I certainly saw them all with the same frame of reference—my needs as a woman in America, teaching film to women— and that is what puts them together in this text.

This book contains many films that deal with sex education. From my own experience and from teaching for two years in a public high school for pregnant teen-agers, I have come to see how desperately our younger women need good sex education and counseling.

I wanted to show my students that if we are to relate realistically to our bodies, if we are to accept the responsibility of our sexual functions, we must be educated to understand our bodies. Consequently in this text I have included films that inform us on abortion, birth control, lovemaking, lesbianism, and childbirth.

VII

Body education is core education. Our bodies are the physical base from which we move out into the world; ignorance, uncertainty—even, at worst, shame—about our physical selves creates in us an alienation from ourselves that keeps us from being the whole people that we could be.
— Boston Women's Health Book Collective,
Our Bodies, Our Selves, p.3

Some of these films may be too sexually explicit in language and image for your situation. You are the judge of what films you are going to screen with your group. So that you can be the judge, I let you know, through the reviews, what is in the films, particularly if they might be objectionable to some administrations, churches, and so on. I don't want you to pay $100 to rent a print and then "get into trouble" or be embarrassed for having shown it. Remember, too, that the reviews are meant to help people in many diferent situations choose films. So perhaps a film like *Judy Chicago and the California Girls* isn't what you want for your eighth-grade class, but it very well might be just the film for a college drama professor. I want you to know what is in the film, so that you can decide.

I have included reviews of five films on childbirth: *The Birth Film, Window Water Baby Moving, Thigh Lyne Lyre Triangular, Childbirth,* and *Kirsa Nicholina*. Each has its own merits. You may want to reinforce all of these films with informative discussions. You will probably be surprised (as I was) at how little your audience knows about childbirth. With some groups you might want to prepare the audience with stills of childbirth and by announcing that though some may be familiar with scenes of childbirth, those who aren't should be prepared to be awed, surprised, and possibly shocked. Time your programming so that the audience can ask questions that arise from watching the film. I have indicated the differences between the films, so that you might choose the one that best fits your group. If you read all the reviews on childbirth, you will be prepared to make the most appropriate choice for your screening situation.

You are going to look for films that aren't here. Maybe they haven't been made or are only now being made. Maybe I missed them or excluded them intentionally. But, along with me, you will probably be looking for films that still need to be made: a good film on menopause, the problems of the careerless middle-class divorcee, the story of a happy middle-aged career woman, and so on. Every month I hear about another film that I have wanted to see made going into production, such as Linda Feferman's film on menstruation and Martha Stuart's studies on women in management and creative parenting. Once you have gotten onto the premise that films like these are available, you will find films on your own. You will discover areas of film neglected on these pages that you will decide to use in your own work.

New films will be made. Some of the filmmakers reviewed in these pages will go on to make more films. Some will never make another film. But all of them give encouragement to young women who want to develop media careers or are looking for good models in screen images to present to their groups.

I have seen every film reviewed here, many several times. Whenever it was possible, I have presented them to my classes.

The film reviews have been designed to fill three needs. First, the review gives the facts or tells the story of the work, so that you know how the film develops. Secondly, the review assesses the film critically, particularly from a feminist viewpoint. Thirdly, it suggests what groups might be most interested in the films. After screenings, I suggest you re-read the reviews to recall some of the critical points given, using them to stimulate your own thinking and group discussions.

In many cases the reviews are followed by a page devoted to the film-maker. Most include a quote, a picture, a brief biographical sketch, and a filmography. Some of the filmographies are more complete than others. I apologize to the filmmakers who appear to have been neglected. In many cases they did not respond to the questionnaire or couldn't be reached.

After many of the reviews there are suggestions for feminist readings. The women's movement has spawned a great many books on women's issues as well as a reassessment of earlier works. It seemed important to me that after screening a film you have other resources on the topics investigated in the film. These books provide that guide. You will notice that in the back of this book there is a list of over seventy books, most of which are referred to after individual film reviews. Turn to this list for publishing information, a brief summary of the whole work, a suggestion of the appropriate reading level, and the book's thematic concern.

Just as I found that the more films I looked at and the more people I met, the more films I discovered, so too, Madeline Warren (who prepared the bibliography) was hearing at the last minute about more books, some of which were just going to press. We both acknowledge that there had to be a cut-off point, and certainly there are films and books we missed. If you know about them, share your information with others. We are saying these are the books that Madeline Warren found (or the films, in my case); if they found favor with her she listed them. Her list is a sampling, not a complete index.

Another entire bibliography could have been given for the films *as* films—a book on Czechoslovakian films would be appropriate for Chytilova's *Something Different;* a book on the compilation film for *I Am Somebody,* and so on. But the filmic aspects of the films have not been my major emphasis in the book. I don't expect as many film professors to be using these pages as I do the many teachers, librarians, and community organizers who are responsible for selecting films to supplement their programs in Psychology, Women's Studies, Modern History, etc. If you do not want to see the women and men with whom you work and live stereotyped into classes—the dainty, precious, female wife-mothers of the future and the strong, daring, male makers of the world—then you will be glad to know that a body of film and literature exists that is trying to correct these stereotyped, role-playing approaches to living.

The films are dealt with alphabetically. You will find that your direction in using the book comes from the indexes. The films are organized in several indexes—by filmmaker, by title, by theme.

I have sometimes listed suggested shorts with features and what I think would make some good double features. I haven't explained these groupings, but if you turn to the reviews it should be pretty obvious.

If you are ordering films for the first time, the following suggestions might help you avoid inconvenience. Most films should be ordered a few months in advance. That does not mean you will never be able to make a last-minute reservation, but generally you should order films a generous amount of time—one term or five months—before you are going to screen them. All film orders must be put in writing, though I usually precede the written confirmation by a phone call. Thus if a film isn't available when I want it I can arrange for another date.

Some films reviewed in this book are remarkably reasonable in rental cost (*Menilmontant*, $10; *Fear Women*, $12.50; *Phoebe*, $14). Others are very expensive ($125 for *Wednesday's Child*). Most of the films rent for about a dollar a minute.

Films arrive a few days ahead of time, special delivery, insured for $200. Unless instructed otherwise, you should return them the same way they were sent to you. When you budget films you might be able to include this expense in your request for funds. Otherwise you are going to end up with the expense of return, which averages $2.00 a film. The distributor assumes the first leg of the shipping cost; you, the return. Always mark post office receipts with the name of the film so that you can identify the insurance number by film if necessary.

Make all of your screening arrangements ahead of time. Have your sixteen millimeter projector lined up with a screen. Check all shades and be sure that you have an extra bulb in case the projector light blows (bulbs have a life of only 15-30 hours). The film should be on the projector and ready to roll before your group arrives. With these preparations you will avoid trying to show an hour-long film to an hour-long class and finding you need an extension cord, the bulb has blown, or the screen won't stand properly.

Your approach to presenting a film will depend on your own temperament and background, the maturity of your audience, and the time available to you before and/or after screening. If the film deals with a controversial subject, you might question the group to air conflicting opinions. If it is an older film, you may begin by placing it in historical context. Films that have an interesting theme can be introduced by asking people to react to the theme on a personal level. For example, I introduce *String Bean,* a film about an old woman, by asking students to describe themselves as old women.

Some films would be more meaningful if the topics were researched before the screening. *Wednesday's Child* will be more provocative if students are acquainted with Laing's theories and the causes of schizophrenia. A screening of *Black Girl* could be preceded by research on the independence of Senegal and its current economic and political condition; *Salt of the Earth,* by research on the mine unions of the Southwest, problems of Chicanos, or blacklisting in Hollywood during the McCarthy era. In any of these cases you could provide information in a prefatory lecture.

As you read my annotations on the films and preview them yourself, you will make your own decisions on how to introduce them. But avoid the pitfalls: don't give away the plot; don't refer at length to scenes from the film; don't tell people how much they are going to like it; don't assign my annotations before screenings.

After some of the annotations I mention activities my students have enjoyed. If you haven't used films with groups before and do have time for discussion, you will find that your group is often mesmerized by the screen images and that your flesh-and-blood appearance is a poor second to a good film. Film teachers are learning to cope with this "drugging phenomenon" of film. You too will find it easier to stay in your own world, now broadened or intensified by the film, rather than motivate a discussion or begin a lecture.

I have approached this problem in many different ways. If I know that for a particular screening there will be only ten extra minutes of class time, I use that time before class for background and motivation. Then as the students are leaving (after the film) I hand them a worksheet or other form of written assignment. The worksheets ask questions that should stimulate revisualizing the film (How did the filmmaker let you know that Phoebe was remembering the past and imaging the future?); relating it to other films we have seen (How does Phoebe differ from Veronica?); relating the film to their own lives (In what way do you feel like Phoebe?).

If a film is very short, I still don't compete with it too much; I merely discuss points about the film and show it again, replaying sections that are relevant to our discussion or that answer questions we have raised. When I am following up a film with discussion, I usually get the students going on whether they liked it or not and why. That frequently leads to conflicting responses, which stimulate almost everyone.

Of course, if you are using these films in a more academic framework (e.g., *Wednesday's Child* with a course in psychology), you will be able to relate the film to previous lecture, readings, and discussions.

Out of the discussions and viewings of the films in this book, I hope that a real picture of women—as they are individually—will emerge. I know how much harm there is in films that present all the stereotypes in films (woman as witch, virgin, bitch) from my own reaction to the films of my teens and twenties in contrast to my students' and older friends' reactions to the films reviewed here. If these films impressed students enough to motivate them to make remarks like those given below, and throughout the text, how wrong it is to show them women in film only as sex symbols or martyrs; somebody's sister, mother, or wife. It is encouraging to me to know that the films reviewed on these pages have elicited responses like these:

On *Women on the March*

"It showed me how women should fight for their freedom. It showed me how a woman can fight, how women did not have legal rights before. It made me stronger and even ready to fight anyone or to protest against any law that would take away women's rights."

"Don't let men think we're weak. No, we should fight for our rights. Don't just stand around, do something about it. I felt good we saw the film because women were proving they could do what a man could do. Your husband hits you or something, don't be afraid to hit him back. Show him you're not afraid, honey, cause if you do he'll take advantage of you and do it more often. Show him you're not afraid. I'm glad this really did happen."

On *I Am Somebody*

"It made me realize that women are just as good as men. I was always saying this, but didn't really believe it completely until I saw this film. To most men a woman is an unpaid maid. She cleans, cooks and raises children. In this film it was shown differently. It emphasized the importance of a woman. The women weren't on the mining payroll, but they still were at work. I liked seeing the women standing fast and not being scared off by a few nights in jail or cars trying to run them off the picket line. Most importantly, not going under when their husbands didn't want their women at the picket line at all. Women are not just maids, bed partners, or babysitters."

"It makes you see that as a woman you could get what you really want if you try hard, without the help of another person. And it makes me feel good that in the future I will try to get what I really want."

On *It Happens to Us*

"It made me realize how great a chance we have when we, as women, can put the final say on whether or not we want a child—now, later, or never."

"It made me feel like I was inside the women who were talking and I could feel exactly the way they felt when they were talking."

On *The Cabinet*

"It helped me to understand that you don't live the same life as your mother."

On *Phoebe*

"This film makes me realize what responsibility you have when you're a girl. I know now when I get ready to have sex, I will be mature enough to get some protection."

index

The Films

A to B—Nell Cox 2

About Sex—Herman Engel 4

Angela Davis: Portrait of a Revolutionary—Yolande Du Luart 6

Anything You Want to Be—Liane Brandon 8

Are You Listening?—Martha Stuart 11

At Land—Maya Deren 15

Bed and Sofa—Abram Room 18

Behind the Veil—Eve Arnold 21

Betty Tells Her Story—Liane Brandon 23

Black Girl—Ousmane Sembene 24

The Cabinet—Suzanne Bauman 27

Childbirth—Maurice Amar 29

Cleo from Five to Seven—Agnes Varda 30

Cover Girl: New Face in Focus—Frances McLaughlin-Gill 34

Crash—David Abramson 37

Crocus—Suzan Pitt Kraning 39

Cycles—Linda Jassim 41

Dirty Books—Linda Feferman 43

Dream Life—Mireille Dansereau 45

Fear Woman—Elspeth MacDougall 48

Films About Women and Work—Kathleen Shannon 50
    It's Not Enough 51
    Luckily I Need Little Sleep 51
    Mothers Are People 51
    Tiger on a Tight Leash 51
    Would I Ever Like to Work 51
    'And They Lived Happily Ever After' 51
    The Powers That Be 51
    The Spring and Fall of Nina Polanski 52
    The Glass Slipper Pinches the Other Foot 52
    Aliette and Pierre 52
    Like the Trees 52
    Extensions of the Family 52
    Our Dear Sisters 52

For Boys Only Is for Girls, Too—Josef Pinkava 54

Game—Abigail Child, Jonathan Child 56

Gertrude Stein: When This You See, Remember Me—Perry Miller Adato 59

The Girls—Mai Zetterling 62

Goodbye in the Mirror—Storm De Hirsch 64

Growing Up Female: As Six Becomes One—Julia Reichert, James Klein 67

Happy Birthday Nora—Linda Feferman 70

How About You?—Bonnie Friedman, Deborah Shaffer, Marilyn Lubois   71

I Am Somebody—Madeline Anderson   72

It Happens to Us—Amalie Rothschild   76

Janie's Janie—Geri Ashur   78

Joyce at Thirty-Four—Joyce Chopra, Claudia Weill   81

Judy Chicago and the California Girls—Judith Dancoff   85

Kirsa Nicholina—Gunvor Nelson   86

Lavender—Colleen Monahan, Elaine Jacobs   87

L'Opéra Mouffe—Agnes Varda   90

Loving Couples—Mai Zetterling   91

Lucy—Alfred Wallace   94

Madalyn—Bob Elkins   95

Maedchen in Uniform—Leontine Sagan   98

Menilmontant—Dmitri Kirsanov   100

Meshes of the Afternoon—Maya Deren   102

Mosori Monika—Chick Strand   104

Nobody's Victim—Vaughn Obern, Alan Baker   106

Park Film—Linda Feferman   107

Phoebe—George Kaczender   108

Ramparts of Clay—Jean-Louis Bertucelli   111

Ritual in Transfigured Time—Maya Deren   114

Salt of the Earth—Herbert Biberman   116

Sambizanga—Sarah Maldoror   119

Schmeerguntz—Gunvor Nelson   120

The Smiling Madame Beudet—Germaine Dulac   121

Something Different—Vera Chytilova   124

Sometimes I Wonder Who I Am—Liane Brandon   125

String Bean—Edmond Séchan   126

Sweet Bananas—Ariel Dougherty   128

Take Off—Gunvor Nelson   130

Thigh Lyne Lyre Triangular—Stan Brakhage   130

3 A.M. to 10 P.M.—Zagreb Film   131

Three Lives—Louva Irvine, Robin Mide, Susan Kleckner   132

Unfolding—Constance Beeson   134

Veronica—Pat Powell   136

A Very Curious Girl—Nelly Kaplan   138

Virginia Woolf—The Moment Whole—Janet Sternberg   141

Wednesday's Child—Kenneth Loach   142

What I Want—Sharon Hennessey   145

Window Water Baby Moving—Stan Brakhage   146

Women Make Movies **146**
    Just Looking—Suzanne Armstrong **147**
    Fear—Jean Shaw **148**
    Domestic Tranquility—Harriet Kreigel **148**
    It's a Miracle—Marie Celine Caufield **149**
    Paranoia Blues—Jane Warrenbrand **149**
    For Better or Worse—Judy Acuna **149**
Women on the March—National Film Board of Canada **149**
Women Up in Arms—United Nations Television **152**
Women's Happy Time Commune—Sheila Paige **154**
Woo Who? May Wilson—Amalie Rothschild **156**

the filmmakers

The Filmmakers

In most cases, page numbers refer to biographies, in some cases to films by that person, or to a mention of the person in the text.

Abramson, David 39
   Crash
Acuna, Judy 149
   For Better or Worse
Adato, Perry Miller 61
   Gertrude Stein: When This You See, Remember Me
Amar, Maurice 29
   Childbirth
Anderson, Madeline 75
   I Am Somebody
Armstrong, Suzanne 147
   Just Looking
Arnold, Eve 22
   Behind the Veil
Ashur, Geri 80
   Janie's Janie
Baker, Alan 106
   Nobody's Victim
Bauman, Suzanne 28
   The Cabinet
Beeson, Constance 135
   Unfolding
Bertucelli, Jean-Louis 111
   Ramparts of Clay
Biberman, Herbert 118
   Salt of the Earth
Brakhage, Stan 130, 146
   Thigh Lyne Lyre Triangular
   Window Water Baby Moving
Brandon, Liane 10
   Anything You Want to Be
   Betty Tells Her Story
   Sometimes I Wonder Who I Am
Caufield, Marie Celine 149
   It's a Miracle
Child, Abigail 57
   Game

Child, Jonathan **58**
    Game
Chopra, Joyce **83**
    Joyce at Thirty-Four
Chytilova, Vera **124**
    Something Different
Cox, Nell **3**
    A to B
Dancoff, Judith **85**
    Judy Chicago and the California Girls
Dansereau, Mireille **47**
    Dream Life
De Hirsch, Storm **65**
    Goodbye in the Mirror
Deren, Maya **17**
    At Land
    Ritual in Transfigured Time
    Meshes of the Afternoon
Dougherty, Ariel **129**
    Sweet Bananas
Dulac, Germaine **123**
    The Smiling Madame Beudet
Du Luart, Yolande **6**
    Angela Davis: Portrait of a Revolutionary
Elkins, Bob **97**
    Madalyn
Engel, Herman **4**
    About Sex
Feferman, Linda **44**
    Dirty Books
    Happy Birthday Nora
    Park Film
Friedman, Bonnie **71**
    How About You?
Hennessey, Sharon **145**
    What I Want
Irvine, Louva **132**
    Three Lives
Jacobs, Elaine **87**
    Lavender
Jassim, Linda **42**
    Cycles

Kaczender, George **110**
  Phoebe
Kaplan, Nelly **140**
  A Very Curious Girl
Kirsanov, Dmitri **100**
  Menilmontant
Kleckner, Susan **132**
  Three Lives
Klein, James **70**
  Growing Up Female: As Six Becomes One
Kraning, Suzan Pitt **40**
  Crocus
Kreigel, Harriet **148**
  Domestic Tranquility
Loach, Kenneth **142**
  Wednesday's Child
Lubois, Marilyn **71**
  How About You?
MacDougall, Elspeth **48**
  Fear Woman
Maldoror, Sarah **119**
  Sambizanga
McLaughlin-Gill, Frances **36**
  Cover Girl: New Face in Focus
Mide, Robin **132**
  Three Lives
Monahan, Colleen **89**
  Lavender
National Film Board of Canada **149**
  Women on the March
Nelson, Gunvor **87**
  Take Off
  Kirsa Nicholina
  Schmeerguntz
Obern, Vaughn **106**
  Nobody's Victim
Paige, Sheila **155**
  Women's Happy Time Commune
Pinkava, Josef **54**
  For Boys Only Is for Girls, Too
Powell, Pat **136**
  Veronica

Reichert, Julia **69**
  Growing Up Female: As Six Becomes One
Room, Abram **18**
  Bed and Sofa
Rothschild, Amalie **77**
  It Happens to Us
  Woo Who? May Wilson
Sagan, Leontine **98**
  Maedchen in Uniform
Séchan, Edmond **126**
  String Bean
Sembene, Ousmane **26**
  Black Girl
Shaffer, Deborah **71**
  How About You?
Shannon, Kathleen **53**
  Films about Women and Work
    It's Not Enough
    Luckily I Need Little Sleep
    Mothers Are People
    Tiger on a Tight Leash
    Would I Ever Like to Work
    'And They Lived Happily Ever After'
    The Powers That Be
    The Spring and Fall of Nina Polanski
    The Glass Slipper Pinches the Other Foot
    Aliette and Pierre
    Like the Trees
    Extensions of the Family
    Our Dear Sisters
Shaw, Jean **148**
  Fear
Sternberg, Janet **141**
  Virginia Woolf—The Moment Whole
Strand, Chick **104**
  Mosori Monika
Stuart, Martha **13**
  Are You Listening?
United Nations Television **152**
  Women Up in Arms
Varda, Agnes **33**
  Cleo from Five to Seven
  L'Opéra Mouffe

Wallace, Alfred **94**
 Lucy
Warrenbrand, Jane **149**
 Paranoia Blues
Weill, Claudia **84**
 Joyce at Thirty-Four
Women Make Movies **146**
 Just Looking
 Fear
 Domestic Tranquility
 It's a Miracle
 Paranoia Blues
 For Better or Worse
Zagreb Film **131**
 3 A.M. to 10 P.M.
Zetterling, Mai **63**
 The Girls
 Loving Couples

the films

A to B

Nell Cox's *A to B* presents a sixteen-year-old as she begins to come to terms with herself in the face of the oppression she feels from school, home, and dating. In several sequences the film shows Penny on the last day of her junior year in high school and the first day of her summer vacation. Her conflicts are those of a conservative middle-class family. Her father doesn't want her to wear pants. Since life depends on the private car, getting a driver's license becomes an initiation rite into "manhood." A neon sign over the drive-in restaurant reads, "Go to church. Don't just talk about it."

Penny also suffers from sexist oppressions. When she asks her father if she can drive to her driving test, he snaps, "I'm not going to be driven by any lady." Her date comments, "It just seems like the girls don't have any real feeling for driving." Another boy says how great life is for his successful twenty-eight-year-old swinging single brother, who has "all the girls hanging on him." As Penny is helping prepare dinner, her mother asides, "If you can't work in the kitchen and cook, you'll never catch a husband."

Nell Cox admits that the tone of the film is autobiographical. As many women artists have gone through the process of shaking off sexist oppression, they study their past and see how yesterday's encounters have influenced their present lives. *A to B* is the product of that kind of retrospective consciousness-raising for Nell Cox.

In the Kentucky town of her childhood, Nell Cox spent some time observing the teen-agers for the lead roles. Penny was chosen from a crowd at the high school dance. The male lead, Wade, was spotted as Nell Cox was driving around one day. The cast was nonprofessional and much of the acting is extemporaneous. Scenes at the hog market, in the drive-in, and at the high school were shot with whoever was there. These authentic locations and the acting style inform the camerawork, which is partly *cinema vérité*. You feel the camera's searching for the next speaker or action, just as your eyes do in ordinary conversation. In all the sequences the camera finds Penny in close-up or shows the scene from her vantage point, heightening your identification with her. Even though you don't see Penny's thoughts (as you do with the girl in *Phoebe*), you certainly can imagine them. The style of *A to B* is very refreshing and honest.

Something real is captured in this film—you see a young woman reaching for maturity in her culture. The closing credits of the film are superimposed over medium close-up shots of Pennys' smug smile in the back seat of the moving family car.

I have found that high school students enjoy this film even if Penny's family problems differ superficially from their own.

A to B (1970): 36 mins., color, rental $40; purchase $400. Filmmaker: Nell Cox. Distributor: TIME-LIFE Films.

SUGGESTED FEMINIST READING
DeCrow, Karen. *The Young Woman's Guide to Liberation.*
Egan, Andrea. *Why Am I So Miserable When These Are Supposed to Be the Best Years of My Life?*
Nunes, Maxine, and White, Deanna, *The Lace Ghetto.*

Nell Cox

I have found that being a woman puts me back about five years at any given point. Minor incidents that have occurred to me would sound like nitpicking—but one only has to look at the number of women in powerful positions of total creative control to see that there is extreme discrimination. In addition, the subject matter of current films is totally dominated by masculine images and male adventure films.

Virginia Woolf said that women poets cannot look to poetry that has been written for inspiration. They must look back to their mothers.

—response to questionnaire, Spring 1973. 3

Nell Cox became interested in film when she was studying in Paris. Her first job was with a *cinéma vérité* team that included Leacock, Pennebaker, Maysles, and Drew.

In 1968 she formed her own company, Nell Cox Films Inc. She produces, directs, writes, and edits her own work. Cox has done advertising spots for AT&T, politicians, and Japan Air Lines, Her feature film script "50/50" was scheduled for shooting in the fall of 1974. Cox describes it as: "a feature film from a woman's point of view about the classic triangle: a couple having a baby, and how this affects their marriage and each of them individually." Currently Cox is making an industrial film for AT&T.

FILMOGRAPHY

Reflections. Twenty-seven-minute film (produced by Maysles Films) for Japan Air Lines to introduce their 747 Jumbo Jet. Filmed in Japan using a Japanese family as non-actors. Also a one-minute commercial on the same theme.

"Fifty-Fifty." Wrote this feature-film script for the Rhombus Film Corporation in 1970. Film to be directed by Cox.

AT&T Scripts. Wrote three scripts for industrial films for AT&T.

Foster Pettit Campaign. An entire television political campaign consisting of twelve spots for Foster Pettit when he ran for mayor of Lexingington, Kentucky, in the fall of 1971. (He won.)

Kentucky Crime Commission Commercial. One-minute spot about a prisoner leaving the state penitentiary.

*A to B. Thirty-six-minute film shot in Kentucky on a grant from the American Film Institute. Identity crisis of a sixteen-year-old girl. Distributor: TIME-LIFE Films.

AT&T Commercials. Four commercials produced in the fall of 1969 for AT&T Network Specials (shown on the Julie Andrews Specials).

Operator. Fifteen-minute film produced for AT&T to recruit telephone operators. Distributor: Modern Talking Pictures, New York City.

French Lunch. Fifteen-minute food orgy in the kitchen of the Caravelle Restaurant. Distributor: EYR Campus Programs, New York City.

*Reviewed in this book.

About Sex

All in all, I would label About Sex *about perfect. I hope it will circulate through schools nationwide. It's exactly what we've been waiting for.*
    —Harriette Surovell, Student Coalition for Relevant Sex Education

"Let's get together and make it better—SEX." So sings the rock group Ghetto Brothers at the opening of *About Sex.* That is what this film sets out to do: make sex better for teen-agers through understanding. The film is divided into two parts. The first is footage of a loose rap session of a group of city teen-agers with Angel Martinez, Youth Programs Consultant for Planned Parenthood, New York City. Martinez has a good

4   rapport with the teen-agers. When they bring up points about masturba-

tion (insecure) or homosexuality (prejudiced), he builds on their comments to give scientific information and display a mature attitude, without putting them down. His efforts are to give as much correct information as possible and to dispel uncomfortableness.

"You *can* get pregnant before, during, or after your period. It's less likely."

"Even if he pulls out, it could be too late."

"Douching is not birth control."

In the second section of the film, Martinez—now facing the camera alone—gives more information around specific topics, which are illustrated by visuals. For the first topic, "Thinking and Dreaming" (It's natural.), you see the flowing ocean and a couple having intercourse on the beach. The next segment is "Body Growth" ("We all develop dif-

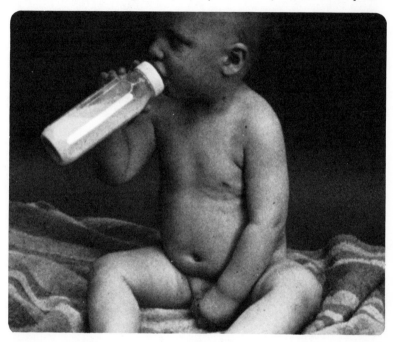

ferently, at different rates. Isn't it nice?"). Then "Masturbation" ("Normal."), "Homosexuality" ("Don't be critical."), "Pregnancy and Birth Control" ("Know what you're doing."), "Abortion" ("Safe, available, quick."), and "Man and Woman" ("Women are being more proud of their sexuality than their sexiness."). The film concludes with the Ghetto Brothers singing, "Let's get together to understand what it is all about."

About Sex may be useful for some classes in sex education and psychology from junior high school through early college. The atmosphere created on the screen will encourage easy discussion in your own groups. Moreover, much of the information the viewers receive right from the screen will dispel fears and help them to start building a healthier and more confident sex life.

About Sex (1972): 23 mins., color; rental $25; purchase $220. Director: Herman Engel. Distributor: Texture Films. Study guides upon request.

SUGGESTED FEMINIST READING
The Boston Women's Health Book Collective. *Our Bodies, Our Selves,* Wierdiger, Paula. *Every Month of Our Lives.*

Angela Davis - Portrait of a Revolutionary

What we see here is not the creature of the FBI nor the caricature of the revolutionary that the gutter press has tried to make. Instead, we meet a young woman of great moral and intellectual character, whose sincerity and purity are immediately apparent.
Philip Bronosky, *Daily World*, January 18, 1972.

Documentary biographies are most frequently made after the events that make the subject "worthy" of biography. This is not the case with Yolande Du Luart's film. When she was a student in Angela Davis's philosophy class Yolande proposed to fulfill a requirement for the film department with a documentary on Angela Davis. Even though her request was refused, she went on with her project with the help of some independent filmmakers in California. Little did she realize how many events would develop during the time of her filming, or how important her footage would be in establishing a public image of the private person so typically obliterated by the rhetoric and editorial viewpoint of the news media.

The film opens with scenes of Angela Davis's arrest on December 5, 1970, but soon turns back in time to her teaching year at UCLA, fall of 1969. She appears kind, strong, and conscientious as she leads a discussion with a class, speaks with students during a break, and studies in her home. Other footage shows her with a downtown community group at the Malcolm X Center, where she states that she won't defend her job, that she has to fight for her people. The arrest of the Black Panthers is shown next, mostly in still photos with Angela's voiceover as an accompaniment. As the film goes on, it alternates between scenes of Angela speaking in and to groups, with close-ups of her talking directly into the camera. The screen is commandeered by a committed revolutionary, never the performer or the charlatan. That Angela's commitment is self-sacrificing and powerful can never be mistaken. Certainly her very bearing contradicts the image of a love-sick girl that the judge tried to portray at her trial.

In footage from the strike on UCLA campus, May 20, 1970, Angela speaks to thousands of striking students after the murders at Kent State, the arrest of the Soledad brothers, and the murder of students in Jackson, Mississippi. She says, "I don't feel very good today. I don't feel very good because I walked down those steps and saw people screaming, jumping up and down, throwing frisbies, when there is a war going on. I just want to know what are people celebrating? What is there to feel good about?" As she continues, her voiceover accompanies scenes of that same campus during the days preceding this rally . . . a campus of tear gas, arrests, national guard, and police brutality.

Angela Davis's single-mindedness cannot be mistaken. One cannot know if Yolande Du Luart knew that the private and public Angela were one before she started shooting and that Angela practices her own dictum: "We have to react as if we were the ones shot down. We have to react collectively, have to overcome the whole idea of individual fulfillment and individual accomplishment . . . [There] has to be only one course, the revolutionary course . . . . My life belongs to the struggle." But certainly she discovered it with her film.

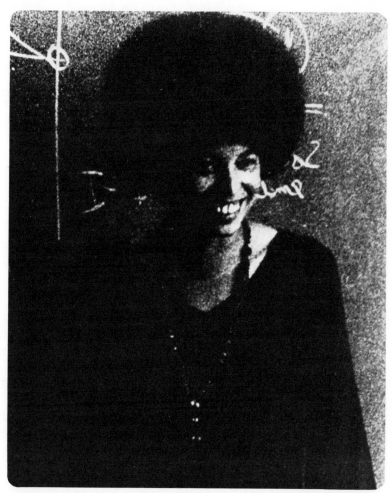

The prejudice of the Board of Regents in firing Angela Davis from the university is explicit in the film. One of the members of the Board of Regents says that Angela was fired because she didn't have the proper credentials. This is contradicted by Max Rafferty, the chairman of the philosophy department. Yet he too is helpless, a pawn of the Board of Regents, so that, despite his respect for Angela and sympathy for her, he cannot save her job.

Through editing, the film parallels the powerlessness of Angela, Rafferty, George Jackson, all of us, to a system controlled by the Ronald Reagans. "Repression comes in many forms . . . I cannot separate my present plight with these more violent forms of oppression . . . we can no longer separate what is happening to Bobby Seale with what is happening in Vietnam . . . or the campuses."

Documentary films are frequently limited in their visual appeal and in technical details. This film has the added limitation of starting with a small humble body of material that is now eminently more important than anyone suspected at the time of shooting. But is it actually a limitation? It seems to me to be one of the special qualities of *Portrait of a Revolutionary*. The simplicity of the camerawork and editing leaves room for Angela to show and reflect her single purpose. The cameras of a few of her students could not possibly be imposing, and they captured moments that CBS would never have thought of capturing or that wouldn't have occurred in front of their imposing camera.

This film is suitable for the upper years of high school and on. Your students, like mine, may be a little disappointed in the absence of drama and emotion. They may also be taken back by the demands that Angela makes on them if they are to be revolutionaries: "Am I going to stay home and get high or am I going to go out to rap with the people to organize? You no longer have that alternative."

I have seen only the original 60-minute film. A 35-minute version is available also.

Angela Davis—Portrait of a Revolutionary (1971): 60 mins., b/w; classroom rental $75; unrestricted $125; purchase $425. 35 mins., classroom rental $40; unrestricted $75; purchase $275. Filmmaker: Yolande Du Luart, made with the help of film students at UCLA. Du Luart was assisted in editing the footage by French TV personnel and Jean Genet. Distributor: New Yorker Films.

SUGGESTED FEMINIST READING
Cade, Toni (ed.). *The Black Woman.*
Davis, Angela. "Reflections on the Black Woman's Role in the Community of Slaves." *Woman: An Issue,* pp. 81-100. Edited by Lee R. Edwards, Mary Heath and Lisa Baskin.
Lerner, Gerda (ed.). *Black Women in White America.*

Anything You Want to Be

Aren't you glad you're a woman? You can be anything you want to be.
—from the film.

"You can be anything you want to be" . . . the great American promise. Between the promise and adulthood there are many contradicting and damaging influences. This short film visually explores these contradictions for a young woman who looks very much like everybody's kid sister. As she describes her high school years, the screen shows her various attempts to be what she wants to be. She runs for class president, but soon learns that she will be more successful running for secretary.

Having decided to be a doctor, she goes into the guidance office, only to walk out in a nurse's uniform, bedpan in hand. Chemistry tubes turn into baby bottles. When she graduates, it is only as the graduation cap becomes a wedding veil that her parents smile. Finally she decides, "I think I want to be a woman. But what is a woman?" The film answers the question in front of a medicine chest mirror. The character appears in appropriate dress and gesture to accompany contradicting stereotyped definitions of woman. One says women are "elegant, sophisticated, suave." The next says they are "simple, sweet, sympathetic, subordinate." Another "sexual, sensual, and erotic" and so on.

The film comes to a frightening, screeching halt as the character screams, putting her hands to her ears. Other hands are pointing to her from all sides of the frame as overlapping voices shout, "Anything you want to be, anything you want to be . . . "

Liane Brandon's film is unpretentious yet successful. I account for this success by the charm of the character, the clear sentiments of the film, and the contrast of animated live figures with the real horror of the final screech.

I would use this film starting in the high school years. As a motivation I asked my group of ninth-graders if, when they were younger, they were told, "You can be anything you want to be." They talked about that promise in terms of real-life situations and what factors were already limiting their free choices. Once we saw the film and discussed it, the students made lists of what they wanted to do, why they wanted to do it, and what they would have to do to achieve their goals.

Anything You Want to Be (1971): 8 mins., b/w; rental $15; purchase $100. Filmmaker: Liane Brandon. Distributor: New Day Films.

SUGGESTED FEMINIST READING
Bird, Caroline. *Born Female.*
DeCrow, Karen. *The Young Woman's Guide to Liberation.*
de Rivera, Alice. "On De-Segregating Stuyvesant High." *Sisterhood Is Powerful*, pp. 366-371. Edited by Robin Morgan.

Dvorkin, Connie. "The Suburban Scene." *Sisterhood Is Powerful*, pp. 362-366. Edited by Robin Morgan.

Egan, Andrea. *Why Am I So Miserable When These Are Supposed to Be the Best Years of My Life?*

Merriam, Eve (ed.) *Growing Up Female in America: Ten Lives.*

Nunes, Maxine, and White, Deanna. *The Lace Ghetto.*

Liane Brandon

Photo by Gilli Terry

I find my films are becoming closer and closer to the real me. I learn an awful lot about myself every time I make a film. Sometimes it's pretty scary.

—to JoAnne Greene, for a paper.

Liane Brandon has interestingly and successfully combined a teaching and a filmmaking career. A teacher since 1964 in Quincy, Massachusetts, she is now Associate Professor at the University of Massachusetts School of Education (media). Her teaching has always been media oriented, and she has worked as a consultant to many media programs and courses.

Brandon's first film, *Gum*, was done with her junior high school students. Later she did a film with high school students, *Le Sujet c'est nous.* She has also shown her students' Super-8 work in a collection entitled *Garbage*.

Brandon is a member of New Day Films, an independent distribution cooperative. Her own independent films (*Sometimes I Wonder Who I Am, Anything You Want to Be,* and *Betty Tells Her Story*) have received justifiable acclaim for their poignancy and humor. Currently she is working on an eight-to-twelve-minute film, *You Haven't Changed a Bit,* based on the fifteen-year reunion of her high school class.

FILMOGRAPHY

You Haven't Changed a Bit (in progress), approx. 8-12 mins. Distributor: New Day Films.

*Betty Tells Her Story (1972), black and white, 20 mins. Distributor: New Day Films.

*Anything You Want to Be (1971), black and white, 8 mins. Distributor: New Day Films.

Clinic (1971), Super-8, 4 mins. Instructional film for medical personnel.

*Sometimes I Wonder Who I Am (1970), black and white, 5 mins. Distributor: New Day Films.

Garbage (1970-71), Super-8, 15 mins. Collection of student work.

Le Sujet c'est nous (1970), black and white, 13 mins. Made with high school students. Documentary to send to France.

R.T.P.T. . . . Developing (1969), black and white, 5 mins. Documentary for Roxbury Photographers Training Program.

Gum (1968), black and white, 8 mins. Made with junior high school students.

*Reviewed in this book.

Are You Listening ?

At this point in time what's wrong with commercialism is wrong with commercial television, only the latter is more personally destructive to more people. Both are saying to people, "You are out of it." The problems seem too big and complicated and the pleasures too glamorous for small people to do anything about or to be a part of so they keep some contact with the outside world by watching more television and living more vicariously.
—Martha Stuart, *Random Thoughts about Television and Our Society.*

We have to look for a new way of communication and get across to people, turn people on to the point where they're gonna really want . . . there's something in all of us that really wants to be happy and when you see somebody happy, doing something glad, well, you want to do it too you know.
I've a really hard time with the words sexism *and* racism *because to me the only thing that really exists is some humanity or lack of humanity.*
—quotations from *Freaks (Are You Listening?).*

Since many titles in Martha Stuart's video-cassette series *Are You Listening?* have been printed on sixteen millimeter film, I am reviewing the series here. Like many people who are currently working in film and video, Martha Stuart feels that television should relate to people's daily lives, helping to break down barriers, rather than feeding unattainable dreams and supporting both role playing and prejudices. In her tapes, Stuart asks you to listen, really listen, to people talking about themselves. These people are grouped by areas of concern and/or experience. For example, you listen to welfare mothers, or prisoners, or judges. The format is the same for all the tapes. After having made initial individual contact, Martha Stuart sits with eight to ten people and introduces them, describing their common concern. The people then carry on a discussion with one another, giving an opportunity for "people to listen to other people who are endlessly talked about and rarely ever listened to."

11

I was impressed by the honesty and directness of the subjects, qualities that I have never been able to associate with television. How many of us feel we are getting "the truth" in a TV special on welfare problems or abortion? Yet those shows frequently have a god-like, problem-solving tone. The *Are You Listening* film/tapes do not try to give "the whole truth" or to solve problems, but they do give glimpses of lifestyles and groups of people we might not otherwise meet. It is a chance to see areas of concern less in terms of problems and more in terms of the people who live with those problems.

The format for these programs is simple—the editing (4:1 shooting ratio) never breaks the time sequence in which the discussions are conducted. Moreover, there is nothing to look at but the people, nothing to listen to but their ideas and feelings. The tapes that I saw (*Prisoners,*

Black High School Girls, Woodlawn Sisterhood, Welfare Mothers, and *Women Who Have Had An Abortion)* were inspiring and could be useful to you in many different situations. Certainly think of using them in sequence with other films which deal with similar concerns. If you decide to show *It Happens to Us* , show *Women Who Have Had An Abortion* first. *Black High School Girls* is a very good companion to *Veronica;* and *Welfare Mothers* goes well with *Janie's Janie.* Since the tapes never end with solutions, but tend more to humanize problems, they should motivate discussion and disagreement in your own group.

• For data on titles see the Filmography following. All titles are available from Martha Stuart Communications, Inc.

SUGGESTED FEMINIST READING
Check for books with similar themes when ordering specific films.

Martha Stuart

We need to say to people fast on television—no other medium is fast enough—"Yes, it's all right to think about yourself; yes, it's all right to disagree and find out about things; yes, it's all right to make our life better and here are some ways that other people like you *are doing just that.*

We need to make the adult classroom an open classroom. We need to revise the adult reader—television—so that we see and hear people with whom we can share experiences—people in the real world.

. . . Television makes it possible to underline the common bonds of human concern so that the differences of age, sex, color, religion, nationality or whatever can be enjoyed not feared.
　　　　　　　—from *Random Thoughts about Television and Our Society,*
　　　　　　　　　　　　　　　Martha Stuart Communications.

　　Martha Stuart is an independent video-tape producer whose series *Are You Listening?* is being introduced on video cassette and educational and cable stations. Before starting this series, she produced photo- 13 graphs, books, booths, radio and television shows, conferences, and change processes for various clients (Planned Parenthood, the University of Notre Dame, Masters and Johnson, the Spanish Pavilion, and the State of Oklahoma). Producing and editing a conference and book called *The Emerging Woman: The Impact of Family Planning* made her decide to concentrate on video tape.

Stuart has had her own company for eleven years and says it specializes in "making social change through human exchange." She is currently developing a series of tapes on women in management, another on medical topics, and a third on parents. In November, 1973, Martha Stuart produced video cassettes with CESI (Centre for Economic and Social Information) for the People of World Population Year. The series, *People of World Population,* was made in India, U.S.A., Japan, and Egypt with students, workers, family leaders and rural women and will be presented at The Tribunal of World Population in Budapest, August, 1974. She lives and works with her two children, Barkley and Sally, at 66 Bank Street, New York.

FILMOGRAPHY
Women in Management (1974)
Creative Parenthood (1974)
Couples in India (1974)
Women in Middle Management (1974)
Shop Stewards (1973)
Cook County Interns (1972), 16 mm.
Freaks (1972).
Women (1972).
Garfield Ridge (1972).
Policemen (1972).
Women Who Have Had an Abortion (1972), 16 mm.
Black P Stone Nation (1971), 16 mm.
Woodlawn Sisterhood (1971), 16 mm.
Welfare Mothers (1970), 16 mm.
Prisoners (1970), 16 mm.
Prison Guards (1970), 16 mm.
Switchboard (1970), 16 mm.
Judges (1970).
Black High School Girls (1970).
Boys with Long Hair (1970), 16 mm.
All of the above are color, 28 min. 38 sec. Sony video cassette: rental/ sale $25/175; 16 mm film: rental/sale $35/350; audio cassette: sale $15.
Vasectomia (1971), black and white, 16 mm, 20 mins. Spanish program.
Mujeres Colombianas (1971), black and white, 16 mm, 20 mins. Spanish program.
The two programs above are Sony video cassette: rental/sale $20/100; 16 mm film: rental/sale $25/150; audio cassette: sale $10.
Programs can be ordered separately or in any combination. Available for broadcast on all video-tape formats (price on request). Cost of rental may be applied to the purchase price.

At Land

At Land has little to do with the inner world of the protagonists. It externalizes the hidden dynamic of the external world. It is as if I had moved from a concern with the life of a fish to a concern with the sea, which accounts for the character of the fish and its life.
                                        —Maya Deren, *Film Culture*, 1965.

The hidden dynamic of the external world that Maya Deren is talking about is exhibited in a realm of no set time and discontinuous space. It is one of an eternal quest for identity and the secret to the life force—a searching out, at any cost, for control over one's own destiny.

In some of the most exquisite shots of all Deren's work, Maya herself is washed up from the sea. She rises to climb up driftwood onto the dining room table of a formal room. While everyone ignores her, she crawls on her belly to the head of the table. She passes through forests and continues to climb the driftwood. Once she is at the head of the table, everyone leaves her. Yet the chess game going on there continues without anyone, except perhaps Maya's will, controlling it. A pawn falls off the table through a hole in the driftwood and into the sea. Suddenly Maya is walking along a road, talking to a man. During alternating close-ups of each of them, the man changes into three different men. Finally it is Alexander Hammid, her husband. As they walk along, he gains distance on her. She chases after him, but ignoring her, he enters a hut. She climbs through a hole under the porch and comes out in a closed house. There she sees a rather gross man in bed, smoking a large cigar. Walking through a door, she comes out on a high rock from which she slides onto the beach. While fitfully gathering stones, she discovers a game of chess on the shore. She distracts the women playing, grabs the pawn and runs. As she runs there are brilliant cuts to shots of herself in various other poses of the film. So you get the image of the persona of the film watching her own life. The last shot is of Maya running—arms up in the air, pawn in hand—down to the beach.

There are very definite sexual themes in this film that align Maya's thinking with recent positive ideas of sexuality in the feminist movement. When Maya crawls up to the chessboard, she watches the game of life being acted out there. At first it seems that the pieces move by them- 15 selves. Then it seems that she is not watching the board but controlling it with her eye movements. Then the pawn, her life in this game, drops off the board. In her search for her life, her pawn, she meets with several men who, in turn, become her husband (representing the traditional heterosexual relationship). She must rush after the husband, walking behind him. When he goes into the house, leaving her behind, she crawls in through the bowels of the building, looking to see if her pawn, her life, is in this relationship. She doesn't find her husband, but an older man smoking that great phallic symbol, the cigar. She leaves, rejecting the subservience of the implied relationship and comes out on the cliff, a free open space, in contrast to the stuffy, smoky house.

The scene of Maya stroking the hair of the women chess players suggests, in my reading of the film, a homosexual love. This, too, she passes by, taking the pawn from the chessboard, leaving the women (lesbianism) and running down the beach with the controls of her own life. It isn't that she denies the role of sex in her life—she is rejecting sex as the ruling dynamic of her existence.

Space is boldly filmed in *At Land*. Close-ups are contrasted with extreme long shots. Editing screams at you: "She *does* have one foot on the driftwood and her hands on the table." Or: "Watch her struggle through the trees as she crawls up the table."

In *At Land*, more than either of her other films considered in this book, Maya Deren conforms to her own dictum:

So the artist, beginning in reality—in that which already exists—starts moving towards a vision, an idea, and, with the cumulative momentum of that dedicated concentration, crosses the threshold from that which already exists into the void where, still moving forward, she creates a plane of earth where her foot has been, as the spider, spinning from her own guts, threads her ladders of highways through the once empty space over the abyss. —Maya Deren, *Anthology Files*.

It seems to me, then, that in *At Land* Maya has not only spun ladders through an abyss of cinematic possibilities, but has also predicted one of the essential premises of the feminist movement—that a woman's life should not be defined and determined by her sexuality, be it heterosexual or homosexual, but she should control and determine her own existence.

College students should find *At Land* thematically interesting and cinematically exciting. If you want to use a Deren film with high school students, however, I suggest *Meshes of the Afternoon*. In either case allow for more than one screening.

At Land (1944): 15 mins., b/w, silent; rental $35, purchase $150. Director: Maya Deren. Distributor: Grove Press.

SUGGESTED FEMINIST READING
Arnheim, Rudolf. "To Maya Deren." *Film Culture Reader*, pp. 84-86. Edited by P. Adams Sitney.
Cornwell, Regina. "Maya Deren and Germaine Dulac: Activists of the Avant-Garde." *Film Library Quarterly* (vol. 5, no. 1), pp. 29-38.

Horney, Karen. *Feminine Psychology.*

Miller, Jean Baker (ed.). *Psychoanalysis and Women.*

Nin, Anais. *The Diary of Anais Nin* (vol. IV). Check indexed references to Maya Deren; Nin writes about her friendship with Deren, the making of *At Land* and *Meshes of the Afternoon,* and analyzes Deren's work.

Vogel, Amos. "Poetry and the Film: A Symposium." *Film Culture Reader,* pp. 171-186. Edited by P. Adams Sitney.

Maya Deren

Sincerity, as the honest conviction in the truth and importance of what the artist has to say, serves to trigger the adrenalin which makes her highest pitch.—from draft of paper on file at Anthology Film Archives

Maya Deren was born in Russia in 1917. Having spent her childhood in Syracuse, New York, she was sent to Geneva for her high school education. She returned to Syracuse to study English at Syracuse University. Her undergraduate education was completed at New York University. Her graduate studies, including a thesis on French symbolist poetry, were done at Smith.

As a poet herself, Maya was frustrated because her mind worked in images, which she would then translate into words. Once she took up the camera there was no more need to translate. The medium was direct. It was through her relationship with Alexander Hammid that she recognized how suitable film was to her artistic and moral intentions.

Part of the Greenwich Village "scene" of the forties and fifties, she was instrumental in the establishment of the Creative Film Foundation and Cinema Sixteen. She made her films in New York and wrote articles on everything from cats in New York for the *Park East* magazine to "Cinematography; The Creative Use of Reality."

In 1946 she won the first Guggenheim Fellowship granted for creative filmmaking in sixteen millimeter. Soon afterward she made the first of three trips to Haiti where she worked on films, made three records of Haitian music, and gathered materials for her *Divine Horseman,* a book on Haitian voodooism.

17

Following three successive cerebral hemorrhages, Maya Deren died on October 13, 1961.

FILMOGRAPHY
The Very Eye of Night (1952-56), 15 mins. Direction, script, photography, art direction, and editing by Deren.
Meditation on Violence (1948). A choreography for camera based on movements from Chinese boxing. Distributor: Grove Press.
*Ritual in Transfigured Time [also entitled *Ritual and Ordeal*] (1945-46), silent, 15 mins. Conceived and directed by Deren. Photographed by Hella Hamon. Distributor: Grove Press.
A Study in Choreography for the Camera [also titled *Pas de deux*] (1945), silent, 4 mins. Conceived and directed by Deren and Tailey Beatty.
*At Land (1944), silent, 15 mins. Conceived and directed by Deren. Technical assistance by Hella Hamon and Alexander Hammid. Distributor: Grove Press.
*Meshes of the Afternoon (1943), 14 mins. Shot in only two weeks by Deren and Alexander Hammid. Score by Teiji Ito. Distributor: Grove Press.

*Reviewed in this book.

Bed and Sofa

I liked the whole film. The plot was so exciting and the ending was so different from any love story that I've ever seen . . . it has taught me that in reality you don't get married and live happily ever after . . . I think a woman should decide whether she wants to be single or married instead of being persuaded into marrying.

—Maritza Cotto, age 15.

What a delicately balanced combination of comedy and drama it is built upon. And how rarely such a combination works! Such material, and in such realistic surroundings, has no comparable sequel in Soviet films, or elsewhere, for that matter.

—Jay Leyda, *Kino; A History of the Russian and Soviet Film,* p. 216.

"Well, it looks like we are rotters," says Volodya to Nikolya at the conclusion of *Bed and Sofa.* That they are rotters isn't surprising. What is unusual is that a 1928 film should show the point of view of an oppressed and unhappy young woman while her male counterparts enjoy her maid and sex services. The consciousness of Abram Room is clear: Throughout the film he shows not only that the men are rotters, but that women should and will take their lives into their own hands.

The story is a *ménage à trois.* Ludmilla and Nikolya live in a one-room flat, circa 1926. Nikolya is a construction supervisor; his wife— a wife. When Nikolya's war buddy arrives to an overcrowded Moscow, the couple give him their sofa to sleep on. After Nikolya goes off on a business trip, Ludmilla and Volodya begin to sleep together. Following his return, Nikolya finds himself on the sofa. The friendship between Nikolya and Volodya is the important relationship to both men. When Ludmilla announces that she is pregnant, the men demand that she get an abortion. She goes to a private hospital but runs out without having an abortion. She leaves a note:

I have decided to have this child, but I don't believe that either of you are worthy to be its father. So I am going out of both of your lives—and try to make my own. We may meet again someday but I hope we shall have learned more by then.
                    Goodbye,
                    Ludmilla

The relevance of *Bed and Sofa* comes from the consciousness of a filmmaker whose liberated and liberating attitude toward people is exposed in the strategies of the film. The jobs of men are shown as exciting. Beautiful shots of Moscow from the roof of the Bolshoi Opera define Nikolya's job as he has lunch at the feet of great statues and runs animatedly from one section of the roof to another, supervising the work

there. Volodya's job as a printer is shown in shots of the factory that indicate the rhythm and design of turning wheels, with endless printed sheets rolling. On the other hand, Ludmilla is bored and disinterested as she limply picks up, washes clothes, and does dishes.

In the scene in which Nikolya gets ready for his trip, Volodya complains about being left with Ludmilla. "People will talk," he says. "I'm not worried," replies Nikolya. "Everyone knows that Ludmilla is crazy about me. She knows I am very fond of her. But when one loves one chastises if necessary. She understands that too." The camera shows Ludmilla's reaction to this exchange. It is an angry face. But she takes out her anger by packing faster and harder, to her husband's benefit. It is partially because Volodya relieves her boredom by taking her for an airplane ride and to the movies ("I seldom have the honor of going out with my husband.") that Ludmilla sleeps with him. But he in turn becomes master of the house.

The scene of the morning after their lovemaking exposes Ludmilla's disillusionment and continued frustration. Waking to see Volodya beside her, she shows as much disgust as remorse. You realize that she is more angry with her situation than guilt-ridden. Volodya, on the other hand, is quick to move his bedding from the sofa to the more comfortable and accommodating bed.

When Volodya tells Nikolya of their adultery, Ludmilla is no part of their discussion. The men decide who will stay, and each night they try to trick one another to see who will get to sleep with her. When Nikolya sleeps out of the apartment for the night, he remembers scenes of the domestic bliss that he has been deprived of, not by his friend but by his wife. He sees shots of himself rocking in a chair. These shots are superimposed on images of him stroking the cat—then, in the same manner, his wife's arm. "Damned woman," he says.

Each evening Nikolya and Volodya play chess. Ludmilla sits looking out the window. Their competitive game over her is but an extension of the game of chess. Ludmilla finally begins to verbalize her distaste for both men: "I am tired of you and your confounded games. I am tired of both of you." And of her new lover she realizes, "His majesty. As loud as the other one and just as bad." When they order her to have the abortion, she asks: "Who is making this decision?"

When Ludmilla finally leaves them, she takes a picture of herself from the wall, carefully replacing the empty frame in its place. As the film draws to its conclusion, shots of Ludmilla on the train (with the wind blowing her short hair as she looks out the window) are intercut with the men's discovery of her absence. They look at their images in the mirror and worry about whether there is jam for their tea.

We are so accustomed to sound films, whose feeling and ideas are as much carried by the sound as by the sight, that seeing a good silent film is a visual treat. It is a double treat when the concerns expressed in the film are applicable to our own times and feelings. Enjoy *Bed and Sofa,* using it with many different groups. My high school classes loved it and were literally cheering when Ludmilla went out on her own. If you work with history or sociology classes, you will be interested to know that *Bed and Sofa* gives a good picture of life in Moscow around 1926.

Bed and Sofa (1927): 72 mins.; rental $40. Director: Abram Room. Distributor: Macmillan Audio Brandon Films.

SUGGESTED FEMINIST READING
Bernard, Jessie. *The Future of Marriage.*
Friedan, Betty. *The Feminine Mystique.*

Behind the Veil

It seems to me that in every story there comes a time when it can be told. Given the right factors, doors open just enough for the reporter to make contact. Once that is done if there is trust on both sides, things work. I fell lucky and things began to work.

—Eve Arnold in a letter to Joe Bernstein, August 25, 1971.

Doors opened for Eve Arnold's cameras into an Arabian harem and the wedding of the Crown Prince of Dubai. Comfortably edited footage presents proof of the inequality of women in Arabian culture. Men buy cloth for the women's wedding dresses because women cannot deal with strange men. Men do all the celebrating for the wedding while the women are secluded indoors. The bridegroom participates in all the fun, while the bride has been sitting in *purdah* (seclusion) for a month. The men attend camel races in their Rolls Royces while the women sit secluded, eating sweets.

The voiceover for the film is a narration that Eve Arnold devised for Noura, the handmaiden of Hind, the Sheik's twelve-year-old niece. Noura quotes the Koran ("The Arab loves first his son, then his camel, then his wife.") and describes the elaborate wedding preparations and celebrations (over 2,000 guests come for over three weeks of partying). With quiet dignity she suggests not only the beginning of change for women in Arabia, but also expresses her support of those changes.

I was completely enchanted and amazed by *Behind the Veil*. The photography is beautiful and well-edited; the narration's soft tones and rhythmic speech patterns are appropriate to the pace of the filmed sequences. It is a film of contrasts—the contrast between the freedom of men and the enslavement of the women, between the East and the West, between the wealth of the Sheiks ($500,000,000 a year for the Sheik of Dubai) and the poverty of the desert Bedouins.

Behind Eve Arnold's unprecedented camera presence at the ceremonies and inside the harem is her acquaintance with Sheikha Suma, the sister-in-law of the ruling sheik. Though still wearing the veil, Sheikha Suma drives a jeep, owns large taxicab concessions, and has a multiplicity of investments in local businesses. Though the bride, her daughter, is never seen on the film (after all, she never appears at the ceremonies either), she did not don the mask on the wedding night. Sheikha Alia, the new bride, told Eve Arnold: "You have your Paris fashions, the midi, the maxi, and the mini. This year we have a new fashion too. We will no longer wear the mask." Eve Arnold's reporting on what she suggests is a disappearing way of life is both historically important and artistically satisfying.

As I watched the lush sequences of *Behind the Veil*, I thought also of the similarities of the situations of Arabian women and American women. Wherever women are considered a possession, the way they look and their ornaments reflect their husband's wealth. And certainly there is some correlation between the rich man's wife in America and the members of the harem. Also, just as in Arabia, a man's standing in the American communities is judged to some measure by the wedding that he gives his daughter.

Use *Behind the Veil* with junior high school age students and older. Not only will your audiences be amazed at the blatant male chauvinism of the Koran and the daily life of the Arabians, but they will also be given a respectful look at the customs and traditions of another culture.

Behind the Veil (1972): 50 mins., color; rental $60, purchase $600. Director: Eve Arnold. Distributor: Impact Films.

SUGGESTED FEMINIST READING
Leavitt, Ruby R. "Women in Other Cultures." *Woman in Sexist Society,* pp. 393-427. Edited by Vivian Gornick and Barbara K. Moran.
Martineau, Harriet. "The Hareem." *by a Woman writt,* pp. 199-213. Edited by Joan Goulianos.

Eve Arnold

Photo by Cornell Capa, Magnum Photos Inc.

This was my first film, but I had enormous experience as a stills woman on film, and I was accustomed to working all over the world under difficult conditions on my own ideas, writing my own stuff, etc. . . . When I returned from Arabia, a Hollywood friend asked me how I felt about directing my first film. I replied off the top of my head that that was the way a celibate must feel when he first discovers sex. Out there all these years there has been sound and motion and I had been working away on that flat, silent page.
—letter to Joe Bernstein, August 25, 1971.

American still photographer Eve Arnold has been living in England for the past ten years. She is a member of Magnum Photos, an international co-op of photographers. Her work has appeared in leading slick magazines of the *Life-Ladies Home Journal* variety and has brought her to such places as Arabia, Afghanistan, Egypt, France, Spain, Russia, and England. She is currently planning a series of films to be made in the Far East in 1974. At the time of this writing, *Behind the Veil* is her only film.

In 1971, when Eve Arnold was making arrangements for her crew for *Behind the Veil,* she tried to find women technicians. Of this experience she wrote:

While my more militant feminist friends kept clucking about my going into the medieval benighted world of the women of the east, I kept worrying about our own benighted world in which I couldn't find even four skilled female technicians. I needed a lighting cameraman, an operator, a combination of focus puller and assistant to the sound recordist, and a sound recordist. I started looking in the U.S. while there last November. I came back to London and looked. I checked in Paris . . . assistants, yes—full-blown, experienced chef du camera, no. I followed up dozens of leads and invariably the girl would turn out to be an editor, or an assistant to an assistant—but not quite right. It was too easy to say—women's lib right are right. Women had not had a crack at the brass ring.

Eventually she found two camerawomen and a soundwoman.

Betty Tells Her Story

Seldom in film does the warmth and human spirit of an individual come across as it happens here; seldom does a person reveal herself so honestly and openly.

—Patricia A. Black, *Film Library Quarterly*, Winter 1973.

One of the critical responses to Kate Millet's *Three Lives* was joy in having women, face to camera, describing their own lives. It was promising suddenly to have film—the medium through which we were bamboozled into wanting to be cutesy Doris Days or kewpie-doll Marilyn Monroes—give respect to real women. Suddenly credibility followed the disillusion of the fifties and sixties.

With *Betty Tells Her Story* the forthrightness and honesty of *Three Lives* is expanded. In Liane Brandon's film Betty tells her story facefront —only she tells it twice. The second time through the facts are the same but the story is different, more troubled and emotional. The newness of camera is gone and there is less effort to make the story entertaining.

Betty's story is simple, even ordinary. She bought a dress for the governor's ball, a dress that was far out of her price range. When she looked in the mirror and tried it on for friends, she felt beautiful for the first time in her life (and the last, apparently). Pathos surrounds the telling because Betty is plain and overweight. Moreover, she lost the dress without even wearing it.

Betty, whose whole life must be haunted by size-five models in perfect dress, bearing, and setting, unwittingly gets to some rather ugly realities of our "beauty culture" when she says:

There weren't too many times I had a chance in a lifetime to feel very special or noticed.

I had a feeling I lost more than the dress—I had lost the feeling that went with it and I knew that I would never have it again.

The film gives Betty undivided, uninterrupted attention with nothing but a slow zoom for camerawork.

Use *Betty Tells Her Story* with high school students through adults. It is particularly useful for psychology classes and college students. I asked students to describe the difference in the two tellings and to explain why the dress was so important to Betty. My students didn't react with the depth of Deborah Rose when she said:

I could see a reservoir of pain, deep pain which startled and frightened me. I wanted to look away. I thought a thousand different thoughts to avoid thinking about Betty. But I was drawn back into watching this woman, whose sincere, incredibly real presence defied all the stereotypes of movie personalities I had grown up with.

—Deborah Rose, *Second Wave.*

I did, and perhaps older students will too.

Betty Tells Her Story (1972): 20 mins., b/w; rental $25, purchase $200. Producer-director: Liane Brandon. Distributor: New Day Films.

SUGGESTED FEMINIST READING
DeCrow, Karen. *The Young Woman's Guide to Liberation.*
Egan, Andrea. *Why Am I So Miserable When These Are Supposed To Be the Best Years of My Life?*
Horney, Karen. *Feminine Psychology.*
Nunes, Maxine, and White, Deanna. *The Lace Ghetto.*

Black Girl

The role of the artist is not to say what is good, but to be able to denounce. He must feel the heartbeat of society and be able to create the image society gives him. He can orient society, he can say it is exaggerating, going overboard, but the power to decide escapes every artist.
—Ousmane Sembene to G. M. Perry and Patrick McGilligan, *Film Quarterly,* Spring 1973, p. 40.

Black Girl, a narrative film by the Senegalese director Ousmane Sembene, describes a young African woman's oppressions as a house servant. The film opens with her arrival on the Riviera, where she is to work as nursery maid for a French family that she had worked with in Dakar, Senegal. She soon realizes that she is expected to do all the housework and cooking. In a series of flashbacks you see how she first began to work for the family and her friendship with a university student.

Diouana's communication with her employers is limited to receiving orders. Unhappy as a servant and embarrassed to go home, Diouana commits suicide. The man of the household returns to Dakar to give her suitcase, a mask, and Diouana's salary to her mother. Her mother silently walks from him into her hut, refusing the money. Uncomfortably and guiltily he walks out of the black section of Dakar, followed by a young boy who wears the mask.

This mask, symbolizing the black identity of the colony, appears several times, setting the characters on a symbolic level as they identify with it, seize it, or discard it. The struggle between the colonizer and the colonized is symbolized in a fight over the mask between Diouana and her white mistress. Diouana had given it to the family, but took it back when she was fully aware of her slave position in their home.

It seems to me that Diouana's position as household servant is determined both by the French, who hire but do not respect her, and by her own culture, which does not educate her so that she might have alternatives in employment. Even if Sembene was not intentionally exposing this aspect of Diouana's oppression, it is clear when you study the film. You also see the limited alternatives for the white woman, who is characterized as the 'white bitch." Sembene uses this white housewife as the symbol for the white colonizer and oppressor—browbeating, demanding, selfish. (How ironic—I hadn't known that French women had so much political power that they should be used as the symbol of established and maintained colonial rule in Africa. Why the female figure? Is it like giving a car, a ship, or a hurricane a woman's name?) I see in *Black Girl* the frustration of limited horizons and expectations for both women.

In style, *Black Girl* shows the influence of the early films of the French "new wave" directors: real locations as opposed to sets, and direct, simple camerawork. In the confinement of the Riviera apartment, Diouana and the family are never seen without the physical restriction imposed on the camera by the four walls. The result is the appropriate feeling of restraint that reflects Diouana's feelings of oppression. The camera assumes Diouana's view. You not only see her thoughts and memories; you hear and see what she hears and sees.

The music alternates between African music and tinny bar music. For the most part the music is used in the appropriate location. But when you hear African music in a French scene, it aptly points up the difficulty Diouana meets in adjusting to her new environment and her failed expectations.

Black Girl is a powerful and effective narrative film. Use it with high school aged groups and older, citing the feminist points that have been made here. It would be a good film for black studies classes and classes that include African area studies.

Black Girl (1965): 60 mins., b/w; rental $75, purchase $650. Director; Ousmane Sembene. Distributor: New Yorker Films.

SUGGESTED FEMINIST READING
Beal, Frances M. "Double Jeopardy: To Be Black and Female." *Sister-hood Is Powerful,* pp. 340-353. Edited by Robin Morgan.
Cade, Toni (ed.). *The Black Woman.*
Leavitt, Ruby R. "Women in Other Cultures." *Woman in Sexist Society,* pp. 393-427. Edited by Vivian Gornick and Barbara K. Moran.

Ousmane Sembene

Photo Gordon Hitchens

Women have played a very important part in our history. They have been guardians of our traditions and culture even when certain of the men were alienated during the colonial period. The little that we do know of our history we owe to our women, our grandmothers.
— *Film Quarterly,* Spring 1973, p. 41.

Ousmane Sembene is now recognized as the father of African cinema. Born in 1923 in a village in Senegal, he was a fisherman, soldier, and dock worker before he started to write in the fifties. He became a writer of first importance with novels and short stories written in French.

In 1960 Sembene turned to filmmaking. He felt that film as an art form is more in keeping with the imagistic orientation of the African society. An apprenticeship in Moscow under the renowned Russian director Mark Donskoi prepared him technically. His films have won prizes all over the world, including the coveted Jean Vigo prize for *Black Girl.*

FILMOGRAPHY
Emitai (1972). Distributor: New Yorker Films. 101 mins.
Mandabi (1970). Distributor: Impact Films. 90 mins.
Tavw (1970). 27 mins.
*Black Girl (1966). Distributor: New Yorker Films. 60 mins.
Nyaye (1964)
Borom Sarret (1963). 19 mins.

The Cabinet

I liked that the daughter didn't live the same life as her mother. It helped me to understand that you don't live the same life as your mother.
—Karen Robertson, age 14

"It's all part of the American heritage," sings a voice in the middle of *The Cabinet*. And indeed this film is a record of an American heritage, the heritage young girls receive from their mothers. *The Cabinet* defines this heritage as Bauman received it from her mother, with all the oppressive forces that women across America have come to identify and express through consciousness-raising groups, psychotherapy sessions, and friendships.

The film sorts out the feelings that Suzanne Bauman has come to realize in her mother. It also indicates the ways that her mother's oppressions influenced the filmmaker. The tools of this expression are the still pictures of her parents' courting and marriage, some recent home movies of her parents, and the animation of Suzanne's childhood dolls. For much of the film the dolls are animated and take on the roles of the characters of the family—an appropriate technique since children use dolls to act out family life as they see it, or would like to see it. Suzanne uses these dolls to replay her early family experiences as she sees them now, in the light of her raised consciousness.

As an example of how the various visuals are mixed, consider the way Bauman now sees her mother's wedding. First there is a close-up of the middle-aged mother's eye going out of focus. As the screen comes into focus, you see a medium shot of a group of dolls, including a few religious statues. A nun doll enters and bows before the Christ figure. A Pinocchio doll enters, his cap twirling, and he jumps on the nun doll. Close-ups of the nun's face show her eyes blinking as the sound track says over and over, "Stop it, stop it." Thunder and rain sounds accompany stills of her parents as a young couple. These fade out and there is a fade-in on a photograph of an infant. Thus Bauman recounts her mother's first experiences of sexual intercourse—the wedding night that was anticipated without knowledge or experience, the impassioned husband and the frightened bride. (And hasn't it been this way for many women?)

Throughout much of the film, the filmmaker expresses anger at men. But her anger is perceived less as, "I hate you" and more as: "I see how I have been treated and how it has affected me. I have to express it, objectify it, so that I can try to understand my feelings and overcome the effects of this kind of relationship." Certainly our culture, the roles we play, and our marriages have been unhealthy and unhappy for men too. But Bauman hasn't time for that here. Besides, she isn't the person to make that film.

The Cabinet requires at least two screenings and much discussion. For my students and me it was worth the effort. The closer your experiences as a young girl and growing woman come to the experiences of Suzanne Bauman and her mother, the quicker you will understand the images and pick up the tone of the film.

27

I would suggest showing *The Cabinet* and *Wednesday's Child* together, or in the same unit. In *Wednesday's Child* Janice cannot integrate the elements of her personality. She is torn between her mother's image of her and her own inclinations. Suzanne Bauman, on the other hand, has been able not only to detach herself from her family and become independent, but she has gone on to review that past, to understand the ways in which her childhood influenced her. She goes even farther and shows how her mother came to the unhealthy and unhappy state that she was in with Suzanne's father. The kind of insight and consciousness-raising process that Suzanne exhibits in *The Cabinet* could have been the saving grace for Janice in *Wednesday's Child*.

The Cabinet (1972): 14 mins., color; rental (apply); purchase $175. Filmmaker: Suzanne Bauman. Distributor: Carousel Films.

SUGGESTED FEMINIST READING
The Boston Women's Health Book Collective. *Our Bodies, Our Selves.*
Chesler, Phyllis. *Women and Madness.*
Herschberger, Ruth. *Adam's Rib.*
Horney, Karen. *Feminine Psychology.*
Miller, Jean Baker (ed.). *Psychoanalysis and Women.*

Suzanne Bauman

Photo courtesy of Carousel Films, Inc.

In the midst of commercial ventures, otherwise known as paying work, a little voice from the world of my dreams keeps nagging: "Make your own films, personal statements, be a poet with the medium." "Shut up, I'm busy," I want to reply. But I'm in this field for love of the art, after all, and usually the integrity of the art is the first thing sacrificed in this business. . . . Do I ever wonder why I make films? All the time. Like right now. Maybe I should have stuck with sculpture. Stone lasts longer than Kodak original. I could be making marble caryatids . . . oh well, they're probably as hard to finance as features these days.

—response to questionnaire, July 1973.

Suzanne Bauman was born on Long Island in 1945, the only child of lonely parents. They moved a lot, so that she attended six public schools before going to Vassar College. By the time she graduated, she was scholastically prepared for graduate school in English Literature or Art History and was somewhat trained as a painter and sculptor. However, after seeing Fellini's *8½*, she decided that she wanted to make films. At New York University's Institute of Film and TV she became a film fanatic and has remained one ever since.

Button, Button was her first experience with stop motion. This technique attracted her because it was cheap and provided instant magic. "Anything, a doll or a button or a puzzle or the furniture in a room can come alive and take on personality. As an animator, I'm like an actress assuming the role of whatever I'm moving."

After making several educational films for ACI, Bauman has been working through Suzanne Bauman Productions and with Gene Searchinger at Equinox Films ("where off-beat documentaries and good will predominate"). She has collaborated with Searchinger on *Manhattan Street Band, Fantasy and Fugue: Rosalyn Tureck Plays Bach*, and her more current projects.

FILMOGRAPHY

The Intruder (in progress), approx. 40 mins. Drama: "a young woman is awakened in the middle of the night by a strange man standing in her doorway.... through her mind flash one thousand unsought memories of facing the unknown."—S.B.

Project for National Park Service (in progress). Film showing how petrified forest in Arizona became that way.

Film about Velasquez (in progress). Portrait of Pareja.

"Sesame Street" films (1972-73). Short animated pieces.

Fantasy and Fugue: Rosalyn Tureck Plays Bach (1972). One-hour special for CBS.

*The Cabinet (1972).

Manhattan Street Band (1970)

Why the Sun and Moon Live in the Sky (along with several other educational films for ACI).

Button, Button. Theatrical short about the campaign and novelty button craze.

The Father. Half-hour modern adaptation of Chekhov's short story. Started under N.Y.U. Institute of Film and TV; finished under grant from American Film Institute.

*Reviewed in this book.

Childbirth

The experience of childbirth is an important one—and should be a positive one as well—for those of us who decide to have children. For some of us it is the first time in our lives we are in touch with all parts of our body. And when we are prepared, it is an experience which demands that our minds and bodies work together and therefore an experience 29

that helps us break out of the mind-body separation that keeps 'women in their place.'
—Nancy Hawley, "Prepared Childbirth," *Our Bodies, Our Selves*, p. 107.

Childbirth is the only film reviewed here that documents a hospital delivery. An eerie musical score emphasizes the strangeness of hospital equipment and the robed, masked staff. The music also reflects on the other-worldliness of those few hours of the unknown that are special, frightening, and unpredictable in the lives of women.

Another contrast of this birth film with the others reviewed here is the absence of the husband-father. This film emphasizes the aloneness of the mother and her expectation of her child. The film opens with a woman walking a small child through deep rooms to a window. The labor scenes are interrupted with scenes of the infant on the mother's flat stomach. After the child's birth the film cuts to shots of the mother sitting, rocking the child; then, walking with the child in fast motion.

The final shot is of the hospital nursery shade being drawn. At the same time that the film explicates the exclusiveness of mother-child relationships, it points out the strangeness and impersonal aspects of hospital and nursery.

Visually strange, yet emotionally realistic, Amar's film is a powerful birth film and can be used interestingly in combination with films of home births.

Childbirth (1968), 10 mins., b/w; rental $15; purchase $100. Director: Maurice Amar. Distributor: Grove Press.

SUGGESTED FEMINIST READING
The Boston Women's Health Book Collective. *Our Bodies, Our Selves.*

Cleo from Five to Seven

In France the hours from five to seven are the time for rendezvous. If someone asks to make an appointment with you between these hours, the intention is clear.

In Agnes Varda's film, Cleo is having a rendezvous with herself, a self that may soon have to face death. For from five to seven are the last two hours that she has to wait before she will receive the verdict from her doctor on whether she has a fatal case of cancer. Cleo, as the film clearly shows, sees herself as the world sees her—a spoiled child. The typical lush blond popular singer, she is coddled by everyone. She even has a female companion, non-threatening in her ordinariness, comforting in her adoration, and helpful in her constant picking-up. "She has everything," says the companion, "but she needs to be comforted like a child."

The viewer is forced to wait, as Cleo must, the exact eighty-six minutes that the film recounts. The film is broken up into chapters that announce each segment of time as Cleo will spend it. We are told every minute that has passed of her waiting and of our watching—for example, "Cleo from 5:13-5:18." This exact rendering of real time in film time intensifies the suspense.

What we learn of Cleo is increasingly depressing. Even though at the end of the film she says, "It doesn't bother me," you know that it does in fact bother her very much and that the only way she will face death is in the coddling way that a child is deluded and comforted. Her image of herself is based on the image created for her by her songwriter, manager, and public. She cannot face the destruction of that facade. "As long as I'm beautiful I'm alive—very much alive."

In this film Agnes Varda does what, to many, is the most brilliant job of her long career as photographer and filmmaker. As in *L'Opera Mouffe,* she shows the scene of the film through the consciousness of the persona, with its attending attitudes and tone. Thus in *Cleo* there

is a constant fluctuation between the shocking realism with which Cleo views the world and the reflection of herself as a beautiful woman. Everywhere there are mirrors and Cleo avails herself of them. Here it is a mirror in her room, there a shop window. Sometimes it is an inadvertent reflection, as she looks through a window. But always it is there—the view that she must maintain for herself and her public. At the same time, she is seeing Paris—its poor, suffering, plain people—in a view that seems to come for the first time. It is as if she is asking herself, "How can they be happy? They aren't beautiful." And then for other views, "How can they stand it? How can they live?"

As she walks along through a cafe, she plays one of her songs on the jukebox. No one listens. Some complain to one another of the loud noise. She walks in and out of the tables listening, watching. We first see her; then we see her view, slightly reeling as she weaves in and out toward an empty table. Her vision rests on fat women with children on their laps, lovers with blank expressions, and old women who gape at her. Finally she sits next to a pillar of mirrors, little rectangles of mirror broken to fit around the pole.

The metaphor is clear: To see herself in the face of death, to see   31 herself in any perspective other than that of a beautiful woman, adored and loved by all, is to destroy her image of herself, to break up the mirrors. "When I think, which is seldom, I only have questions. Today everything is new, faces of others and mine."

As the minutes tick on, she goes to visit a friend who is a nude model for sculptors. This brief scene is the kind of moment in film that could come only from the camera of a person conscious of the exploitation of women in the arts. The camera, as Cleo's view, enters the studio and passes through a room of sculpture on the way. As the camera progresses it looks through the legs of reclining nude figures. Then we see artists chiseling away at blocks of stone, creating life-size statues, and there in front of them is the soft form of a nude woman. When Cleo later asks her friend how she can model nude, she says she doesn't think about it. "Besides," she says holding up a handful of bills, "I get paid."

Cleo gets more disturbed and finally goes to the park. There she sees children in a playground, swinging as she does on her own apartment swing. She then does a musical number of the "Stairway to the Stars" variety down the long set of stairs to a lower garden. There she is "picked up" by a soldier who must go back to Algeria that night. Evidence that she is no more mature, no less dependent than at five o'clock is that she finds her support from this soldier who refers to all the mythological and romantic connotations of her star name, Cleopatra, and her real name, Florence. Hand in hand with one more person who will support her painted self, Cleo accepts the news that her doctor will give her two months of radiation treatment and see what happens, a clear diagnosis that there is nothing that he can do.

Music is used very ironically. In a Judy Garland tradition Cleo sings a sad new song. As she starts to sing, the background is darkened, the camera comes in for a close-up, a full orchestra breaks out of the piano, and histrionically she sings, "Dead, alone and ugly without you, without you, without you . . . All my love is dying. There is no love to replace it." And when she finally comes to the park to "commune with nature," symphonic music accompanies her stroll. These are the contrivances of the musical-comedy melodrama that are appropriate to a woman who was brought up to see herself in those terms and is comfortable only in that cinematic, Technicolor illusion.

Although Cleo is not a positive image for women, she is a realistic one—an image of a woman who has been so manipulated and conditioned, used by her culture, that she truly cannot live, thus clearly cannot die.

Use this film with college and adult groups. Since it is entertaining and feature length, it makes a good festival film.

Cleo from Five to Seven (1962): 90 mins., b/w; rental $50. Director: Agnes Varda. Distributor: Contemporary Films/McGraw-Hill.

SUGGESTED FEMINIST READING
Alta. "Pretty." *Woman in Sexist Society,* pp. 35-36. Edited by Vivian Gornick and Barbara K. Moran.

Greer, Germaine. *The Female Eunuch.*

Horney, Karen. *Feminine Psychology.*

Oakley, Ann. *Sex, Gender and Society.*

Stannard, Una. "The Mask of Beauty." *Woman in Sexist Society,* pp. 187-206. Edited by Vivian Gornick and Barbara K. Moran.

Agnes Varda

The image of women is crucial, and in the media of movies that image is always switching between the nun and the whore, the mama and the bitch. We have put up with it for years and it has to be changed. It is the image that is important, not so much who is making the film. However, if men are not ready to change the image of women, the women will have to make films to change it. But everybody, men as well as women, has to participate.

—to Barbara Confino, *Saturday Review,* August 12, 1972.

Born and reared outside of Paris, Varda currently lives on the Left Bank with director Jacques Demy. She has been making films since 1954. Varda admits that even after she felt "strong and complete and liberated" she was still "buying a lot of the ordinary clichés." That has changed, however, and her most recent films reflect her raised consciousness. *Mon Corps est a moi,* her most recent effort, is a humorous feature film about France's abortion laws.

About women directors Varda has said:

You ask me, is it difficult to be a woman director? I'd say that it is difficult to be a director period! It's difficult to be free; it's difficult not to be drowned in the system. It's difficult for women, and it's difficult for men, the same way. We have a lot of women in the French film industry—a lot of producers, a lot of assistant directors, and most of the editors (85 percent) are women. Women hold a lot of positions; it is in terms of consciousness that we have not got it right.

—to Barbara Confino, *Saturday Review,* August 12, 1972.

FILMOGRAPHY

My Body Belongs to Me (in progress). Feature-length narrative.

Lions Love (1971), 115 mins.

Black Panthers—A Report (1969), black and white, 26 mins. Distributor: Grove Press.

Loin de Vietnam (1967). Anti-war. Varda directed a segment of this film with Resnais and Godard.

Les Creatures (1966). Feature film.

Le Bonheur (1964). Feature film.

Salut Leo Cubain (1963). Short film.

* *Cleo from Five to Seven (1962),* 90 mins.

* *L'Opéra mouffe* (1959), 19 mins. Semi-documentary.

Uncle Janio (1958). Short film.

O Saisons O chateaux (1957). Short film.

La Pointe-courte (1954-55). Feature film.

*Reviewed in this book.

Cover Girl: New Face in Focus

The American Woman's Fantasy may have begun a long time ago with the Declaration of Independence. America renounced its allegiance to the British monarch, but it was replaced with a devotion to Pickle Princesses and Auto Parts Queens. Now, only God and the rhinestone-tiara manufacturers know the full extent of the American aristocracy of orthodontia and uplift bras. But we are all pretenders to the throne, and very few of us can't sing along with Bert Parks when he oozes once again: "There she is, Miss America/There she is, your ideal . . . ."
—B. J. Phillips, "The Beauty Queen," *MS.*, September 1972, p. 35.

I'd walk down the runway in those swimsuits, and I'd see all those women with rollers in their hair, their children all around them, looking at me, gritting their teeth, hating me. They had to believe there was some idealized existence, some perfect life, and that I was living it. I'd feel so much sympathy for them. Afterward, when I was signing autographs, I would try to tell them that it wasn't true, it wasn't real, but they wouldn't believe me. They had to believe in the myth of the beauty queen. I was just another way that people used to run away from their problems, just another means of masking what is wrong with our lives. They needed the fantasy, but they hated me for living it.
—Wendy Long, Miss USA 1969-70, *MS,* September 1972, p. 37.

Fashion photographer Frances McLaughlin-Gill has made a documentary film on *Mademoiselle* model of the year (1968) Elaine Fulkerson—a project sponsored by Noxema ("Cover Girl" is their foundation makeup). But what Gill has produced is an amazing piece of double-edged documentary. At the same time that Noxema and modeling schools use *Cover Girl: New Face in Focus* for promotional purposes, many people (including the filmmaker), see it as an exposition of the ironies of the model-of-the-year position and, ultimately, of the ironies of being a woman in a culture that considers women as a beauty commodity.

Elaine is seen first in stills from grammar school and high school. Then she is seen in film, tearfully accepting her award as model of the year. "I was never elected as any kind of queen . . . the whole big scene was beautiful." Later you see her on the streets of New York with the two runners-up. In documentary footage you see them keeping appointments with the agency, then makeup, hair, and exercise specialists. Later Elaine is seen being dressed by Bill Blass and photographed by David McCabe. In these scenes I sensed the phoniness of these beauty culture attendants to Elaine. And since they know they are being filmed, that phoniness becomes accentuated. This masked attitude toward being filmed is in sharp contrast to the personality dynamics in documentary films where the process of filmmaking and the rapport between the filmmaker and subject make for more honesty and self-revelation, rather than adding one more level of phoniness.

Watching the film is akin to watching a Miss America contest with a raised consciousness. I came away from seeing it with feelings of nausea

and amazement. Nausea that because of our beauty culture so many of us are still wrestling with the order of things when dealing with the importance/unimportance of clothes, makeup, good figure. Amazement that Noxema, *Mademoiselle* magazine, Bill Blass, and particularly Elaine Fulkerson don't see the way it all really is.

Cover Girl: New Face in Focus documents the isolated big business of our beauty culture whose lipsticked, mirrored walls show surfaces which are accepted as real and then presented to us as models.

I haven't had a chance to screen *Cover Girl* for an audience, but after seeing it myself I would suggest it for late high school through adult.

Cover Girl: New Face in Focus (1971): 28 mins., color; rental $150.
Part of "The Best of the New York Festival of Women's Films."
Director: Frances McLaughlin-Gill. Distributor: New Line Cinema.
"The Best of the New York Festival of Women's Films" is a package
of films made by women, available through the distributor, New Line
Cinema. It includes *Crocus, Cycles,* and *Cover Girl: New Face in
Focus* (which are reviewed in this text) as well as *Opening/Closing* 35

by Kathleen Laughlin, *The Gibbous Moon* by Nancy Ellen Dowd, and *Commuters* by Claudia Weill (not reviewed here). *Cover Girl: New Face in Focus* is available only through this package.

SUGGESTED FEMINIST READING

Alta. "Pretty." *Woman in Sexist Society,* pp. 35-36. Edited by Vivian Gornick and Barbara K. Moran.

Shulman, Alix Kates. *Memoirs of an Ex-Prom Queen.*

Stannard, Una. "The Mask of Beauty." *Woman in Sexist Society,* pp. 187-203. Edited by Vivian Gornick and Barbara K. Moran.

Frances McLaughlin-Gill

Photo by Kathryn Abbe for *Glamour Magazine*.

Film work is a discipline, a madness, a challenge. There is nothing on earth that I would rather do. The camera gives visual form to the idea; it conveys the message, tells the story. In film, a turn of the head, a glance says more than a hundred words. The material from life around us, real and imaginary, is the source of emotional memory. The sound track, the editing, timing all these are important. Technique must not fall victim to the message.

—response to questionnaire.

Frances McLaughlin-Gill was born in New York City and spent her childhood years in Connecticut. She was trained first as an artist, working with Yasuo Kuniyoshi and Reginald Marsh, and received a B.F.A. degree at Pratt Institute. Photography, first a hobby, became a passionate pursuit when she was eighteen. She feels her early exposure to the films of the thirties was a strong influence on her later work.

In 1945 she won the Vogue Prix de Paris contest, a competition open to college seniors in the U.S. This led to a photography career. One year later, she was working full-time as a photographer at the Vogue studios of Condé Nast publications. Travel, beauty, personalities, fashion, family stories, and features of all sorts became her regular assignments.

In 1954 she opened her own free-lance photography studio in New York City, doing editorial and advertising assignments for magazines like *Glamour, Vogue, Town & Country, Good Housekeeping, New York Times, Seventeen, Elle, Life.* In 1964 she started a film unit, the FMG Production Company, working as a director and consultant. One year later she produced her first sixteen-millimeter documentary in black and white, *College,* for *Glamour* Magazine. In 1968, on assignment for the Noxell Corp., Ms. Gill produced and directed a sixteen-millimeter color film, *Cover Girl: New Face in Focus,* with camerawork by Juliana Wang.

Frances McLaughlin-Gill was married to Leslie Gill, the well-known photographer and originator of American still-life photography, who died in 1958. Their daughter, Leslie, is now sixteen years old.

Ms. Gill has two full-length projects in work, both to be shot in black and white, scheduled for production in early 1974. At the same time she is experimenting with the Super-8 camera for narrative documentary work.

FILMOGRAPHY

Miscellaneous TV-commercial work (1964-73). Photography and direction of film footage for various products (Johnson and Johnson, Ivory Soap, Banks, Lever Brothers, Revlon, Breck, Noxell Corporation, etc.).

* *Cover Girl: New Face in Focus* (1968), 28½ min. and 14½ min. versions. Revised 10-minute version (1970) also available.

College (1965), black and white, 16 mm., 13½ mins. Documentary for *Glamour* Magazine. Produced and directed by McLaughlin-Gill.

*Reviewed in this book.

Crash

If he knew something hurt me he would keep these things and use them later on . . . . The girls he dates are all mixed up and they need to lean on him . . . he needs to have a childlike woman that he can dominate.
                                        —Jan in *Crash.*

Crash presents Jan Summer, born October 3, 1950, in Elgin, Illinois. Sitting comfortably on a couch, Jan talks about herself, her boyfriends, her memories, and an abortion. The visuals that are intercut with shots of her add to the information on Jan. These shots are unrelated and frequently repeated. When they are repeated you are so much more informed about Jan that the images take on added meaning—just as Jan's experiences take on new meaning through her memory process. We see a staged scene of a group of young women in a hotel sitting room. They look severe and nervous. Eventually we realize that each is waiting for an illegal abortion. Later Jan, reflecting on her experiences with an illegal, expensive abortion, says how much better it is to have legal abortion and free contraceptive information available.

We see a young man, John, standing in the open. Later we see him by the water, in a stance and setting of freedom and independence which fits Jan's feelings about him. He is free; she is confined by fear of pregnancy and a future of kitchen and kids.

Jan is frank about her sex life and family background. Visuals show the contrast between where she is now and her childhood. There are shots of midwestern families leaving church in their Sunday best. The 37 icons of stained glass windows contrast with the icons of advertising in a magazine that one of the girls is looking through in the hotel room. They both have influenced Jan. But the icon quality of the advertising isn't obvious until that image has been repeated several times, with the church windows in between.

Technically *Crash* is fascinating—especially for its use of repeated images. Abramson also exposes the process of the film form. At the end of the film you hear "cut" and see a figure pass between the camera and Jan. After this Jan says, "The thing I admire most would be honesty and sincerity." The filmmakers are being honest and sincere, too, by exposing their form.

My classes enjoyed *Crash*. They appreciated Jan's modernity and openness. They also enjoyed the element of suspense as visual pieces developed significance and added meaning. A good biographical film. Use *Crash* with high school students through adult groups. Plan on showing it twice, with discussion in between.

Crash (1971): 18 mins., b/w; rental $25; purchase $150. Director: David Abramson. Distributor: Grove Press.

SUGGESTED FEMINIST READING
The Boston Women's Health Book Collective. *Our Bodies, Our Selves.*
Gutcheon, Beth Richardson. *Abortion: A Woman's Guide.*
Schulder, Diane, and Kennedy, Florynce (eds.). *Abortion Rap.*

David Abramson

I became involved with filmmaking because I had very strong feelings about the failure of love in our society (still do). Film is the way for me to cope with this.
—response to questionnaire.

When he was fifteen, David Abramson was making political films with Charles Guggenheim. As a student at the University of Iowa, he made *Girl on a Landscape*. Like *Crash*, it points up feelings of alienation and shifting values in contemporary life. A long-time admirer of Antonioni, Abramson finally tracked down the director for a job interview. Antonioni's reaction to Abramson's films was: "Work for yourself."

When funds are available, Abramson wants to edit several thousand feet of Jan Sommer (subject of *Crash*) shot in Sausalito, California, a few years after *Crash* was made.

FILMOGRAPHY

Columbia College (1973), 13 mins. What it is like to be going to Columbia College in 1973; response of students to diversity of New York; alienation.

Proud New Yorkers (1970), 22 mins. Peckham Production.

* *Crash* (1970), 22 mins.

Girl on a Landscape (1967), 21 mins. Alienated coed being hurt by Svengali-type boyfriend. Distributor: Grove Press.

Two Families (1961), 28 mins. Fund-raising.

Duster (1957). Satiric western set in Ladue High School (suburban St. Louis); barroom beauties in the snack bar.

*Reviewed in this book.

Crocus

Though the story line of *Crocus* is simple and familiar to most parents, I haven't seen it on the screen before. As a couple gets into bed together and become involved in lovemaking, a two-year-old voice rings out, "Mama, Mama." After giving baby a drink of water, mama 39 returns to papa and the lovemaking resumes, illustrated in lovely cut-outs of cucumbers, roses, birds, Christmas trees, and butterflies that go over the couple's heads and out the window.

Suzan Pitt Kraning's film is a fine example of a painter who, when turning to animation, hasn't sacrificed either art form for the other. On the contrary, she has used the one to enhance and develop the other. The painterly qualities of her figures and backgrounds—muted colors, homey patterns, selected details, expressive faces—are suitably displayed in the slow-moving, stylized animation of her cutouts. The almost staccato movements are timed to enhance the artwork, giving the viewer time to notice the details.

After the organ grinder music for the credits, there is no music until the mama puts on the radio as she comes back from getting a drink for the baby. The only other sounds are giggles and sighs from the lovers and the child.

Kraning indicates the autobiographical quality of the film by showing a double of the woman in the bed taking a picture from the mirror. Then as the last fantasy cutout comes out the window, the view is suddenly from the outside and the shades of the room are drawn. Our view of Kraning's private life is interrupted.

Crocus is a fine animated film. I would use it with high school classes through adult groups, for it shows the passionate, yet warm, attitudes of the partners toward one another. At the same time, it admits the place of parental responsibility within that scheme. This film is particularly suitable for classes in sex education and family living.

Crocus (1971): 7 mins., color; rental $12; purchase (apply). Director: Suzan Pitt Kraning. Distributor: Canyon Cinema. (Also available as part of "The Best of the New York Festival of Women's Films," New Line Cinema; see *Cover Girl* annotation.)

SUGGESTED FEMINIST READING
Bernard, Jessie. *The Future of Marriage.*
de Beauvoir, Simone. *The Second Sex.*
Friedan, Betty. *The Feminine Mystique.*

Suzan Pitt Kraning

Minneapolis Star and Tribune

I always have more ideas than I can actually see realized. My brain is constantly conjuring up fantasies and I am running after them trying to catch them.
—*Minneapolis Tribune Picture Magazine,* February 18, 1973, p. 31.

Suzan Pitt Kraning's animated films are being shown and enjoyed all over the world. Like many animators, Kraning was first a painter. She studied art in the midwest and was a painting instructor in Detroit and Des Moines. Eventually she decided that she wanted to see her pictures move, and so she became involved in filmmaking. Later she taught filmmaking in Minneapolis at Walker Art Center, in the public schools, and at the local colleges.

Kraning has won many scholarships and awards and is frequently invited to present one-artist shows and to participate in festivals. When her work was criticized for erotic content, her reaction was:

Sex is just as worthy a topic [to film] as any other . . . pornography is boring and crass; there is nothing at stake other than making money . . . . However a film of people making love to each other because they love each other is entirely different.
—*Minneapolis Tribune Picture Magazine,* February 18, 1973, p. 23.

FILMOGRAPHY

Whitney Commercial (1972), color, 16 mm., 2½ mins., sound. Animated film commissioned by the Whitney Museum, New York City.

Cels (1972), color, 16 mm., 6 mins., sound. Animated film directed by Kraning and made with students at Minneapolis College of Art and Design.

A City Trip (1972), color, 16 mm., 3 mins., sound. Directed and animated this film made with children's drawings.

* *Crocus* (1971), color, 16 mm., 7 mins., sound. Animated film.

Bowl, Theatre, Garden, Marble Game (1970), color, 16 mm., 7 mins., sound. Animated film.

Cleaning, Giving Birth, Trying to Dance and Not Being Able To (1969), black and white, 16 mm., 3 mins., silent. Animated film.

Walker Art Center (1968), color, 16 mm., 23 mins., sound. A commissioned work documenting the collection, history, and philosophy of the art center. Produced by Walker Art Center.

All the above films available for rental from Canyon Cinema.

*Reviewed in this book.

Cycles

Terror is an integral part of the oppression of women. Its purpose is to ensure, as a final measure, the acceptance by women of the inevitability of male domination. The content of terror includes the threat of death, destitution, and/or inhuman isolation for the female . . . . There is no sign that designates a rapist since each male is potentially one.
—Barbara Nehrhoff and Pamela Kearon, "Rape: An Act of Terror,
Notes from the Third Year: Women's Liberation, p. 79.

The fear and nightmare of being raped or otherwise physically abused is a familiar trauma for women in a culture where the sexual exploitation of women is a common attitude. *Cycles,* a dance film, shows a nightmare of rape. The female dancer's fright and physical violation by a group of men are dramatized by the forceful, harsh movements of the dancers; the quick cuts from one shot to another; the luscious, deep shades of red, purples, yellows; and the discordant sounds of a moog synthesizer. The shots that isolate parts of the intertwining bodies are particularly frightening, since frequently you can't visually arrange the fast-moving parts into the total picture.

As the protagonist is being raped, men are seen floating into the warm red of a womb. Next we see a large pregnant body, then the woman in a body-sized plastic womb. She struggles determinedly, but hypnotically to break through to the outside—to be reborn. This sequence is particularly involving for the viewer because the camera shows this struggle not only from outside the membrane but also from within the womb, as if the viewer were the woman. When she finally breaks through, the woman ascends again and again in a repeated shot.

Cycles is disturbing and beautiful. For me it produced a catharsis, expressing deep fears of physical abuse and the strong primal desire to return to the sea, the womb. Use *Cycles* with mature audiences.

Cycles (1971): 10 mins., color; rental $15; purchase $150. Director: Linda Jassim. Distributor: Creative Film Society. (Also available as part of "The Best of the New York Festival of Women's Films," New Line Cinema; see *Cover Girl* annotation.)

SUGGESTED FEMINIST READING
The Boston Women's Health Book Collective. *Our Bodies, Our Selves.*
Notes From the Third Year. "Men and Violence" (pp. 39-43); "Rape: An Act of Terror," by Pamela Kearon and Barbara Mehrhof (pp. 79-81).

Linda Jassim

Photo by Joan Churchill.

At first it was difficult to accept the idea that I could be a director. I felt very isolated as a woman as I tried to fit myself into the male-authori-

tarian, competitive-director role. That didn't work. I soon found several talented and technically trained women with whom I could work in a different way. We were all more equal—and although there is a director, she is human, allowed to make mistakes, not the whip-cracking, aloof, ego-centric sort of director. We all worked together as a family, more of a unit. From several of these experiences now, on both student films and professional films with all women crews, I have devised a way of working with women and men that tries to eliminate the competitive atmosphere, where everyone is working for the good of the film. This comes in the selection of certain types of people—people that have a sensibility similar to my own.

—response to questionnaire, June 1973.

Linda Jassim's interest in filmmaking grew out of her work as a ballet dancer and still photographer. ("I wanted to express my emotions, feelings in a purely visual way—through movement.") An eight-millimeter film class got her started. Then she earned her B.A. in cinema at U.C.L.A. and partially completed an M.F.A. in cinema.

She is currently making a documentary film on a prostitute (under the sponsorship of an AFI grant). Of this work Jassim says, "I followed her around on film for several months, becoming close to her on film and in real life. I want to show—from her point of view—the feelings and experiences she lives with, being a hooker!"

FILMOGRAPHY
Documentary about young streetwalker (in progress).
* *Cycles* (1971), 10 mins. Experimental film.
For sales of Linda Jassim's films, contact filmmaker directly. (See list of distributors.)

*Reviewed in this book.

Dirty Books

Dirty Books opens with a blue screen and a narrator reading pornography. This is not, however, the blue movie you might expect. In the first shot you see it is the voice of a young woman and that she is reading the pornography to two pre-school children. There is a cut to home movies, obviously of the porno reader as a child herself. Now the voice-over tells that she really doesn't like writing porno. A seedy male voice (the porno voice of the credits) reads an erotic scene as Ellen types it. While the voice gets more and more excited, you see the author checking porno literature for ideas, referring to a list of porno terms, and typing. Finally, at the climax of the porno scene, she falls exhausted on her typewriter. The telephone rings. As the voiceover of the call asks Ellen to come to California to work on a small magazine, you see her sick in bed, cuddling a stuffed animal. "You can cook, can't you?" the telephone voice asks.

As the film continues, the dilemma that faces Ellen in choosing between going to California or staying in New York is developed. The 43 questions that come up in making the move are clarified in scenes with her father, her friends, her boyfriend. "I can't believe I was going to stick around here for that hippie," she says.

The sound is unusual in that you hear Ellen's voiceover constantly interrupting itself as she tries to work out her problems. This—mixed with the porno voice, dialogue with her friends, and some guitar music— is always in balance or contrast with visuals from the old home movies, black and white sequences with her friend in the park, and a sequence with her father in his hotel room.

Dirty Books is a very funny movie. One of the funniest scenes is of Ellen describing her parents' reaction if they found out that she was writing pornography. Her voiceover, accompanying sequences of home movies of her childhood, takes on the frenzied tone and simple-sentence structure of pornography.

This film gives us a chance to see a young woman making decisions on her own life, in the reality of the indecisions that hassle many of us.

Some high schools may take exception to narrated pornography and quick flashes of photos and drawings from porno magazines. Certainly it is an appropriate film for the college and adult level, where the questions that we face at each change in our lives can be recalled, related, and explored.

Dirty Books (1971): 17 mins., color; rental $35; purchase (apply). Director: Linda Feferman. Distributor: Linda Feferman.

SUGGESTED FEMINIST READING
DeCrow, Karen. *The Young Woman's Guide to Liberation.*

Linda Feferman

Being a woman filmmaker has allowed for my film to be shown more now that there are so many "women's films" showings. However, I feel that this is discriminatory. I would like to be recognized as a filmmaker, not a woman filmmaker. If my films are good enough, they should be able to be shown as films, not just as a woman's films.

—response to questionnaire, Spring 1973.

Linda Feferman started making films in college. Now, only a few years later, she has an interesting group of films, independently made and distributed. Her latest project, a semi-narrative film on menstruation, is being done under a grant from the American Film Institute.

FILMOGRAPHY

Film on Menstruation [untitled at time of publication] (1973-74). Educational film that describes not only the hormonal-medical aspects of menstruation, but also presents good attitudes. Includes animated how-it-happens segments, explores myths, and has humorous narrative structure.

* *Dirty Books* (1971), color, 17 mins., narrative.
* *Happy Birthday Nora* (1970), black and white, 6 mins., narrative.
* *Park Film* (1969), black and white, 2 mins., narrative.

*Reviewed in this book.

Dream Life

The film has no aim of revolution, but if it could give women an idea or two, that would be a good aim.

—Mireille Dansereau.

Isabella and Virginie, both in their twenties, work together in a film company and become close friends. The joys and fun of their friendship and shared times are refreshing. As I watched their good times, I realized how little I had seen women in film having genuine, satisfying times without men. Virginie enjoys herself as she eats her lunch alone on the roof of her building, runs along a street, or watches children play stickball. On a picnic, Virginie and Isabella dash through a cemetery, have lunch in the nude, and then have a fine time swimming and playing in the water.

They share their dreams too—joining in one another's fantasies. The fantasies are mostly based on Isabella's dream of Jean-Jacques, a married man from the film studio. Isabella dreams of the four of them—Virginie, Jean-Jacques, a child, and herself. Later Isabella frees herself from her obsession for Jean-Jacques enough to say that she doesn't care how long it lasts; she just wants to be his lover and have his child. After all, she and Virginie will raise the child. Her fantasies of Jean-Jacques are intercut with fantasies of herself with her father, of her as a young girl offering herself to Jean-Jacques, and of her as a six-year-old raising her dress and licking her lips.

Finally Isabella gets up her courage and calls Jean-Jacques. In the style of slick advertising, the two of them are shown walking arm in arm, looking in shop windows, sitting in a cafe, and finally in bed—all of this to appropriate Mancini-type music.

The lovemaking cuts to a silent shot of the two nude figures in bed, under the sheets, looking mildly bored. "I'm worn out lately," says Jean-Jacques, "better make it another time." When Virginie comes in, Jean-Jacques is embarrassed and covers his crotch as he goes to dress. It is all very funny and truly liberating for Isabella. After he has left, she shouts, "He's a fake. Now I'm free. I'm through with dream life." The girls then tear off all the slick-magazine-ad pictures around the flat. As the images are torn away, the credits for the film appear on the white wall.

At the same time that the film is fun, it relates troubling fantasies particular to women. Isabella's desire to repeat her relationship with her father through a lover is reiterated in her dreams. Home-movie shots of her as a little girl with daddy are intercut with her sexual fantasies of Jean-Jacques. The image of the six-year-old raising her dress is repeated several times. In one longer sequence she is dressed as a little girl and Jean-Jacques becomes her father.

There is little to laugh at except (perhaps nervously) when Isabella is "excessed" from her job. She is the one to go because she is young and female. The boss says, "For a woman it is not all that important. I'm sure you'll find a husband without any trouble." It is hardly funny when you see nude women audition for a modeling job in front of a fully clothed man, complete with hat, sunglasses, and a cigar.

Nonetheless, *Dream Life* isn't an angry film. It gaily pulls at the myths that Madison Avenue promulgates, and it is basically a lot of fun.

I haven't had an opportunity to screen *Dream Life* for an audience, but I expect you might use it as an entertaining, yet provocative, film with mature high-school-age through adult groups.

Dream Life (1972): 80 mins., color; rental (apply to Faroun Films regarding U.S. distribution). Director: Mireille Dansereau. Distributor: Faroun Films.

SUGGESTED FEMINIST READING
de Beauvoir, Simone. *The Second Sex.*
DeCrow, Karen. *The Young Woman's Guide to Liberation.*
Firestone, Shulamith. *The Dialectic of Sex.*
Lessing, Doris. *The Golden Notebook.*

Mireille Dansereau

What I am saying is stop identifying with the images in Vogue *and* Elle, *stop making ideal images of what should be happiness. Work with reality . . . . You should always have images and myths, but from within. Not from men or newspapers. You should be in contact with your own imaginary world.*
—Mireille Dansereau to the *Gazette* of Montreal.

Mireille Dansereau makes French-language films in Canada. After completing an undergraduate degree in literature from the University of Montreal, she earned a master's degree in cinema and TV from the Royal College of Art in London. She became a filmmaker because "it was the most satisfying expression I found after dancing during several years." She never thought that being a woman affected her career until a London newspaper responded to her prize for *Compromise* with a headline that insisted, "Woman gets first prize" (underlining added).

Dansereau's current work, *Marriage,* is a portrait of four women and will be distributed by the National Film Board of Canada as part of a women's series, *En Taut que femme* (producer: Anne Claure Poirier).

FILMOGRAPHY
Marriage (1973), 90 mins. Four portraits of women interviewed by filmmaker.
* *Dream Life [La Vie revée]* (1972), 80 mins.
Markets (1970), 20 mins. Documentary on meat and fish markets in London.

Forum (1969), 60 mins. Video transferred onto film. Psychodrama with Steve Ben Israel from the "Living Theatre."

Compromise (1968), 30 mins. Dramatic film. Lack of communication and of love between a French girl and an English boy.

Moi, un jour (1967), 10 mins. Dramatic essay.

*Reviewed in this book.

Fear Woman

Fear Woman *is a good movie, but must be understood as one reaching for a goal and not already there. It isn't as we all would like it to be . . . . The dance of the young girl as she enters womanhood is enough to show change as being hard to come by, but what the other women are doing makes that change a slight easier.*

—Linda Bright, age 15.

I liked the way this film showed women's talents, not only in the house, but also in business and other important jobs. It helped me to realize that as I grow up to be a woman I'll expect to be treated with respect and equality and participate in any kind of business, disregarding my sex.

—Cornellia Francis, age 15.

United Nations TV, International Zone, offers *Fear Woman* as evidence that the women of Ghana are independent and forging ahead in the demand for equality. Shown as representatives are Esther Ocloo, the founder of a food processing plant and a consultant to the government on nutrition; Nana Lkosampa VI, chief of the community of Atwia, 70 miles out of Accra; and Mrs. Justice Jiagge, a Supreme Court Judge and one of the authors of the "United Nations Declaration on the Elimination of Discrimination against Women." Each of these women is seen and heard in close-up monologues and voiceover scenes at her work. A male narrator takes care of the rest of the sound, accompanied by appropriate Ghanaian music. Scenes with each woman are interwoven so that you meet each almost simultaneously. Their film portraits show not only a common strength and courage, but the strong individual character each possesses.

Some of the most effective and revealing footage is seen as a "background" for the narration—the street scenes, the marketplace, the village. In one sequence Esther Ocloo's red Mercedes goes into the distance, passing a village kept in the tradition of past centuries. The narrator frankly admits that the women interviewed do not have the average lot of Ghanaian women, that still the "awesome proportion of the world's drudgery falls on the shoulders of womankind."

Justice Jiagge reminds us that it took two decades of fighting by women in the UN to get the Declaration on the Elimination of Discrimination against Women to pass the General Assembly. She also makes the point that until women have political power they have no real strength or protection. The film shows that Ghanaian women do not have political power. When the chief meets with her council, they are all male. When Esther Ocloo goes to meet with the committee that runs her political campaign, all are male.

48

In one of the last sequences, we see high school students voicing their opinions on women's liberation. Only eight percent of the boys go on to high school and only two percent of the girls. Several girls are asked what they would like to do when they get out of school. "Dentist," "doctor," "teacher," come the replies. A few of the girls say that they think they could run a house and work too. After one of them says that she expects her husband to share in the running of the house, the off-camera interviewer asks a few of the boys what they think of that. "I want my woman to stay at home," says one. "I want a housewife," says another. One of the girls retorts, "If all women are of this mind [the last girl's] then the men aren't going to have anyone to marry."

The film closes with the scene of a young girl, encircled by her tribe, doing a dance that acknowledges her entrance into womanhood. As the camera zooms into a close-up of her young, beautiful face the narrator admits, 'The odds are stacked against her just because she is a woman."

Fear Woman, like the other two United Nations TV films *(Woman Up in Arms)* reviewed in these pages, is not a radical film. It was made to be understood by as many people as possible, so feel comfortable in using it with conservative groups.

Fear Woman (1971); 28½ mins., color; rental $11, purchase $260. Filmmaker: Elspeth MacDougall, International Zone, United Nations TV. Distributor: Contemporary Films/McGraw-Hill.

SUGGESTED FEMINIST READING
Beal, Frances M. "Double Jeopardy: To Be Black and Female." *Sisterhood Is Powerful*, pp. 340-353. Edited by Robin Morgan.
Diner, Helen. *Mothers and Amazons.*
Leavitt, Ruby R. "Women in Other Cultures." *Woman in Sexist Society,* pp. 393-437. Edited by Vivian Gornick and Barbara K. Moran.

Films About Women and Work

Films about Women and Work was planned as an hour-long documentary on "working mothers." As Kathleen Shannon interviewed the individual women, she began to see and feel the diversity of jobs that women hold and how their individual work situations affect and are affected by their families. Consequently she acted on what the material demanded and made a number of short separate films centered on the theme, mothers and their work.

These short films, as described below, are forceful in themselves, as each woman speaks with Shannon in her own home environment, with its attending physical force and demands (particularly of children). One irons, another sews, still another tends seven children. You rarely see the interviewer, but only hear her occasional questions. I sense that each woman feels comfortable with Kathleen Shannon, her questions, and the cameras. I never feel that the subjects are being exploited. What I frequently feel in these films is awe—awe at the power of our customs and role playing to impose so many hardships on women who must work or want to work outside the home as well as in it.

The brevity of each film leaves you wanting to see more—to know this person better, to look deeper into her problems, and possibly to talk about solutions. Since each interview ends, rather than being intercut with others, there is time at the end to discuss the films, exploring how the woman's information and feelings fit into what the viewer already knows and feels.

The films can be ordered in any grouping. There is a printed discussion guide—a road map of the series that will aid people in deciding what kind of package would be most appropriate for their purposes. Because of the separate packaging and simplicity of style, some of the films could be used from fifth or sixth grade on.

The descriptions below are written by the director-producer of the series, Kathleen Shannon. (Times are approximate.)

1. *It's Not Enough*—15 mins.

   Covers a wide range of "why women work outside the home" questions and their feelings about it; statistics about the average income of women, the number of women in the labor force who have young children, the astonishing number of those children for whom no regular care is available. It is the best film to start with in any of the various packages possible.

2. *Luckily I Need Little Sleep*—10 mins.

   The problems aren't discussed explicitly in this film, but quite a number are there implicitly. It is a monograph of a nurse, trained in Greece, who makes the point that life is easier for a professional woman there than in Canada. She works forty hours per week at her job, another sixty at home (she and her husband are doing full-time farming). Two quite conservative men have reacted, "He couldn't manage without her, though she could manage without him," and "I'd rather be him than her." I think the film can be useful in certain groups. It demonstrates the commitment most women have to their families.

3. *Mothers Are People*—7 mins.

   A research biologist feels this society has a long way to go in its attitudes toward women and children. She feels that in many respects, Canada is behind Jamaica.

4. *Tiger on a Tight Leash*—10 mins.

   The chairman of the language department in a Maritime university has three young children and faces the same mundane daily problems of all employed mothers: The babysitter quits suddenly, or one morning you get up and the children don't have any clean or mended clothes for school. She remarks that society still feels that women belong at home; that if they work outside of it as well, the situation is acceptable only if they do *both*. She feels that society has to take more responsibility toward children and suggests a model system that would benefit a number of groups.

5. *Would I Ever Like to Work*—10 mins.

   A deserted woman on welfare, the mother of seven children, will not be able to work until there is a subsidized day-care service nearby. Then, when her youngest is old enough to go (another two years), she will get off welfare and support herself and them. Her face shows that there's just a chance that she will last that long, and one wonders about the children too.

6. *'And They Lived Happily Ever After'*—13 mins.

   Deals with how people end up like the woman in *Would I Ever Like to Work*, how and why women don't grow up preparing themselves to compete in the job market. "I'll get married and everything will be all right" is not an attitude that equips one for life in the present world.

7. *The Powers That Be*—10 mins.

   Grace MacInnis talks about the lack of interest on the part of all levels of government in the whole question of the family and its well-being. The film ends with the message that unless groups of concerned citizens get together and make their wishes known, nothing will ever change (day-care legislation, etc.).

8. *The Spring and Fall of Nina Polanski*—4 mins.
Gentle animation about a housewife-mother. (Made by Louise Kerrigan and Joan Hutton for Kathleen Shannon.)

9. *The Glass Slipper Pinches the Other Foot*—15 mins.
A fun treatment of the breadwinner and houseworker roles when reversed.

10. *Aliette and Pierre*—15 mins.
Aliette is a secretary; her husband an engineer with an oil company. They are a conventional nuclear family with one great difference: Pierre takes a full half-share of household and family tasks. They and their three children work as a team. This has been one of the best received of all the films. Different people get different messages from it.

11. *Like the Trees*—15 mins.
A Metis woman describes the course of her life, during which she suffered discrimination, difficulties finding and keeping jobs, alienation, troubles with alcohol—the whole gamut. Then she spends some time time as an activist, helping others with court cases and treaty rights, but again finds that her traveling is keeping her from her children and changes are taking place so slowly. She begins to find her own identity as a Metis and goes with others back to a traditional tribal way of life.

12. *Extensions of the Family*—15 mins.
Here is a group of middle-class people who have pooled their resources and child-care functions. They see day care and their household as extensions of the family. They feel it could be possible to achieve a community which is an extension of the family.

13. *Our Dear Sisters*—13 mins.
A single woman with an adopted child is a performer and must travel a great deal. Whenever possible, she takes her young daughter and tries to find old people to care for her since she believes this society bankrupts itself by segregating the very young and the very old. A folk festival is the scene for part of the film, and it ends with a group of women singing, 'Where are our dear sisters?" with visual material reminiscent of the other films.

Films about Women and Work (1973): 13 films, prices and times vary (apply). Director: Kathleen Shannon. Distributor: National Film Board of Canada.

SUGGEST FEMINIST READING
Check for books with similar themes when ordering specific film.

Kathleen Shannon

Good films are made, I believe, by emulating the Eskimo sculptor who studies a rock until he understands the image waiting within it to be released, rather than the person who decides what he is going to sculpt and then proceeds to hack a rock until he forces it to conform to his preconceived idea.

—statement to National Film Board, 1973.

Kathleen Shannon was a high school dropout at a time "when it was assumed that only the absolute failures or shameful pregnancies dropped out." Like most of her contemporaries, she got into film by accident. Her opportunity came when she cataloged stock music for a small film company. By the time she left the company in 1956, she had edited all the music for over 100 films.

She has been working for National Film Board of Canada ever since, working her way up from sound editor to researching, writing, directing, editing, and producing her own work. Discrimination? Looking over the statistics in 1972, Shannon came to the conclusion that women film-makers of English-language films at the NFB made an average of $4,100 less a year than their male colleagues.

When asked why she works in film, Shannon responded:

"Because I've always done so—it's 21 years now. I don't have paper "qualifications" to do anything else. Maybe, in intellectual hindsight, one strong reason was that it was creative work not hampered by all kinds of academic ritual and lore (at that time). It was still direct, genuine, communicative activity, untrammelled by degrees and esoteric mystique (well, yeah, it did seem rather glamorous—one man wore a scarf and dark glasses at all times—but I think the real glamour was adult work).

—letter of July 1973.

FILMOGRAPHY
1970-1973
*Films about Women and Work. Research, writing, directing, editing, producing.

*Reviewed in this book.

Goldwood. Twenty-minute theatrical short. Memories of childhood in Northern Ontario wilderness illustrated in paintings compared with the reality thirty years later. Writer, director, editor. National Film Board of Canada.

I Don't Think It's Meant for Us. One-half-hour documentary on public housing made from the tenants' point of view. Researcher, director, editor. National Film Board of Canada.

For Boys Only Is for Girls, Too

Wonderful. I liked to look at how good Vicki can do things.
                                                    —Nicole Betancourt, age 5.

As I saw this film I knew exactly what a girl has to go through just because she is a girl. The ending is the part that had the most effect on me, because I'm sure that Vicki will not stay on that team because she's a girl. Her parents, her friends, and teachers will all pressure her into leaving the soccer team. The statement that she made, "Do you think I'll be as pretty as the new teacher when I grow up?" that statement is what every girl that has a traditional family thinks about. I've thought about it too, and I've decided that you can't make a good career by being beautiful.
                                                    —Maritza Cotto, age 15.

You will be just you.
Do what you want to do.
And I will just be me. —from the film.

Do you want a matinee for children in your film series? Are you having difficulty finding nonsexist materials for your children's literature course or a course in education? Are you sick and tired of films for children with wispy princesses and strong knights? *For Boys Only Is for Girls, Too*, a sixty-minute feature film from Czechoslovakia, is a film for you.

Vicki and her brother, both in the seventh grade, play soccer with a passion. When a famous player offers to coach their backyard team so that they can enter competition, Vicki is excluded because she is a girl. An unfortunate decision, since Vicki happens to be their best player. Unhappily she ends up watching TV, getting her mother to kick to her, and using a doll on a pail as a substitute goalie. School doesn't relieve her miseries, as the new teacher, a feminine model to the other girls, doesn't think girls (or boys) should play a rough game like soccer.

Eventually one of the boys is hurt in a game and Vicki, with shorter hair and a boy's medical card, is offered by the team as his replacement. Of course she wins the game for them and is the hero of the day.

Wisely, Vicki doesn't feel like a winner. She knows that if she had this much trouble just getting to play soccer, then being a girl is never going to be very useful. After the big game she sits morosely under a bridge, picking her fortune from a daisy. She counts off, "Marriage, husband, babies, bad luck, sorrow, disease, death, marriage ..."

Back home she asks her mother how she feels about being a woman. When the mother asks Vicki what is wrong, she says, 'Boys are taken a lot more seriously than we are." After her mother assures her that there are some nice things about being a girl too, Vicki asks her mother if she (Vicki) will ever be as pretty as the new teacher.

That last line limits the impact of the film, though it doesn't nullify it. It may be realistic to acknowledge the place of real role models that girls do have today. But why couldn't they be shown the growing number of exceptions? For instance, it is clear from his tools and the office work at home, that the father does drafting. But why are we never told, even visually, what the mother's outside job is? This and other weaknesses in the "feminism" of the film should be pointed out to students. I regret, for example, that Vicki cries twice, but her brother never does; that the girly girls are shown as gossipy shrews (at twelve?); and that Vicki is posed as smarter than her brother. And why doesn't Vicki have female allies, friends who feel as she does and help her?

On the other hand, I am delighted that Vicki's brother is compassionate with his sister and even offers to carry her silly purse on a family outing. And, though the mother and father don't share housework, the brother and sister do dishes together. In one scene the boys talk among themselves about how the competition rules that eliminate girls from the field are illegal.

As you might expect, the dubbing of this film is wretched. The visuals, though ordinary, are pleasant. I suggest that you start the projection after the credits, as they are dreadful.

Use *For Boys Only Is for Girls, Too* with children from five or six through adult groups. It is perfect for a family film night at the library.

For Boys Only Is for Girls, Too (1972, U.S. release): 61 mins., color; rental $30, leasing (apply). Director: Josef Pinkava. Distributor: Xerox Films.

SUGGESTED FEMINIST READING
DeCrow, Karen. *The Young Woman's Guide to Liberation.*
Moberg, Verne. *A Child's Right to Equal Reading.*
Nunes, Maxine, and White, Deanna. *The Lace Ghetto.*
Stein, Gertrude. *The World Is Round.*

Game

I think man is bigger and badder.
I'm a woman. He's a man.   —Tina, from the film.

Abigail and Jonathan Child, New York filmmakers, document two lives in the prostitution game on the lower east side of Manhattan. Through friends, the Childs met a prostitute and her pimp, with whom they first developed a friendship and whom they later filmed. The result is not a "document on prostitution," but a brief look at the personal lives of two people in the "game."

In the film you see the prostitute, Tina, dressing for the street, looking for "tricks," playing with two of her steady customers, and talking with her lover and pimp, Yogi-Slim. Slim says, "I tried being square and saw how hard I was hurting . . . . I got into the game strictly on the economic side." Tina says, "Slim's really together. I went with him three weeks before I knew he was a pimp . . . . I dig playing on men and getting their money." Tina and Slim are both physically at ease and comfortably verbal as they speak in voiceover narrations and directly to the camera in close-ups.

There is nothing big, bad, or ugly about Tina and Slim's game. It is small, short-lived, and ridden with risks. It is seen for what is is without editorializing by the Childs' camera or editing. As Slim's pimp friend says, "It's a way to make a lot of money without killing nobody or dealing no dope." Tina says, "If I can do it with a clear conscience, then it's cool . . . as long as I'm not hurting anyone then it's got to be cool."

There is a pride and searching in Tina, qualities that Abigail Child said continued to develop during the filming. As with other independently made documentaries reviewed in these pages, the experience of making the film was a growing process for both the subject and the filmmakers, a process that gives the film a feeling of honesty. You also sense that Abigail, Jon, Tina, and Slim were comfortable with one another. Before the shooting started Tina and Slim signed a contract with Abigail and Jon that they would share fifty percent of the profits after meeting the cost of the film.

Game gave me a chance to meet people I might otherwise never know. I feel that it should be used that way with high-school-aged groups and older. In a follow-up on the film, probe more into the social and economic inequities of the prostitution game (see "Who Pays for Prostitution," by Gail Sheehy, *MS.* magazine, June 1973, p. 59) and the ways in which it victimizes many people, starting with the prostitute.

Game (1971): 40 mins., b/w; rental $35, purchase $275. Directors: Abigail Child, Jonathan Child. Distributor: Radim Films.

SUGGESTED FEMINIST READING
Millett, Kate. *The Prostitution Papers.*
Strong, Ellen. "The Hooker." *Sisterhood Is Powerful,* pp. 289-297.
    Edited by Robin Morgan.

Abigail Child

My mother told me recently she always thought of herself as Cinderella and was very happy being that way. Some of her romanticism comes out in the film I made of her marriage at the age of sixty-three. Nonetheless I gasped when she told me, for I'm right in the middle of struggling to shed myself of those myths: to really know that there is no man, no role, no fairy-godmother that will suddenly step off the fire-escape outside my window and provide me with the life I want. The difficulty is a lack of role models for being a woman and a creative energy. If you're   57

not Cinderella, who are you? Who do you want to be? And will you live happily ever after? Does anyone? . . . There is much more to say, but I keep coming back to the core thing of taking responsibility for myself.
—response to questionnaire

Abigail Child received her B.A. in history and literature from Radcliffe in 1968 and an M.F.A. from the Yale School of Art and Architecture in 1969. Starting as a free-lance designer and photographer, Abbie Child soon found that what she really wanted to do was make movies.

She has experience in all of the technical aspects of filmmaking, having worked as a sound-person, camera-person, sound editor, editor, and so on. As director she does much of the technical work on her own films. Like many of the filmmakers whose work is reviewed on these pages, Abbie Child was awarded an American Film Institute grant. With it she is making *Angel Baby*, a half-hour dramatic film about a woman going mad.

FILMOGRAPHY
Will You Still Be a Mother (1973), 30 mins. Documentary for "New York Illustrated," WNBC. Writer-director.
Mother Marries a Man of Mellow Mien (1973), color, 7 mins. Documentary of mother's marriage, March 1973.
*Game (1971), 40 mins. Co-directed with Jonathan Child.
Except the People (1970), color, 20 mins. Documentary of East Village non-community. Shown at Film Forum, MOMA, The Whitney Museum. Excerpted for NBC News. Co-directed with Jonathan Child.
Alphabet Soup (1968). Animated class project at Carpenter Center, Harvard University.

*Reviewed in this book.

Jonathan Child

Every individual understands "reality" in his own way. The most interesting thing for me in documentary filmmaking is getting into someone
else's sense of reality and translating it into film in such a way that it

can draw a diverse audience into experiencing that potentially alien understanding of reality as "real," viable at least within its context, and more than something just to look at or judge.

—response to questionnaire

A Harvard graduate in architectural sciences, Jon Child is a free-lance photographer, musician, and filmmaker. As a recording engineer he has worked with The Band, Paul Butterfield, Linda Ronstadt, Howard Tate, and Valerie Simpson. As a cinematographer he has free-lanced at WCVB-TV in Boston and produced for Kenyon and Eckhart Advertising.

In addition to co-writing, directing, shooting, and producing *Game,* he performed the music for the film. Child's latest film is *Polka in the Park*—a documentary of the Susan Brody and Company dance troupe performing in Central Park.

FILMOGRAPHY
Game (1972), black and white, 40 mins. Documentary.
Except the People (1970), color, 20 mins. Documentary about East Village non-community. Distributor: TIME-LIFE Films.
Bartending HSA (1967), color. Promotional for Harvard Student Agencies.

*Reviewed in this book.

Gertrude Stein: When This You See, Remember Me

She provides an exemplary model for us all in her rigorous pursuit of her own individuality and creativity.
—Saunie Salyer in Women and Film magazine, Vol. 1, No. 2.

Gertrude Stein's individuality and creativity are recorded in her works. In media, however, she was recorded in only a few minutes of silent home movies and on some radio tapes. Not many of those with whom she lived and worked in the early years of the twentieth century are still alive. Perry Miller Adato has included the few that remain (or were living at the time of her filming) in this eighty-nine-minute biography-compilation film on the great Stein. Among them are composer Virgil Thompson, sculptor Jacques Lipchitz, writer Janet ("Genet") Flanner, publisher Bennett Cerf, and couturier Pierre Balmain. They tell their anecdotes which help fill in a background of the flourishing of the arts in the twenties and thirties in Paris.

The rest of the narration is culled from Stein's own writings and the written comments of her now-deceased contemporaries (among them Hemingway, Picasso, Matisse, Alice B. Toklas). During the film, the camera makes frequent reference to Stein's magnificent art collection, old photographs, newspaper clippings, and other cherished belongings. Two of her works are shown in production: Al Carmines's jazz-rock version of *In Circles* and *Four Saints in Three Acts,* an opera that Stein wrote in collaboration with Virgil Thompson.

The facts of the writer's life in the years between 1905 and 1930 are well documented here. Her relationship with her brother Leo is ex- 59 plained by their friends. As the art dealer Bailman says, "The great man of the family was Gertrude Stein." Her frequent arguments and broken friendships (with Hemingway, Picasso) are not ignored or glossed over. Adato skillfully edits all of these isolated materials by dissolves, pans, and zooms so that continuity and a sense of wholeness are always present.

Use *When This You See, Remember Me* with high school classes and older. It is particularly well suited for art, humanities, literature, and history classes. For people unaware of the importance of Gertrude Stein and the nature of her work, this is a good introduction that places her in an historical context. For those familiar with her works and with Paris between 1905 and 1930, this film provides a well-organized and sensitive reminiscence.

Gertrude Stein: When This You See, Remember Me (1971): 89 mins., color; rental (apply), purchase $850. Director: Perry Miller Adato. Distributor: Contemporary Films/McGraw-Hill.

SUGGESTED FEMINIST READING
Stein, Gertrude. *Selected Writings of Gertrude Stein. The World is Round.*
Wilson, Ellen. *They Named Me Gertrude Stein.*

Perry Miller Adato

I wanted to give people a cultural experience, an emotional experience, entertain them while I am learning something—and film is the only way to do this that interests me.

—response to questionnaire

Reared in Yonkers, New York, Perry Miller Adato first came to Manhattan to study acting. She worked in theater until the late forties, when her interest shifted to film. At the New School for Social Research she did three years of independent study in economics and social subjects. For many years she was a "documentary film expert," serving as a film coordinator for TV programs on CBS and for museums. She searched out films of a cultural, scientific, or social nature from all over the world to put on television.

In 1967 she finally made a film herself. It was the Emmy Award winner, *Dylan Thomas: The World I Breathe*. Since then she has been a producer and director for NET (National Educational Television).

In response to my question, "How has being a woman affected your career?"—Perry wrote:

I have two children, thirteen and sixteen years old, and I consciously held back for four or five years trying to be a producer or director . . . . I also doubted my ability to do all that this implied . . . . I was and still am constantly subject to conflicts between my duty to my husband and family and my responsibility to my work. I always feel I am skimping on one or the other or all. I also have been paid less than a man doing the same job would have received, until action by the woman's committee at NET prompted adjustments, and the success of my films forced management to raise my salary. Because I am a woman I felt reluctant to push for more money myself. I felt I was lucky just to be doing films.

FILMOGRAPHY
Film on Charles and Ray Eames (in progress).
The Great Radio Comedians (1972), color, 90 mins. The lost art of radio
comedy with all the greats. For NET.

Norman Corwin's 'Untitled' (1972), color, 20 mins. Documentary on radio drama. For NET.

*Gertrude Stein: When This You See, Remember Me (1971), color, 90 mins. Distributor: Contemporary Films/McGraw-Hill. For NET.

The Film Generation and Dance (1969), color, 60 mins. Work of four filmmakers who have done important work in the field of dance films (Norman McLaren, Shirley Clarke, Hilary Harris, and Ed Emshwiller). For NET.

Dylan Thomas: The World I Breathe (1968), black and white, 60 mins. The life and poetry of Dylan Thomas. For NET.

*Reviewed in this book.

The Girls

It is ruefully comic, like a majorette marching bravely down the street with a banner saying, "we the people" while turning to see if anyone is following .... The film's anger finally is directed not so much at inequality as at indifference; its call to arms is also a cry to despair, which has only its own echo to keep it company.
—Molly Haskell, Village Voice, June 29, 1972, p. 67.

As a Broadway and Hollywood star turned filmmaker with a feminist voice, Mai Zetterling knows well the ironies of being a woman in a culture that treats women as empty-headed, pretty things. *The Girls,* more than her earlier feature-length films (*Night Games* and *Loving Couples*), shouts angrily at the inequities of being a woman.

Three women go on tour with Aristophanes' play, *Lysistrata* (the story of Greek women who forced their men to sign a peace treaty by denying them sexual favors). From the start Zetterling indicates how closely the play is related to the lives of the actresses. The more the women get into practicing and performing the play, the more they see the oppressive situations of their personal lives. The lines of the play go through their heads as one has her hair done, another brings her dogs to be groomed, and a third buys makeup.

The more the actresses get involved in the play, the more they become aware that their audiences aren't relating to it the way they do. Yet *The Girls* doesn't resolve the issues of the actresses' oppression, for they are unsuccessful in applying the lesson of the Aristophanes play to their own lives. The film repeats the confrontation that occurs in the middle of the play when Lysistrata asks her audience to remain and talk about the play. "I thought that you'd like to talk about what we've seen . . . Is it possible to change the world? . . . Aristophanes wants us to stop thinking we're as good as we are."

No one responds, and so too the actresses don't really respond to the moral of the play, even though they have the impetus of intensive creative action to motivate them. The actresses (and possibly we) are too absorbed in guilt, comfort, and the attitudes of those around us to put our dreams into effect.

The further you get into the film, the more difficult it is to tell what is fantasy and what is real. In the end, when Lysistrata announces to her husband and the crowd at a cast party that she is getting a divorce, one doesn't know if she really said it, if she imagined it, or if she said it as an empty, ironic gesture.

The Girls is successful in many ways: the camerawork is lively; the story line absorbing; the politics complex. I was able to screen the film only once, but from that screening I feel that many people would find it interesting. It seems particularly suitable for students who are interested in comparative literature and women who have been involved in the women's movement. But consider Marjorie Rosen's warning:

The Girls *is self-conscious and self-indulgent in its repeated use of flashbacks, fantasies, and rhetoric; too often these tools distract and confuse. Yet it is rich, exciting political work that just may be trying to say too much too vehemently.*

—Marjorie Rosen, "Women, Their Films, and Their Festival," *Saturday Review*, August 12, 1972, p. 32.

The Girls (1972): 100 mins., color; Director: Mai Zetterling. Distributor: New Line Cinema (rental, classroom use: $100)

SUGGESTED FEMINIST READING
Bernard, Jessie. *The Future of Marriage.*
Davis, Elizabeth Gould. *The First Sex.*
de Beauvoir, Simone. *The Second Sex.*
Diner, Helen. *Mothers and Amazons.*
Ellmann, Mary. *Thinking About Women.*
Firestone, Shulamith. *The Dialectic of Sex.*
Millett, Kate. *Sexual Politics.*
Morgan, Elaine. *The Descent of Woman.*

Mai Zetterling

In Sweden we ban films of violence and war, not those which portray sex in life with honesty.

—to *N.Y. Times*, Sept. 15, 1966. 63

Swedish by birth, Mai Zetterling became a popular actress on the Broadway stage and the Hollywood screen in the fifties and early sixties. She made her Broadway debut as the tiger tamer in *Tonight in Samarcand* in 1954. After a move to England with her writer-husband David Hughes and her two children from a first marriage, Zetterling gave up acting and began collaborating with Hughes on five documentaries for BBC.

Her first feature-length film, *Night Games,* also appeared in novel form. When it was shown at the San Francisco Film Festival, Shirley Temple Black stormed off the panel in protest. With such lively critical review, Zetterling was motivated to go on to make *Loving Couples.* The acclaim for this film was widespread. (However, black and white posters advertising *Loving Couples* at Cannes were criticized for frontal male nudity and had to be modified.) Zetterling's most recent film, *The Girls,* is the angriest of the three.

FILMOGRAPHY

Visions of 8 (1973). Documentary on 1972 Olympics by eight international directors. Zetterling did portion on wrestlers.

*The Girls (1972). Feature length.

*Loving Couples (1964). Feature length.

Night Games (1963). Feature length.

*Reviewed in this book.

Goodbye in the Mirror

Do you know what you want?
Why did you come here?
Don't you know what you want?   —from the film.

I, myself, belonging to the Spies for Beauty, Inc., and the humble monk of the Order of Fools, was allowed to peek at this film, and I couldn't believe what beauty struck my eyes, what sensuousness.
                              —Jonas Mekas, *The Village Voice.*

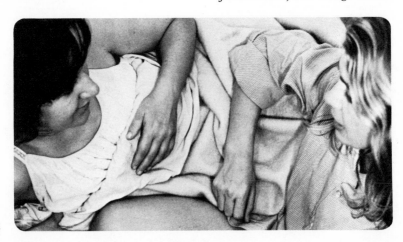

Goodbye in the Mirror, the only "narrative" film by avant-garde film-maker Storm De Hirsch, describes the lives of three single women sharing an apartment in Rome. Two of them, a Swedish singer and a British whore, rent rooms from Maria, an American who teaches English to Italian men. The story line is simple. Some may even find it slow-moving as it sets forth Maria's conflicts with her roommates, her hunt for a man, and her ultimate decision to refuse her knight in shining armor.

The tone of the film is satirically at odds with the musical-comedy myth of the *Three Coins in the Fountain/American in Paris* variety. Maria is not pretty or young. In fact, by popular standards the man whose marriage offer she refuses is handsomer and sexier than she. The girls aggressively and unabashedly go after their men, as opposed to being pursued by them. The camerawork is unconventional and the little bit of music is horrid. Maria sings "Oh, Marie" completely out of tune. The whore screams her song, "I wish I were a fascinating bitch instead of an innocent child."

The scenes of the film provide a pleasant view of Rome, particularly at night and in the rain. Through Storm De Hirsch's camera, I got a chance to see Rome with her sensuous, indulgent eye—off-angle shots, quick cuts, luxuriously long views of the streets, the tilting, moving views of a pedestrian.

I feel that *Goodbye in the Mirror* is a good film to use with college-age groups and older, groups interested not only in the women's liberation movement, but also in film as an expressive, changing art form.

Goodbye in the Mirror: 80 mins., b/w; rental $50. Director: Storm De Hirsch, 1964. Distributor: Impact Films.

SUGGESTED FEMINIST READING
de Beauvoir, Simone, *The Second Sex.*
Lessing, Doris, *The Golden Notebook.*

Storm De Hirsch

Photo by Louis Brigante.

Each film is for me a voyage into buried continents of the self, an exploration into out-of-bounds areas of no-time, new space.

—response to questionnaire

Storm De Hirsch, poet and filmmaker, is a leading independent avant-garde filmmaker. Her award-winning works have been presented at numerous international film festivals, art museums, and universities here and abroad. She was a recipient of the American Film Institute's first independent film grant in 1968. Over the past seven years she has been conducting lecture-screenings of her work at various universities. During this period she has also appeared as a guest filmmaker at seminars and symposia on film as a creative art form.

De Hirsch is the author of several books of poetry, including *Alleh Lulleh Cockatoo* and *Twilight Massacre*. A collection of her recent writings was scheduled for publication by 1974.

FILMOGRAPHY

River-Ghost [Hudson River Diary: Book IV] (1973), color, 8 mins. Reflections on a haunted area along the banks of the Hudson.

Wintergarden [Hudson River Diary: Book III] (1973), color, 5 mins. A seasonal study of colors and textures; rain, snow, and ice on the Hudson.

September Express (1972), color, 5 mins. (also available in Super-8). Rome to Venice; an experiment in time.

Lace of Summer (1972), color, 3 mins. (also available in Super-8). Impressions of Venice; still life and landscape on the Lido.

An Experiment in Meditation (1971), color, 18 mins.

The Tattooed Man (1969), color, 35 mins.

Third Eye Butterfly (1968), color, 10 mins.

Cayuga Run [Hudson River Diary: Book I] (1966), color, 12 mins. "The eye locks the lens, registers epiphanous moments in time, inscribes fragmented contemplations celebrating the seasons and the river Hudson."—S.D.H.

Sing Lotus (1966), color, 18 mins., silent (24 frames per second). With music of Manipur, Kashmir, and Nepal. "Eighteenth-century Indian miniatures enact a traditional wedding ceremony of a Hindu prince and princess. An exotic landscape of the mind; fable-fantasy images of childhood/manhood."—S.D.H.

Newsreel: Jonas in the Brig (1966), 5 mins., silent. A newsreel of Jonas Mekas shooting his filmed version of "The Brig" on the set of the Living Theatre production.

Shaman, A Tapestry for Sorcerers (1966), color, 12 mins. "For the magic makers of the world, those who enter the atlas of the soul and rummage through the refuse and flowers of time to weave a talisman for man's rebirth in his house of breath."—S.D.H.

Peyote Queen (1965), color, 8 mins. Music: Haitian voodoo drum ritual and electronic organ rock 'n roll.

Divinations (1964), color, 6 mins. Music: Ritual chant of Maori medicine man and Sicilian tarantella on a mouth harp.

66 *The Color of Ritual, The Color of Thought* (1964), color, 26 mins.

Trilogy including *Divinations, Peyote Queen, Shaman.* "A trilogy encompassing multiple voyages into buried continents of the self, exploring out-of-bound areas of no-time, new space."—S.D.H.

Goodbye in the Mirror (1964), 80 mins. (also available in 35 mm.).

Journey Around a Zero (1963), 3 mins. A phallic invocation; an abstract of image and sound. Photography by Giorgio Turi. Music by Storm De Hirsch.

*Reviewed in this book.

Growing Up Female: As Six Becomes One

Seeing Growing Up Female: As Six Becomes One *is one of those painful experiences that's good for you. With a minimum of comment, the film shows how female human beings are brainwashed into passivity, mental sluggishness, and self-contempt. I wish every high school kid in America could see this film.*

—Susan Sontag.

Growing Up Female *charts the channel from the nursery to the breakfast nook. The children, the black and white women, speak clearly and simply, while we, the audience, eavesdrop and learn about the mechanics of oppression they never name, but feel constantly. We are almost embarrassed that we can't warn them of what lies ahead. This is a unique and beautiful film and I strongly urge everyone—men and women—to see it.*

—Flo Kennedy, attorney-at-law and author of *Abortion Rap.*

Julia Reichert and James Klein set out on an ambitious and difficult task when they started their documentary, *Growing Up Female.* Their success is evident in the sixty-minute film that resulted. They present a popularly-styled, palatable documentary exposing the biases and propaganda that family, school, industry, and media effect in the lives of growing girls. Common themes show through six superficially diverse lives—a nursery school girl, an eleven-year-old "tomboy," a sixteen-year-old in a vocational high school, a "liberated" suburban single, a black teen-age mother (now twenty-four), and a disenchanted housewife. By the end of the film, six do become one. And perhaps even seven, eight, nine will become one as women begin to recognize the common pressures upon them and start to see through those biases in their environment.

The first stage, nursery, shows nursery school children already playing out female and male patterns of behavior. Their teacher laughingly describes the differences between little boys and little girls, whose role-playing behavior she encourages by her own prejudices. "Girls tend to fritter their time away . . . girls tend to be jealous . . . they have these little ways about them that are nasty."

Next, a sixth grade teacher describes the difference in girls from the beginning to the end of the year. This educator is pleased to announce that girls develop (?) from acting like boys to adoring them. The father of eleven-year-old Jennel describes feminine as "a mother with a house and children." Her mother wants her to wear dresses and play with dolls. Jennel? She likes to play, run, and enjoys her growing strength.   67

A line from the film describes her best: "She is on the brink of femininity, sensing more than knowing that it will limit her."

The next four women are united by their tendency toward marriage, their competitiveness with other women, and their desire to please men.

Teri, a sixteen-year-old in a vocational high school for cosmetology, plans her whole life around her boyfriend and marriage. Yet this same girl unwittingly admits that her boyfriend is dominating in their relationship and that she wants to be free.

Tammy, twenty-one, is a secretary. She says that to be free is the most important thing. Yet she is controlled by the media image of the "free woman" and buys, buys, buys. As a remarkably blatant advertising man tells us in the film, "We created her—the flower child, the free woman, the hip woman . . . . We make them think they are free. The illusion of freedom is illusory. She'll go down with the others. Soon we'll sell her on the wife-mother image."

Jessica is a factory worker. She quit high school when she became pregnant. Scholarships to college had to be sacrificed and she supported her husband until he was sent to jail. Yet she still defers to men. "A woman shouldn't worry about what she likes and what she wears. She should dress to please her man." Or: "I can only be as strong as the man that's there." And this is a woman who has raised a child single-handedly and supported herself since she was sixteen!

The thirty-five-year-old housewife has left her career to raise her three children. "My thoughts of me as an individual are dominated by my thoughts of myself as a wife and mother . . . if I had my life to live over again right now . . . if I hadn't married and was just getting married today, would I do it the same way? Boy, I doubt it."

Reichert and Klein frequently edit together the voiceover of the subjects with visuals that search out the details of the women's lives. Tammy talks about how important her freedom is to her while the camera shows her carefully placed jewelry and "mod" clothes. Teri describes her school with its discipline and nice teachers while the camera pans over the carefully lined curlers and the identical mannequin heads. Music is important to the film and is frequently used satirically. "The Girl That I Marry" accompanies stills of ads that stress the little-girl bride, with captions like, "He chose you and you chose Thomas china." "I remember every face of every man that put me here . . . any day now I should be released" chants the film as you watch Teri go off into the car with her boyfriend.

Growing Up Female paints an image of the modern woman as one who "seeks approval rather than self-definition . . . her potential robbed from her by constraints and false values, her future uncertain, her identity unknown." (from the film).

Designed as a classroom film, *Gowing Up Female's* open-endedness can lead to much expansion and discussion. I wouldn't suggest it before the high school years because so many concepts and experiences are set into a short time. I preceded the film with an assignment for the students to describe the ways in which they were raised to be women (differently, perhaps, from their brothers).

Growing Up Female: As Six Becomes One (1971): 60 mins., b/w; rental $60; purchase $375. Filmmakers: Julia Reichert, James Klein. Distributor: New Day Films.

SUGGESTED FEMINIST READING
Bird, Caroline. *Born Female.*
DeCrow, Karen. *The Young Woman's Guide to Liberation.*
Merriam, Eve (ed.). *Growing Up Female in America: Ten Lives.*
Miller, Jean Baker (ed.). *Psychoanalysis and Women.*
Nunes, Maxine, and White, Deanna. *The Lace Ghetto.*
Oakley, Ann. *Sex, Gender and Society.*
Shulman, Alix Kates. *Memoirs of an Ex-Prom Queen.*

Julia Reichert

I cannot separate my being a filmmaker from being a woman from being part of the women's movement. And I can't separate any of that from being part of the movement for Socialism. —response to questionnaire.

Julia Reichert has gone through many changes since her childhood in rural New Jersey. Her years at Antioch College helped shape both her personal and political attitudes and her interest in filmmaking. Beginning as a still photographer, Reichert came to "realize the limitations of still photography as a medium for conveying social criticism and moving people toward personal and political change." When her young film teacher, underground filmmaker David Brooks, died in a car accident, she became firmly committed to filmmaking. Through consciousness-raising groups at Antioch College, Reichert realized more and more that she wanted to combine her personal feminist interests with her dedication to filmmaking.

Growing Up Female was the result.

We [Reichert and James Klein] made it to bring some of the new awareness about women's oppression to a broad audience. We specifically wanted to reach beyond the women's movement, to housewives, poor women, black women, high school kids, etc.

Julia's latest projects are also with James Klein. One is a documentary   **69** on methadone; the other a documentary that explores the lives of women who are or have been "criminals." Julia Reichert is a member of New Day Films.

James Klein

Born in Long Island, New York, in 1949, James Klein entered Antioch College expecting to develop his musical talents into a full musical career. Instead, after writing a score for a student film, he became interested first in radio work and then in film. Collaboration with Julia Reichert on *Growing Up Female* came after a period of personal searching and adjustment. "As we (Reichert and Klein) grew closer it became more difficult and painful to look at myself, my attitudes toward women and my actions toward them. Like most men I have met I first rejected Julia's new consciousness, but through struggle over the next year I came to believe that the women's movement was one of the most important and valuable forces moving toward social change in the U.S."

In 1968 James Klein did ten one-hour radio programs concerning student activists, their personal feelings, their backgrounds and their relationships to their parents. These programs were distributed through a tape network that included the Pacifica Stations. He is currently working on two programs with Julia Reichert, one a documentary on methadone, the other a documentary that explores the lives of women who are or have been "criminals." James Klein is a member of New Day Films.

Filmmaking to me is a very expensive but effective way to reach many people with an important message. My goal in filmmaking is to make films that are both innovative and interesting in style and content.

—response to questionnaire.

Happy Birthday Nora

Linda Feferman's films find the common denominator in personal experiences, and through her wry humor and surrealistic cinematic touch she reminds the viewer of how each of us shares in them. In its six minutes, *Happy Birthday Nora* shows how Nora reacts to being twenty. Popping through the paper credits of birthday cake and title, Nora wakes up to the new year of her life as the announcer on the clock-radio wishes her a happy birthday. After checking an empty mail-box, Nora watches an impromptu street band march for her with "Happy Birthday Nora" signs. Later she is caught up with ten-year-olds who are running through the halls of her building. She runs with them and pins the number "20" tail on the donkey. Scenes of her third birth-day follow. Later she watches herself on a late-night talk show, stam-mering and breaking out in spots, not handling her big chance very well. A special delivery package from mom and dad breaks the depression as the talk-show moderator quizzes, "You do agree that the twentieth birthday is no different than the nineteenth?" "Auld Lang Syne" comes from on high while confetti and streamers fall over her.

Haven't you had a birthday like this? When all the expectations for a special day fall short and you get caught up in self-reflection until something small, but special, pushes you over your melancholy?

This film is touching without being sentimental. It has a strong element of suspense, since the shifting between the real and the imagined is never signaled until the sequence is well under way. Off-angle shots, slow motion, fast cutting are all used within the imagined sequences, but so subtly that it is after the fact that we know that it was imagined. And by then we are back in the real, or are we?

It was the combination of this element of suspense, the good musical score, and the exposition of real (but unmentioned) feelings that made the film so successful with my students. I introduced the film by asking what feelings they associated with birthdays. Then we watched the film to see what feelings about birthdays it expressed, and how it reflected upon or expanded our own. This is a good film to use as a short with *Dream Life*.

Happy Birthday Nora (1970): 6 mins., b/w; rental $20. Director: Linda Feferman. Distributor: Linda Feferman.

SUGGESTED FEMINIST READING
DeCrow, Karen. *The Young Woman's Guide to Liberation.*
Egan, Andrea. *Why Am I So Miserable When These Are Supposed to Be the Best Years of My Life?*

How About You?

A man who has a lot of sex is a real man. A girl who has a lot of sex is a tramp.
—from the film.

Perhaps with a new consciousness and a continued effort to minimize role playing in our lives, people will stop using sex as a standard for a man's manliness and a woman's "trampiness." *How About You?* sets out to help young people in their sex lives by providing them with in- 71 formation and correcting some damaging popular notions about sex. During the film there is documentary footage of two different discussion groups, one all girls, the other co-ed; scientific information which is intercut on statistical cards; and instructions by the young women who are monitoring the discussions. Birth control information is presented with plastic molds of a woman's sex organs, so that when the monitor talks about clitoral orgasms, she shows where the clitoris and vagina are inside the model. When she shows how a diaphragm works, she inserts it.

The questions, attitudes, and responses of the boys and girls to one another and to the moderator show both an honesty with their own feelings and a search for information. Some girls admit being pushed into having sex for the first time by peer pressure. They ask the boys how they would feel if the girls told them what they would like when they are having sex. One of the girls shows that she has gone beyond the "keep up with the Joneses" attitude about intercourse common to many young people when she says, "I'm waiting for the right person . . . and when that person comes along I'll be ready."

This film is not slick or sophisticated. In black and white, without any fancy score or camerawork, it speaks very simply—a quality that can be a distinct advantage in motivating discussion and response in a group. As your class goes on to discuss and question after the film, hopefully they will be continuing the realism and honesty that they saw in it.

How About You? (1972): 25 mins., b/w; rental $35; purchase $290. Directors: Bonnie Friedman, Deborah Shaffer, Marilyn Lubois. Distributor: Texture Films.

SUGGESTED FEMINIST READING
The Boston Women's Health Book Collective. *Our Bodies, Our Selves.* Weirdiger, Paula. *Every Month of Our Lives.*

I Am Somebody

The black working woman is perhaps the most discriminated against of all the working women—the black woman.
—Coretta King, in the film.

I Am Somebody is a film about the 1969 strike of Local 1199 of the Drug and Hospital Union in Charleston, South Carolina. What makes this 100-day strike particularly notable is that of the 400 strikers, 388 were women and all were black.

Since the financing for the film came one year after the strike occurred, Madeline Anderson had to develop a compilation film. (A compilation film is composed of footage shot by other people at another time and re-arranged by the filmmaker to form an interpretation of the event or idea.) Through the cooperation of the major networks and some local Charleston stations, she was able to collect roughly fifteen hours of footage.

Much of the film demonstrates the assistance that the strikers were given by people from all over the country. Parts of the speeches of Ralph Abernathy, Andrew Young, Coretta King, Governor Robert Mc-Nair, and national organizer of the AFL-CIO, Bill Kircher, were used. The solidarity of the workers is emphasized in this remark of Abernathy: "We are going to be saved together as *brothers* or perish as fools." (Italics added.) Anderson, more sensitive than Abernathy to the fact that this was a women's strike, found only one line in all of the speeches that related to the workers as women. That was the comment by Coretta King that opened this review.

Even though the strike provoked violence, Madeline Anderson avoids too many strong scenes of the opposition that the strikers met. Her editing concentrates on the spirit of the people who won the strike.

The narration of *I Am Somebody* is its most interesting and innovative feature. When Madeline was in Charleston, she met Claire Brown, one of the more active strikers. This is what Madeline had to say about the film's narration:

In a film of this type you usually use a narrator, but I felt that conventional narration would fail to project the emotional climate I was trying to create. I wanted someone involved in the strike to talk about 73 *it. When I went to Charleston, I met Claire Brown, who had been very active in the strike and who had a very poetic way of talking. When I was ready for the narration I invited her to New York to come and live with me for a week. She came to the cutting room with me every day and I would say, "What do you think of this?" and she would tell me what she thought. After four days I got her to come to the sound studio and talk about the film in just the same way she had been talking in the cutting room. I had her look at the screen and tell how she remembered things about the strike as their images appeared. Certain images would come up and she would speak out of her own feelings about them. That's how I got the narration on the film.*

—Film Library Quarterly, Winter 1972, p. 41.

Claire Brown's comments show the women of the strike. In a clear, patient, but determined, voice she says, "More than 1,000 of us were in jail . . . My kids were in jail too . . . The strike was the most difficult and important period of my life." Since Madeline didn't have any footage of Claire at the strike, she took some new film of her working in her home and interviewed her with her family.

In one scene Claire speaks about how the strike affected her family's life, how her husband had to do all the shopping and chores. "Sometimes it would get difficult and we would have to have a talk. I would try to make him understand that this was my thing. It was something I had to do."

The most impressive footage of Claire are shots of her, in soft focus, walking along the Charleston waterfront—alone, mature, pensive. Her voiceover says, "If you are ready and willing to fight for yourself, other folks will be ready and willing to fight for you."

Another scene that was shot after the strike was a restaging of high school students striking and organizing in a park. It is surprising that the media did not cover this event, since Claire Brown says, "Of all the people that helped us, I think the students did the most to really help us win."

Besides the unusual narration, the film has other interesting cinematic qualities. Madeline says that her editing is emotional, intuitive, that she does what looks and feels right to her. Just as her approach to the problem of narration shows the warmth of her work, so does the editing. In one scene Andrew Young talks of the boycott to be begun in the shopping district of Charleston. There is a medium shot of him on the steps of a shack. As his voiceover continues, you see a quick medium shot of a very old, worn, yet strong, black woman on the steps of another shack. The image of the old woman haunts the next minutes of the film experience.

The continuing of a speech as voiceover, after the speaker has been seen, is a frequent device in the film. Not only does it give Madeline a chance to give visual interpretation and contrast to the speeches, but it also helps to unify the work (since the narration of Claire is almost always voiceover).

Madeline Anderson avoids one of the biggest weaknesses of the compilation film by her use of music. Many compilation films have a strong narrative accompanied by an overwhelming musical score. In *I Am Somebody* there is little music, mostly the songs of the strikers. The other sounds that accompany the narrative are the sounds of marching feet, police sirens, and the city.

Audiences love *I Am Somebody*. It is powerful and hopeful. Since it is easy to follow and inspirational, use it with any group above the seventh grade.

I Am Somebody (1971): 28 mins., color; rental $30, purchase $360. Producer: Madeline Anderson. Financed by American Foundation for Non-Violence. Distributor: Contemporary Films/McGraw-Hill.

SUGGESTED FEMINIST READING
Beal, Frances M. "Double Jeopardy: To Be Black and Female." *Sisterhood Is Powerful*, pp. 340-353. Edited by Robin Morgan.
Flowers, Estelle; Cooper, Luanna; and Smith, Moranda, "Organizing at Winston-Salem, North Carolina." *Black Women in White America*, pp. 265-274. Edited by Gerda Lerner.
Jones, "Mother" Mary. "Excerpts from her Autobiography." *Growing Up Female in America: Ten Lives*, pp. 211-232. Edited by Eve Merriam.
"Madeline Anderson on 'I Am Somebody'." *Film Library Quarterly* (vol. 5, no. 1), pp. 39-41.
Martinez, Sabina. "A Black Union Organizer." *Black Women in White America*, pp. 263-265. Edited by Gerda Lerner.
Norton, Eleanor Holmes. "For Sadie and Maude." *Sisterhood Is Powerful*, pp. 353-359. Edited by Robin Morgan.

Madeline Anderson

Photo by Gale Ross.

I am a black filmmaker. My blackness is a part of my identity as a human being. I am ideologically committed to recording the black experience in films which show the reality of black folks, not showing old stereotypes or creating new ones.

—response to questionnaire. 75

Madeline Anderson was the second black woman to be admitted to the film editors' union. (Hortense Beveridge was the first.) At this writing she is making efforts to be admitted to the film directors' union.

She began her public work in film in the sixties as a producer for Richard Leacock. That first effort, *Integration Report,* was a follow-up on the civil rights struggle. Next she was assistant to director Shirley Clarke for the successful semi-documentary *The Cool World.* After she had been editor and occasional producer of NET's "Black Journal," she made *I Am Somebody.*

Currently Madeline Anderson is making films for "Sesame Street" and "Electric Company" of Children's Television Workshop. She likes this work because of the challenge to make a statement in a one-minute film and a chance to motivate inner-city children to read. Anderson is also teaching a graduate course in documentary filmmaking at Columbia University. Her next film will be about Clemintine Hunter, an eighty-seven-year-old, black primitive painter from the south. Like *I Am Somebody,* this film will give her the opportunity to record the black experience through an individual situation.

Madeline Anderson lives in Brooklyn with Ralph Anderson and their four children.

It Happens to Us

This film helped me mature by facing reality. I learned that abortion isn't what everyone, with no experience, has said. Through this film I now realize that abortion isn't as terrible as I thought.

—teen-age mother.

In *It Happens to Us* Amalie Rothschild shows many women speaking about abortions they had either before or after abortion was legalized in New York State. In the opening sequence a young woman describes the tragedy of two unwanted pregnancies—one that was endured in a "home for unwed mothers" and ended with the adoption of the child; the other, a series of harrowing episodes with an illegal abortionist.

The woman had been denied contraception by local doctors because she was not married. The emotion and tragedy of her testimony is distressing, but don't let that keep you from seeing the rest of the film.

Other women—from different age, economic, and racial groups—are interviewed. The interviews are closely edited for the clearest and most informative effect. "What kind of abortion procedure did you have?" "How old were you?" "What kind of birth control were you using when you became pregnant?" "How did you feel when you found out you were pregnant?" Speaking directly into the camera, some of the women tell of the terrible effects their untimed pregnancies and subsequent abortions had on their families. These yesterdays contrast sharply with Dr. Felicia Hance's explanations of the methods of abortion to a group of young women in a high school. Throughout the film, statistics are flashed on the screen to clear up misconceptions people have about abortion and birth control. Thus the film presents statistics, personal experiences, and clinical information to convey honesty and feeling and maintain interest. Watching it brings a woman away with the sentiments of the seventeen-year-old interviewed at the end: "It was my body, I was going through it. I am alone . . . I can take care of myself."

Careful preparation and follow-up should accompany this film. Don't take for granted that your audiences know about the mechanics, safety, and reliability of birth control methods. Many people have gaps in their understanding of their own bodies. The screening of *It Happens to Us* provides an opportunity to clear up misunderstandings and develop healthy concepts.

It Happens to Us (1971): 35 mins., color; rental $30 (plus $2 handling), purchase $325. Director: Amalie Rothschild. Distributor: New Day Films.

SUGGESTED FEMINIST READING
The Boston Women's Health Book Collective. *Our Bodies, Our Selves.*
Gutcheon, Beth Richardson. *Abortion: A Woman's Guide.*
Schulder, Diane, and Kennedy, Florynce (eds.). *Abortion Rap.*

Amalie Rothschild

Photo by John K. Chester.

I have a theory that all really strong, lasting works of art, in any field, survive because they all have something in common: they're all linked closely to something personal, something strong and meaningful in the life of the maker. It's a connection that all good works have, a spark of life from the artist's innermost being . . . I'm not sure if I'll always make women-oriented films, for I consider myself basically a filmmaker, not a women's filmmaker. But there are millions of films to make. What I work on is an organic outgrowth of my immediate life interests. What interests me at the time determines the direction I'm heading. It's tied in with my individual struggle as a person—as a female person."

to Kay Harris, *Mademoiselle*, February 1973.

After spending her early years in Baltimore, Maryland, Amalie Rothschild received a B.F.A. (1967) in still photography and graphic design from the Rhode Island School of Design. While she was on an honors program in Rome, Rothschild's love of films suddenly developed into a will to make her own films. As a student in the M.F.A. program in film production at New York University, she began her filmmaking career. *Woo Who? May Wilson* was her thesis project there.

Admitting that her attitude toward herself has always been affected by her sex, she says that when she was a child she wasn't taken seriously as a person because she was a child. When she was older people would take her seriously she thought. But then she wasn't taken seriously because she was a woman, not a man. Amalie Rothschild takes herself and her filmmaking seriously; so do her audiences. She is a member of the distribution cooperative New Day Films. (See list of distributors.)

FILMOGRAPHY

My Grandmother, Nana. AFI grant.

It's Alright to Be a Woman. Channel 13 filming of feminist theater. All-woman crew.

* *It Happens to Us.*

* *Woo Who? May Wilson.*

*Reviewed in this book.

Janie's Janie

I told Janie that people would like to see someone like her. "Good," she said, "because I never saw someone like me in the movies."
—Geri Ashur at First International Festival of Women's Films, June 1972.

Before I was my father's Janie,
Then I was Charlie's Janie,
Now I'm Janie's Janie.
I have to be my own boss. —from the film.

Geri Ashur presents fifteen minutes of Janie, a white welfare mother of five children. At age fifteen, Janie admits, she got pregnant in order to get married and thus escape from her father's house. Five children later she threw her husband out and finally started to manage her own life. "He was never here. We never talked. We never went out . . . He'd hit me, but say I deserved it, cause I got fresh with my mouth. He should hear my mouth now. He should hear it now."

Janie's "mouth" now tells of a self that is growing in strength and awareness. She proudly describes how she wallpapered and painted her kitchen with five kids underfoot. As she talks, the film shows her doing other parent chores like fixing bikes, making sandwiches, preparing supper. Even when Janie talks directly to the camera, she is interrupted by child demands. She has developed the most subtle of mother arts, carying on a serious conversation that is punctuated by "wipe me," 'take the pits out," and "Johnny hit me." Janie is aptly placed in this context of home and children because that is the constant reality and demand of her life as Janie's Jane.

One of Janie's complaints is her isolation from other women. During the time that Geri Ashur made the film, however, Janie came to meet other welfare mothers and set up a day-care center. You see these other women hanging clothes and working with their families in the center.

Even though Janie is disturbed about the treatment that she received from her father and husband, she is aware of the pressures that men face. As Janie's voiceover mentions how much many men hate their jobs, Ashur shows men doing repetitive factory work. "So much of that frustration is brought home," comments Janie as Ashur shows Janie getting three kids off to school and dressing the two that stay at home. If Janie didn't see then that her job, like "men's work," can lead to understandable frustration, she must have when she saw the rushes of the film. As Geri Ashur indicated at the First International Festival of Women's Films, the filming process and the film itself helped Janie's changing consciousness toward new self-respect. At the same time, knowing Janie brought Ashur to new respect for other women and their lifestyles.

Although Ashur is not a seasoned filmmaker, there is a freshness and excitement about her shots and editing—something that came out of Janie's changing consciousness, the respect between filmmaker and subject, the realization that they were presenting a "revolutionary" message.

Many different groups from high school age and older would respond to Janie. It is particularly interesting for welfare mothers, consciousness-raising groups, sociology and psychology classes.

Janie's Janie (1971): 15 mins., b/w; rental $20, purchase $200. Filmmaker: Geri Ashur. Distributor: Odeon Films.

SUGGESTED FEMINIST READING
Glassman, Carol. "Women and the Welfare System." *Sisterhood Is Powerful*, pp. 102-115. Edited by Robin Morgan.
Friedan, Betty. *The Feminine Mystique*.
The Milwaukee County Welfare Rights Association. *Welfare Mothers Speak Out*.

Geri Ashur

*Editing a film for me is like playing the bass—giving rhythm and struc-
ture to a song—to try to suck the spectators into the center of the experience so they can feel it from the inside. This is a very anti-intellectual
attitude and it has taken me a long time to believe that filmmaking isn't
about teaching justice but about making magic.*

—response to questionnaire, June 1973.

Raised in Jersey City, New Jersey, Geri Ashur says she was brought
up to be a Jewish man and woman at the same time, "to be competitive,
creative, academically excellent and sweet, passive, obedient, a good
cook." Wanting to be a filmmaker from an early age, she studied language at Barnard because "film was a language and that seemed to me
a way of getting close to thinking in another grammar without disturbing my parents too much." Eventually, however, she went to N.Y.U.
film school and married a filmmaker.

In the next few years she edited the footage others had shot. When
she tried to go off on her own, the response to her resume was, "Oh, a
chick who can do a man's job." At Newsreel (a political collective that
made and showed films about peoples' struggles in North and South
America, Vietnam, Africa) she was part of a women's filmmaking crew.
It was during her two years there that she made *Janie's Janie*. ("I left the
group no longer married, the Jane film finished, the political climate in
America changed, and my belief that films were a direct way of changing
political consciousness badly shaken.") The following year she organized
and taught in an alternative high school in Newark.

Ashur is currently involved in four projects. The first is a long documentary about an old woman blues musician. The other three are proposed features "about the same contradiction—the difference between
how we live and what we know. The moment when the difference is
perceived is like the world cracking open, liberation—but then you have
to live with the knowledge of both worlds." One of these features is
about a young middle-class marriage, another about a young white
working-class girl in Newark. "Both these films are rooted in the lives
women live, their kitchens and washing machines, how they relate to

the spaces they live and move in and what other women (mothers, movie stars, liberation fighters) mean to them." The third feature, which has just started production, is about a generation of young white people "who are in the process of stretching their consciousness to include ways of thinking and living that are nonobjective, scientific, western."

FILMOGRAPHY

Artists in Residence (1973). With Nick Doob and Peter Schlaifer. For Connecticut State Council on the Arts.

Village by Village (1972). With Janet Mendelsohn. Medical aid for Indochina.

Make Out (1971). With Newsreel Women's Caucus. Newsreel.

* *Janie's Janie* (1971). With Peter Barton, Marilyn Mulford. Odeon Films.

*Reviewed in this book.

Joyce at Thirty-Four

One of the rare documentaries that is neither propaganda nor putdown; a film that loves both the people it portrays and the truth.
                                                              —Gloria Steinem.

I had been waiting to see *Joyce at Thirty-Four* since my daughter was born six years ago. Or had it been since seventh grade when the nuns told me that a mother's place is to be at home . . . and mothers should work only "if it is necessary"?

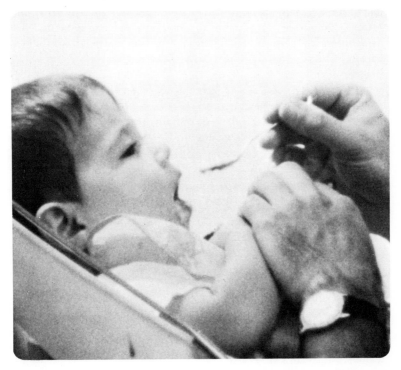

The twenty-nine minutes of *Joyce at Thirty-four* documents fifteen months in Joyce's life, beginning with the ninth month of her pregnancy. Joyce is shown waiting for the baby to come, giving birth to her daughter, and going to New York to work on a film. These and other sequences define not only Joyce's frustrations and guilt as a working mother, but also those of other mothers in her life—her mother, her grandmother, her friends, and her mother's friends. As one of her mother's friends reminisces, "Whether we worked or stayed home we were wrong. Whatever we did was wrong."

The film also includes home-movie scenes of Joyce's "sweet sixteen" party eighteen years ago. As the frames freeze, Joyce describes her school friends. "That's Adrienne—she married a doctor. Tonie—she has three children now; the oldest is thirteen," and so on. Looking back on our teens and twenties with a raised consciousness and new empathy is an attitude of many of us who were raised in the oppressive fifties of pink carnations, proms, and *American Girl* magazine. This attitude is particularly valid in the context of this film which, in effect, explores the destruction of the "motherhood" myth on which we were raised. It puts motherhood in the realism of an independent woman's life, be it harsh or sweet, depending on the moment of the day, the day of the week. But certainly it is not "ever-sweet" as the media are wont to put it. Finally a filmmaker has given us a realistic picture.

Joyce's husband also appears in the film. Just as Joyce is frustrated in her effort to edit a film with a squirming baby in her arms, so he has difficulty collaborating on a writing job as he feeds the baby. Yet Joyce is the one who feels the guilt at dividing her time between child and job, and her husband plays upon her guilt. When he and the baby meet Joyce at the airport after she has made a business trip alone to New York, he says, "Oh, she doesn't recognize you. She is your mommy, Sara."

With great relief I saw real feelings—a woman's feelings—a working mother's feelings demonstrated on the screen. *Joyce at Thirty-Four* is a film that should be used with almost any group in women's studies, sociology, health education, sex education, and so on, from high-school age on.

Joyce at Thirty-Four (1972): 29 mins., color; rental $35, purchase $350.
Directors: Joyce Chopra, Claudia Weill. Distributor: New Day Films.

SUGGESTED FEMINIST READING
Bernard, Jessie. *The Future of Marriage.*
Bird, Caroline. *Born Female.*
de Beauvoir, Simone. *The Second Sex.*
Epstein, Cynthia Fuchs. *Woman's Place.*
Firestone, Shulamith. *The Dialectic of Sex.*
Friedan, Betty. *The Feminine Mystique.*
Nin, Anais. *The Diary of Anais Nin* (vols. I-IV).
Oakley, Ann. *Sex, Gender and Society.*

Joyce Chopra

*When I went to work in film, it was as an apprentice with Richard Lea-
cock and D. A. Pennebaker. I smiled my way into the job and then
worked harder than anybody to prove that they should keep me on.
These were exciting days—the techniques of the* cinema verité *style documentary were first being worked out and I learned a great deal. But
looking back, I realize that I couldn't have become more than a production assistant, had I stayed on, unless I was willing to convert myself into
'a pushy broad'.... So long as a woman accepts a male frame of reference she is bound to be at a disadvantage.* —response to questionnaire.

Joyce Chopra began work in films in 1960 with Richard Leacock and
D. A. Pennebaker. During a long apprenticeship with them, she worked
in many different aspects of filmmaking, from production planning to
final editing. Since 1965 she has produced and directed her own films.

Chopra is at work (with Claudia Weill) on a film about Radcliffe College's young president, psychologist Matina Horner. Ms. Horner is
noted for her theory that many bright women fear success because they
perceive it as a threat to finding a mate and associate it with the loss of
femininity. The film attempts to deal with this question.

Joyce Chopra is a member of New Day Films.

FILMOGRAPHY
Matina Horner—Radcliffe 1973 (in progress). color.
* *Joyce at 34.* Autobiographical film. Sponsored by WNET-TV, New
    York.
Present Tense. Directed film based on a Thomas Mann story. For NET
    Playhouse.
Portrait of Tyrone Guthrie. NET Creative Person series.
Room to Learn and *New Lease on Learning.* Films on the influence of
    environment in learning. Sponsored by E.F.L., Ford Foundation.
Wild Ones. Feature-length television film.
Water. Film for "Sesame Street."

*Reviewed in this book.

83

Twenty-First Century: Home of the Future. Part of CBS television series.
Essays: I. M. Pei. Four short films for WGBH-TV.
Eye-Opener. Exhibition film for Metropolitan Museum of Art.
A Happy Mother's Day. Co-directed by Chopra for ABC-TV. Awarded Bronze Medal at Venice Film Festival.

Claudia Weill

After graduation from Radcliffe in 1968, Claudia Weill went on to study still photography at Harvard. She says that she became involved in filmmaking "unconsciously" ("stills were too static—I wanted an excuse to meet and talk with other people"). Besides shooting, directing, and editing her own work, Weill has run a film workshop for city children and does free-lance editing.

One of her projects is a film about a delegation of twelve American women (headed by Shirley MacLaine) and their visit to mainland China. Claudia Weill is incorporated with Eli Noyes as Cyclops Films, and is a member of New Day Films.

FILMOGRAPHY
Matina Horner—Radcliffe 1973 (in progress), color. Inquire: Cyclops Films.
* *Joyce at 34.* Co-directed with Joyce Chopra. Distributor: New Day Films.
Commuters, Yoga-Great Neck, Roaches, Marriage Bureau, Subway Lost and Found, Belly Dancing Class (1972-73), color, approx. 5 mins. each. Films produced as feature pieces for the "51st State" WNET-13 and deal with the subjective quality of life in and around New York. Distributor: Texture Films.
"Sesame Street" films (1971-72). Fifteen live-action films on numbers (Mad Painter series, Number Detective) and two animated films on letters.
Inca, 1970 (1971), color, 20 mins. Film about the twentieth annual Aspen Design Conference: the questioning of a liberal institution by young radicals. Co-directed with Eli Noyes.
This Is the Home of Mrs. Levant Graham (1970), black and white, 15 mins. Documentary about a black family in Washington, D.C. Made

for the New Thing, a Street Organization. Co-directed with Eli Noyes.
Distributor: Pyramid Films.

Putney School (1969), color, 23 mins. Documentary about a progressive
school in Putney, Vermont. Co-directed with Eli Noyes.

Radcliffe Blues: Fran (1968), black and white, 20 mins. Interview with a
woman radical. Made at Harvard. Co-directed with Tony Ganz. Distributor: American Documentary Films.

Metropole (1968), black and white, 4 mins. Film about go-go dancers;
how they feel about their work and the people watching them. Distributor: American Documentary Films.

*Reviewed in this book.

Judy Chicago and the California Girls

I am an artist *and a feminist (not a producer, etc.) and the film is a personal vision by Judith Dancoff of the Fresno Art Program—a program to
educate women as artists, using performance as a tool in that education,
as a way to reach subject matter for art. This program is part of my aim
of developing a female art community in Los Angeles where I and other
women artists can be ourselves.*   —Judy Chicago

Judy, the subject of this documentary, is an art teacher in an all-
women class. She created the class because: "So many women came into
the art school and didn't leave it as professionals." During the class, the
women act out—in drama, dance, and discussion—the oppressions that
they must overcome to get to the point where each of them can "take
over her own cunt and declare, 'I shall say what cunt is. I shall decide my
own life.' "

The beginning and the end of the film show the students acting out a
play by Judy, in which a "sweet young thing" asks why she must do the
dishes since he dirtied them too. He says because of cunt; cunt is round
and so are dishes. The play ends with the man (who is actually a girl doing role playing and using a falsely low voice) beating the sweet young
thing to death as he says over and over, "You'll castrate me with all these
demands." She just asked if she couldn't come once in a while too. The
whole play is stylized, with the lines spoken in sing-song fashion.

Other parts of the film show similar exercises devised by Judy
Chicago for her classes. She is also shown answering questions, and frequently her voiceover narrates scenes of her in her apartment and at the
school. One segment shows Judy Chicago and Ti-Grace Atkinson argu-
ing about the place of men in the liberation of women. (By the way, Ti-
Grace is satirically greeted at the station by bobby-socked cheerleaders
with shakers and megaphones.)

Judy Chicago might be used for mature audiences as a good model
of an independent woman artist. Because of the drama exercises used
for her group the film is also good for drama classes.

Judy Chicago and the California Girls (1972): 25 mins., color or b/w;
rental $35, purchase $300. Director: Judith Dancoff. Distributor:
Judith Dancoff.

85

SUGGESTED FEMINIST READING
Bird, Caroline. *Born Female.*
de Beauvoir, Simone. *The Second Sex.*
DeCrow, Karen. *The Young Woman's Guide to Liberation.*
Epstein, Cynthia Fuchs. *Woman's Place.*
Herschberger, Ruth. *Adam's Rib.*
Morgan, Elaine. *The Descent of Woman.*
Oakley, Ann. *Sex, Gender and Society.*

Kirsa Nicholina

Deceptively simple film of a child being born to a Woodstock couple in their home is an almost classic manifesto of the new sensibility, a proud affirmation of a man amidst technology, genocide, and ecological destruction . . . . birth is presented as a living through of primitive mystery a spiritual celebration, a rite of passage.

—Amos Vogel, March 18, 1971.

Gunvor Nelson waited with David and Ellis Woeller for the home birth of their child. The first sequence of the film is of a nude couple walking on the beach. The woman is pregnant. The man is present throughout, playing his own music on the guitar as the woman goes through the labor and delivery of their baby. There are other sustaining familiar sights and sounds for the laboring woman. She is in her own home, her pregnant friend assists her, she wears her own smock. As her labor progresses, the viewer sees her growing discomfort and increasing need for support. Her roars frequently drown out the constant guitar music. Finally her water breaks and soon a head appears, inch by inch. In the most astounding moment I have seen in a birth film, the mother, who has been propped by pillows throughout her labor, reaches over, takes the emerging infant by the hands, and assists her out of her body. The mother then lays the child on her shrinking belly, while they are still attached by the umbilical cord. If you have to choose one birth film, and the brief scene with male nudity in the opening sequences isn't a problem to your situation, choose *Kirsa Nicholina.*

"Do I love my baby?
Yes indeed!"

—David Woeller, from the film.

Kirsa Nicholina (1970): 16 mins., color; rental $20. Director: Gunvor Nelson. Distributor: Canyon Cinema.

SUGGESTED FEMINIST READING
The Boston Women's Health Book Collective. *Our Bodies, Our Selves.*

Gunvor Nelson

The fluidity of motion in time using light and sound offers me endless discoveries into the media itself and life and especially the self.
—response to questionnaire, Spring, 1973

Gunvor Nelson was born and reared in Kristinehamn, Sweden. After studying in Stockholm, London, and San Francisco, she completed an M.F.A. in painting at Miles College (California). While married to Robert Nelson, also an avant-garde filmmaker, Gunvor made her first film, a description of their life for her parents in Sweden.

As she continued to work in film, Nelson found that it "offered so many more levels to work with than painting." Her films, most under a half-hour, explore levels of consciousness through experimental use of film. Nelson recently received a Guggenheim Grant to make a film about her parents in Sweden. She is also working on a film based on dreams.

FILMOGRAPHY
Moons Pool (1973), 15 mins.
One and the Same (1973), 4½ mins.
* *Take Off* (1972), 10 mins.
Five Artists: Billbobbillbillbob (1970-71), 70 mins.
* *Kirsa Nicholina* (1969), 16 mins.
My Name Is Oona (1969), 10 mins.
Fog Pumas (1967), 25 mins.
* *Schmeerguntz* (1965-66), 15 mins.
All of Gunvor Nelson's works are available at Canyon Cinema.
*Reviewed in this book.

Lavender

At the beginning of the film I felt embarrassed and uncomfortable. I had never seen women like that—but by the end of the film I understood better and was more comfortable.
—middle-aged librarian. 87

Lavender is a short film that shows a lesbian couple in the ordinariness of their lives. It opens with stills from their respective family albums. Background narration is by each of them describing her own childhood and feelings toward other women as she was growing up. This is followed by snow scenes showing a mature female couple running, hugging, and kissing. The photography and heavy music of this scene seems self-conscious to me. But for people who have uncomfortable (threatened?) feelings about seeing women sexually attracted to and sexually active with one another, it is a soft-sell beginning—a conscious effort on the part of the filmmakers not to alienate the audience before the film has had a chance to make its point.

Understand from the beginning that this film is specifically intended as a "propaganda" film to help women and men to understand homosexuality as a variation, not a deviation or perversion. Throughout the brief snow scene the women speak of how they feel for one another: "Kissing you is a whole different world for me."

In the next scene you hear the voiceovers of the two women reminiscing over their first meeting as you see them eating dinner, doing dishes, holding hands. "Most of the lesbians we know are not butch. They love being a woman and loving a woman."

In another scene one of the women is shown in a library, describing how she was dropped from seminary after she had admitted being gay. The other is shown in her office while she explains that she has not "come out at the office."

Later there are scenes at a gay bar and party, with dancing and fun. As the film comes to its closing sequences, the couple speak of the process of making the film—how it has affected them and how they hope it will affect their audiences. "If they understand a little bit better maybe they won't be so frightened about us and less oppressive." Then one affectionately says to the other, "Are you tired of being a star?"

For the closing shots and credits Colleen Monahan sings her own song, "Baby it isn't easy to say I love you." The qualities of openness and gentle conversation had to have come from a very comfortable working relationship between the subjects and the filmmakers. You will also notice that the process of making the film was a developing-maturing experience for the women who were in it. "It's funny how emotionally involved we've gotten in making this film. We're trying to be honest about our feelings even though its sort of frightening to be this exposed."

This film might be helpful for conservative groups that have prejudices against homosexual relationships.

Lavender (1971): 13 mins., color; rental $17, purchase $170. Filmmakers: Colleen Monahan, Elaine Jacobs. Distributor: Perennial Education, Inc.

SUGGESTED FEMINIST READING
See suggested readings for *Holding*.

Colleen Monahan

I enjoyed making films and had a knack for it, so I pursued it. Any need and desire to "say something meaningful" came through and grew through the development of my craft. As I could do more with film, I found I wanted to project more with film.

— response to questionnaire.

Raised in and around Chicago, Illinois, Colleen Monahan first studied film in high school where, among other projects, she made a fifteen-minute Super-8 film highlighting the activities of the senior class. After high school she majored in film for two years at Columbia College in Chicago.

Since making *Lavender,* Monahan has been free-lancing as a director and editor in Chicago, doing industrial and private projects for friends and acquaintances.

L'Opéra Mouffe

It is a film that could only have been made by a woman in that it is refreshingly chauvinistic and meaningful to other women, in that it is marked by a keenness of vision, an intellectual rigor and an originality of point of view that will hopefully characterize 'women's films' in a new sense of that phrase.

—Susan Rice, *Take One*, February, 1972.

L'Opéra Mouffe shows a pregnant woman's view of Quartier Mouffetard of Paris. A very lyrical, non-narrative reflection, it often employs filmic metaphors and violent symbols with documentary footage of the poor section of Paris.

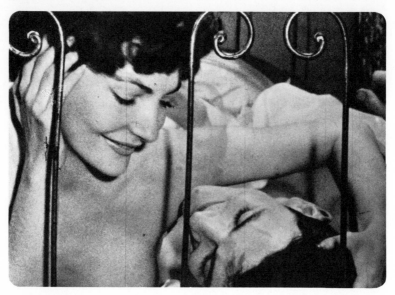

The film opens with a back view of a woman. As she turns to the side, you see her very pregnant form profiled from the neck down. As she lies down, you see the moving fetus in close-up. This scene cuts to a close-up of a full pumpkin, which is cut and scooped out. Close-up slow pans of the other produce in this market lead to medium and close-up shots of old neighborhood people talking and gesturing. Most don't seem to notice the camera.

The several segments of the film are introduced by hand-written intertitles. "Lovers" is in sharp contrast to the shots of the poor streets. It is a contrived scene of nude lovemaking interspersed with visual metaphors of the individual feelings of the lovers. The segment ends with metaphors for sex: a sliced lemon, a half of a revolving cabbage, a tree with branches.

Metaphors for pregnancy appear in the next sequence—a hen in a glass bubble; a girl running in slow motion; then the revolving cabbage half with a new sprout coming up. Next you see the middle half of a wire doll with a metal belly encircling a small plastic doll.

The following segment flashes one tragic, lonely face after another. (It gave me the embarrassed feeling I have on the New York subways—of seeing too much private sorrow on the faces of other passengers.) The instrumental music of the film here takes on a very playful, lyrical tone. At times it mimics the rhythms of the awkward walks of the old and deformed.

"Holidays" has the only view of children in the film. They are presented with masks on—the masks representing the absurd and the ugly that they will be one day. In the midst of masked children and the faces of the old, the young lovers meet and kiss.

"Drunkenness" is the next topic. Shots of sleeping bums are followed by a hammer breaking light bulbs. On a piece of shattered glass you see a small premature chicken; this cuts to a shot of the chicken in a glass, struggling, then dying. The metaphors here are frightening, accurately mirroring the fears of a pregnant woman.

The last sequence is of "Desires." Shots of meats, intestines, hearts, in a meat shop; cut to a medium shot of the pregnant woman coming out of a flower shop. She eats two flowers in her hand. Is eating the flower a quirky desire of pregnancy or is it an effort to assume as much beauty as possible in the face of the ugliness and poverty of the world that the child will enter?

As a reflection of a pregnant woman, this film stands in sharp contrast to the fluffy soap ads and the popular image of motherhood. As an experimental film *L'Opera Mouffe* is exceptional.

Use it with mature high school students and on. Be sure to plan your screening so that it can be seen more than once.

L'Opéra Mouffe (1959): 19 mins., b/w; rental $35, purchase $95. Director: Agnes Varda. Distributor: Grove Press.

SUGGESTED FEMINIST READING
The Boston Woman's Health Book Collective. "Pregnancy." *Our Bodies, Our Selves*, pp. 157-228.

Loving Couples

An unsentimental examination of the search for woman's independence, the film coolly, graphically, but quite unsensationally reports in the course of its action the fornication of two dogs, disposal of a three-month fetus, lesbianism, homosexual play in a church, attempted rape of a thirteen-year-old, nudity, and the emergence of a child from its mother's womb.
　　　—Cynthia Grenier, *New York Herald Tribune*, May 30, 1965.

As a Broadway and Hollywood actress, Mai Zetterling acted out on stage and screen many familiar feminine stereotypes. Her reaction to the illusion of these roles was to show her view of women in her three major directorial efforts: *Night Dreams, Loving Couples,* and *The Girls*.

Loving Couples is a blatantly angry film. In the days before World War I, three women from the same Swedish estate are confined to a　91 maternity hospital. During labor each of them recalls childhood incidents and sexual experiences that established her cynicism toward men, her position in the castelike order of the manor, and the circumstances surrounding the intercourse that conceived the child that she is bearing.

The first woman, Angela (Gio Petre), was left a wealthy orphan to be cared for and loved by a "maiden aunt." Angela's flashbacks show why she disdains men, heterosexual love, and marriage. The men of the family are shown to be particularly gross and unfeeling. For example, after her father's funeral, the twelve-year-old Angela hides under a table as the "men of the family" discuss the most expeditious guardianship for her. The camera shows her view as one man takes off his shoes, another scratches his ankles, while a third flicks ashes under the rug. At eighteen, now "free to enter holy wedlock," Angela goes to boarding school to learn womanly virtues. Once back to the family estates, Angela returns to her love and guardian, Petra, staunchly declaring, "Marriage is like falling asleep for the rest of your life . . . I shall never marry." Nonetheless, she falls in love and becomes pregnant by an old love of her Aunt Petra. Since he leaves Angela, as he had Petra fifteen years earlier, Petra and Angela will raise the child.

The second woman is a servant in Petra's household. Adele (Gunnel Linblom) has known from childhood that "men cannot be trusted." Deserted and left destitute by her father, chased by boys, deserted by a lover, Adele takes out all her anger on her meek husband. Her jealousy of the other two women and her personal grief are heightened when a three-month fetus is removed from her womb.

The third woman, Agda (Harriet Anderson), is first seen eating sweets as she hops up the long stairs of the hospital with her "heavy load." Her memories as a thirteen-year-old show her being bribed into a classic "dirty old man's" room. She avoids his rape, but not before he puts on his white gloves (gynecology?) and dances with her under a clothesline full of white gloves. Agda has all the "happy whore" qualities of more conventional film characters and becomes almost a caricature. Through that caricature there are brilliant moments, like her flippant return of money that she accepted before having intercourse with an aristocrat.

Men are treated with little or no sympathy. Zetterling seems to be settling some old accounts. The innuendos of male chauvinism in Hollywood-style movies are blatantly blown up. For example, cigars and driving as symbols of the phallic ego are played up as two gynecologists leave the hospital. One complains, "They [women] are like a lot of brooding hens, you have to be everything to them." The other agrees, "You trade thirty seconds of heaven for thirty years of hell." Their attitude toward their work? "The women are let out. For us it's a life sentence . . . we are tied to them by the umbilical cord." Cigars lit, they announce, "We are even God to them," and drive off in their huge cars.

Flashback as a major device often gives a film either a banal or a contrived tone. In *Loving Couples* the flashbacks of the three women are interwoven; therefore the pitfalls are multiplied. The satiric, angry tone of the film, however, counterbalances the sentimental, contrived flashback form. Many other familiar techniques for referring to the past are used. One of the best is an instance of shot-by-shot interweaving of past and present. When the second woman, Adele, tries to run from the hospital, her race through the corridors is intercut with a run through the woods to her lover. When the nurses grab and detain her, their gestures are intercut with her lover's caresses. In another particularly good transition from past to present, a relative turns to Angela at her father's funeral, but the view given us is of Angela on the labor bed.

Loving Couples has brilliant moments that cause one to pause and realize how much of woman's experience has not been put on film. When Adele visits the gynecologist's office, she is shown, in medium shot, through the stirrups that will hold her legs up and open while she is being examined. Many women have strong negative feelings about these stirrups, but I had never before seen that on film. Nor had I seen a woman's view of ceilings as she is being rolled prone and defenseless down the hospital corridors to the labor rooms.

When Angela speaks of her unborn child during her early pregnancy she says, "My artist, my explorer, my girl." In the closing shots of the film Angela's child is born. The camera closes in on the new-born with a narrowing rectangular frame, reflecting limitations the real world places on our young girls.

Loving Couples is entertaining and fun at the same time that it is blatantly feminist and dramatically serious. Because of the combined demands of reading subtitles and keeping track of flashbacks, most high school groups would probably find it difficult.

Loving Couples (1964): 113 mins., b/w; rental $65. Director: Mai Zetterling. Distributor: Macmillan Audio Brandon Films.

SUGGESTED FEMINIST READING
The Boston Women's Health Book Collective. *Our Bodies, Our Selves.*
de Beauvoir, Simone. *The Second Sex.*
Firestone, Shulamith. *The Dialectic of Sex.*
Frankfort, Ellen. *Vaginal Politics.*

Lucy

*My name is Lucy. I'm sixteen years old and I'm going to have a baby
. . . It's not the end of the world I guess, but it sure is different from the
way I wanted it to be.*

—from the film.

*The film Lucy shows you that it could happen to you if you don't know
what you are doing. You should use protection if you are going to have
sex. I know. I made the same mistake as Lucy.*

—Pearlie England, age 16.

Lucy is a Puerto Rican girl from New York City. When she finds out
that she is pregnant, she rejects abortion and—with the help of her
mother, a social agency, and her boyfriend—faces the realities of her
pregnancy.

The scenes of her early love with Joe are shot in pretty settings with
the soft color, out-of-focus shots, and fresh scenes that you associate
with advertising and films such as *Elvira Madigan* and *A Man and A
Woman*. These scenes contrast strongly with the scenes of her early
pregnancy. Screeching brakes, honking horns, and street voices are the
background for the young couple's park-bench fight over Lucy's situation. The atmosphere surrounding a screaming fight with her sister in
their tenement apartment and the windy walk with her mother to the
prenatal clinic signify the change in Lucy's feelings about herself and
her future.

Notice the attitudes reflected in this film. There is no indication that Lucy was "guilty" or "wrong" for having intercourse, just that she wasn't smart enough to use protection. "If only Joe and I hadn't been so dumb." The assistance provided by her mother, her counselors, and the birth control clinic show a positive guidance for Lucy (though one can't help asking why it hadn't come sooner). Also, Lucy clearly realizes that her life will never be the same. "I did a lot of thinking, like how different my life would have been if this hadn't happened . . . Things would never be the same for either of us now." She isn't excited about having a baby and doesn't have sweet illusions about motherhood. She is also aware that she has three choices for her child—a foster home until she is ready to take care of it, adoption, or taking care of the baby herself from the start.

My students loved *Lucy* and it led to some mature discussion and questions. We talked about why Lucy probably didn't choose abortion. They also got into how different Lucy's life would have been if she had had birth control information or had an abortion. I think that the overall impression that Lucy's life will never be the same will stick in the minds of my students for a long time.

Consider showing this film with sex education classes from before junior high school. (*Many* girls get pregnant when they are in junior high school.) Plan your time well because students will want to see it more than once, and you will want to get into all the valuable discussion that *Lucy* initiates.

I sure hope my kid sister learns something from this and not the hard way like I did.

—Lucy, from the film.

Lucy (1972): 13 mins., color: rental $25, purchase $200. Director: Alfred Wallace. Distributor: Pictura Films.

SUGGESTED FEMINIST READING
Pierce, Ruth I. *Single and Pregnant.*
Rains, Prudence Mors. *Becoming an Unwed Mother.*

Madalyn

If you succeed?
Don't you know I'd find another cause. That other cause would be the continuing militancy directed toward freedom for women, intellectual and physical freedom for women, political freedom for women, monetary freedom for women, and of course I'm an anarchist.

—from the film.

Madalyn O'Hare is already something of a legend. An atheist, she has almost single-handedly kept the American people aware of the tendency toward alliance between Church and State in this country. As a graduate project at the University of Texas, Bob Elkins documented Madalyn on film. He shows sequences of her answering his questions

95

and those of other students in lecture halls. (These sequences have been cross-edited according to topics.) You rarely hear the questions, but the topics are flashed on the screen. Because of the vibrant, energizing personality of the subject, this conspicuous segmentation does not make the film seem too fragmented.

Some of the topics. What is an atheist? ("If we can question the idea of God, we can question any authority.") Why Texas? ("I didn't come here, I was brought . . . your jails are not a very nice place.") Your parents? ("I hated my mother's guts.") Hippies? ("I like to think that I am a flower child, even an aged one or an unblooming one.") Your bag? ("Don't just sit on your ass.")

Madalyn's direct manner is disarming and the film's cataloging of her responses enforces that quality. Humor and a strong sense of moral responsibility are frequently present in her "drive to action." You chuckle with her when she describes her arrest, which was based on the accusation that she had single-handedly beaten up fourteen policemen. You also laugh when she discloses that the astronauts, who so "spontaneously" quoted the Bible as they whirled around the moon on Christmas Eve, had program notes to guide their religious fervor. But there is no humor in the energy and money she organizes to fight her cause in the courts.

Documentary films by students and filmmakers with limited finances (this was shot with a 4:1 ratio) have two special features. First, there is the sense of discovery; the filmmaker is learning about the subject too. Second, because the subject and the filmmaker are on a one-to-one basis, there is a particularly relaxed and friendly mood on the part of the subject, a faith in the good will of the filmmaker.

Madalyn is a good film portrait of an independent, strong woman. This film is suitable for high-school-age students on. I would, however, precede the screening with some background on Madalyn O'Hare and atheism.

Madalyn (1970): 29 mins., color; rental $45, purchase $350. Filmmaker: Bob Elkins. Distributor: Bob Elkins.

SUGGESTED FEMINIST READING
Daly, Dr. Mary. "Women and the Catholic Church." *Sisterhood Is Powerful,* pp. 124-138. Edited by Robin Morgan.
Doely, Sarah Bentley (ed.). *Women's Liberation and the Church.*

Bob Elkins

Photo by Melinda Wickman.

I'm not sure why I became involved in filmmaking. I like the wide range of possibilities in terms of lifestyles. I like people and find filmmaking a good excuse to learn about people. I think I can be a good filmmaker when I apply myself.

—response to questionnaire.

Bob Elkins was born on Christmas 1945 in Bryan, Texas. He received a B.A. in history from Texas Tech University in 1968 and an M.A. in communication from the University of Texas at Austin in 1970. As an instructor in the Department of Radio/Television/Film, he taught film production at the Austin branch from 1970 through 1972. In June 1972, he left teaching to make films in documentary film and television advertising.

Elkins is doing free-lance work and trying to get funding for films dealing with the world of two Bolivian Indian tribes.

FILMOGRAPHY
Careers in Nursing and *Careers in Carpentry* (1973), 15 mins. Soundman.
Hill Country Happening (1972), 30 mins. Documentary of the Texas Arts and Crafts Fair. Producer/assistant editor.
Ralph Yarborough for U.S. Senate Campaign (1972). Five TV commercials and two five-minute films.
Acromantic (1971), 10 mins. Animated film. Production assistant.
Egg Shells (1971). Feature-length dramatic film. Associate editor.
Glasswork (1971), 15 mins. Documentary film about a glassblower. Produced for PBS.

97

The Future Is Now (1970), 30 mins. Film of an encounter group. Cameraman.

Andrew Sarris (1970), 30 mins. Film about film critic. Production assistant.

* *Madalyn* (1970), 30 mins.

Physics Today (1970), 30 mins. Soundman/second cameraman.

The Love Girl (1969), 15 mins. Interview with a five-year-old boy concerning the effects of TV upon children.

*Reviewed in this book.

Maedchen in Uniform

You must make up your mind that you will be happy here.
—Elizabeth Von Bernberg to Manuela.

Leontine Sagan made *Maedchen in Uniform* just before Hitler came to power. Set in Potsdam in 1913, the film exposes an authoritarian boarding school for the daughters of Prussian officers. The physical structure of the school, its rules, and the effect of the rules on the girls are a metaphor for the strategies of Hitler throughout Germany or of any oppressive authoritarian system.

In the story, Manuela, a motherless girl, is brought to the school by an aunt to be taught some discipline in the tradition of her captain father. As the principal prophesies, "These girls are the daughters of soldiers and, God willing, they will be the mothers of soldiers."

Manuela, highly emotional and sensitive, does not fare well under the strict structure of the school. She cannot and does not hide her affection and need for one of her teachers, Elizabeth Von Bernberg. Elizabeth is caught in the compromising position of functioning in the rigid authoritarian system of the school and feeling the needs the girls have for a freer, more individualized life. She questions the system by her behavior with the girls—kissing them good-night, giving Manuela a much-needed slip, speaking to Manuela after it has been forbidden. Yet she tries to make this behavior fit the system. "You disobeyed my order," the principal accuses Elizabeth. "But I believe I kept the spirit of your order," she counters. Elizabeth Von Bernberg's efforts to make a bad situation bearable only succeed in keeping the girls in the system, thus perpetuating it.

Because Manuela publicly announces her love for Von Bernberg, she is isolated from the other students by order of the principal (whose initial reaction was to shout: "A scandal!"). Overwhelmed and despairing, Manuela prepares to jump the incredible distance of the student stairwell. She is stopped by the other girls who, in the solidarity of revolution, go about the building shouting her name, breaking the rules of silence and order.

In this world of stone, shadows, and empty hallways, the emotional needs and desires of the girls are constantly thwarted. Touching scenes of these needs are in sharp contrast to scenes of the girls marching in line (even in nightgowns and slippers), the two neat rows of iron beds, the angularity of the building, and linear shadows of balustrades on the wall. The evening ritual of getting ready for bed is one of the only times they find to relate to their own bodies. In soft focus, medium shots, and close-ups, you see girls washing one another's hair, looking in the mirror, looking at their skin.

Leontine Sagan was an established theater director when she made *Maedchen in Uniform*. However, she has a sense of the power of film to communicate on its own terms. For example, light and shadow, the creative use of black and white are used to point up the sharp contrast of the needs of the girls and the reality of their situation.

Censorship delayed *Maedchen in Uniform*'s first screening in the United States. It is difficult to imagine why, since Manuela's need for Elizabeth von Bernberg is much more related to her needs for a mother figure than for a lover. The film was made with an all-woman cast of drama students. Rather than receive fixed salaries, they were given a permanent interest in the success of the film.

Maedchen in Uniform is one of the very best early sound films (incidentally, don't make the mistake of ordering the less interesting 1958 remake with Lili Palmer). This film can be used with many different groups. It easily holds the interest of teen-age audiences. After I showed it to my classes, I gave the students the choice of writing diaries for any one of the film characters or letters that any of the characters might have written.

Maedchen in Uniform (1931): 89 mins., b/w, German with English subtitles; rental $50. Director: Leontine Sagan. Distributor: Radim.

SUGGESTED FEMINIST READING
de Beauvoir, Simone. *The Second Sex.*
DeCrow, Karen. *The Young Woman's Guide to Liberation.*
Horney, Karen. *Feminine Psychology.*

Menilmontant

Kirsanov's films can be understood only in terms of themes and counter-themes, built up visually by artifice, that is, by nonnaturalistic means, using image, design, and metaphor. The camera, with all its possibilities and limitations, is supreme, but it is exploited only in so far as the adumbrations of the theme require and permit.

—Walter S. Michel, "In Memoriam of Dmitri Kirsanov."
Film Culture Reader (Praeger Publishers, 1970, pp. 39-40).

The opening shots of *Menilmontant* record a double murder—murders that orphan two young girls. It is quickly established that the sisters, as young women, must make a living doing factory work and boarding in a room in Menilmontant, the lower-class section of Paris. As the story develops, one sister flirts with a young man. He later invites her to his room, where she stays overnight. In the next scene she is waiting for her young man, only to see him meeting her sister. Unseen, she follows the couple and watches them go into his apartment. Time passes unrecorded by the film. The next time you see the young woman she is standing in front of a maternity hospital, a child in her arms. She wanders around the city, finally settling in a dark corner. Suddenly she spies her sister, now obviously a prostitute. Amazed at each other's fate, they embrace and go off together. The young man, who witnessed their reunion, is violently murdered by a prostitute, and the film ends with the close-ups of women working in a flower factory.

Menilmontant is impressive for the strong poetic qualities of its purely visual form and the universality of the problems that face the two sisters as women. The rhythm with which the images are presented is the music of this silent film. The speed of the opening and closing, scenes of violence, coupled with a remarkable use of hand-held camera, produces a sense of intensity. The editing provides you first with what the assailed sees and then what the assailant sees—a complete view of the action. Kirsanov again uses carefully calculated timing and camera placement in the bedroom sequence. The kind of slow, cold realism that the scene held for the young woman is attained by having the camera in the fourth wall and on tripod for most of the sequence. It is only in the imagination of the older sister that it assumes proportions of nudity and excitement, with close-up and angled shots superimposed on very fast moving shots of city life (which earlier in the film had been equated with glamour).

The symbolism used in the film, while suggestive and exploratory, doesn't become clichéd and staid. You see the water of the Seine when the younger sister leaves her first night of sex, a waterfall in her remembrances of childhood, the Seine again when she considers drowning her child. In addition, there are shots of trees reflected in water when she first sees her dead parents. Feet are seen in upper-angle close-ups as women walk away from their day's work; when the young man first appears; as the younger sister goes by the Seine; when the older sister taps her foot as a prostitute; as a prostitute watches the fight between her assistant and the pimp. In screening the film these repeated symbols provide a rhythm and unify the elements of the story. Water and feet are used suggestively and emotionally, not as labels.

With the same delicacy and sensitivity that Kirsanov uses symbolism, he introduces repeating shots and similar sequences. Superimposed shots of the city, violent scenes, women working in the flower factory, clocks, and long shots of the streets are repeated with rhythm, adding to the total impact of the film's emotion.

The content of *Menilmontant* is well geared to the experiences of many women—poverty, difficult family situations, violence causing irreversible developments in family relations, mediocre job opportunities, infatuation with sex but inadequate sex education, pimps in the street conning them into work, unplanned motherhood. These same subjects, when treated by the media, are frequently so sensationalized and portrayed with so little sensitivity to a woman's point of view that young women haven't had much chance to identify with literary or film characters. What do women gain from seeing more women like themselves being victimized? Well, for one thing, by noting the universality of the situation they can realize more fully the need for supporting one another.

In *Menilmontant* the sisters find strength in their mutual support. Once they reunite, the younger can raise her child with more dignity; and the older can leave prostitution, since she has affection and love at home. Kirsanov shows the tyranny of assembly-line work at the flower factory, but sisterhood is there, even in the repressive economic system. There are further implications of the strength women can find in themselves and one another in the violence of the prostitute against the pimp.

Use *Menilmontant* with confidence from high school years and older. It is an unusually well-made film with a feminist sensibility.

Menilmontant (1924): 35 mins., b/w, silent; rental $10. Director: Dmitri Kirsanov. Distributor: Universal Films or Museum of Modern Art ($18).

SUGGESTED FEMINIST READING
The Boston Women's Health Book Collective. *Our Bodies, Our Selves.*
Pierce, Ruth I. *Single and Pregnant.*

Meshes of the Afternoon

Deren made a paean to its [the body's] strength and grace, suggesting that it was the one constant in a world of changing space and time.
—P. Adams Sitney, Ed., *Film Culture Reader* (Praeger Publishers, 1970).

Dreams take place in a world devoid of space—as we experience it daily—in a time in which seconds become hours, hours seconds. When one wakes from a dream of the world of no set space, no ordered time, the only sure thing is that you have been there physically and emotionally, feeling that world of transfigured time and space. *Meshes of the Afternoon*, Maya Deren's first film, depicts the world of the trance, the dream.

A flower is dropped, a woman picks it up and drops her key. Eventually she enters a house. Having let herself in, she sees signs that the resident has been there recently but is now away. She sits down to wait and falls asleep. In her daydream she sees herself enter the house three times, until there are three of her. Also inhabiting the world of her daydream-trance is a figure dressed in black, with a mirrored face, who enters and awakens her. At this point one can no longer distinguish between outer and inner reality; and given two endings, it is not clear which, if either, is the "real."

Among the qualities of dreams recognized by all of us is the lack of coherent, continuous space. Through editing, the movie camera can follow a step that originates in one locus by its fall in a completely different geography. When the persona of the film is walking, knife in hand, to murder herself, she starts on the beach; her foot falls in grass; again it falls in a different grassy area; then onto a sidewalk; and finally, onto a carpet. This rendering of dream space, through cinema, is quickly recognized. But to Maya it is more than that. It also indicates the aspect of universal ritual that is inherent in all her works.

What I mean in that four stride sequence was that you have to come a long way, from the very beginning of time—to kill yourself, like the first life emerging from the primeval waters.
—Maya Deren, *Film Culture*, Winter 1965.

She returns to these primeval waters later on in the film. When she strikes her husband's face with the flower-key-knife, his face crashes as a mirror. As the mirror falls, we see the sea behind it. The mirror falls from the upper part of the frame onto the beach, and the sea slowly and rhythmically rolls over it. Later, in the second ending, the husband comes in to find the broken mirror on the floor. The persona is in the chair with a cut throat and, instead of blood, seaweed drips over her.

The dreamlike quality of the space and time is reminiscent dreams where running gets you nowhere—no matter how hard or fast you walk, you can't catch any person or goal. As her dream figure, Maya approaches the staircase within the house. She climbs in slow motion, as we watch in close-up from below. Then, from middle staircase, we see her climb farther, coming up in slow motion. Earlier she was running after the black, mirror-faced figure. She gained no distance on her even though she ran and the figure walked in slow motion. The stairs also serve to demonstrate the dream-fall, where you catch yourself just in time. Here Maya starts to fall back, back, backward through the window, only to catch herself on an interior stair. There are many more examples of this strategy in the film, always used with thought and balance. Every film device is related to Maya's intention. What could appear as hackneyed and labored, or just pure exhibitionism in the film of another director, is critically essential in the Deren films. Because dreams, or trances, are so confounded with reality, are so imposing on our daily existence, are so bizarre, they require a rare treatment for their exposition, a treatment exclusively possible in cinema.

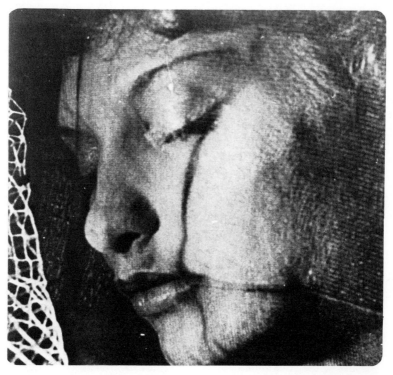

Maya used many opportunities to relate vision, exterior-interior, as a metaphor for the camera. As she is falling asleep in the chair, there is a close-up of her eye. The eye starts to close. Cut to a long-shot view that she sees out the window from the chair. This scene darkens as though a filter or mesh curtain is falling over it. Now we see the eye closed. Then back to the filtered view, which zooms out to include a cylinder that leads as a tunnel, the tunnel of a telescopic lens. The draped figure enters from the right into the long-irised shot. The cylinder, so clearly a camera part, relates directly to the fact that this interior vision, this view of her dream, is possible only through the strategies of the movie camera. This eye-camera metaphor is later elaborated. When her dream image is about to kill, there is a close-up of her eye which cuts to a close-up of her husband coming from her face. She sees that it isn't herself that is there, but him. The camera-eye can change what is there. As she lies on her bed, her husband is again over her—there is a close-up of her eye. The eye looks to the flower next to her on the pillow. The flower turns to a knife as she looks at it.

At other times the eye imagery is used to represent reflection, (as mirrors), suggesting that what one sees through the eye-camera is reflective of life, the real life which confounds inner and outer realities. The black-robed figure has a mirror face. Maya never gets to it, not until she kills her husband. But even if she had, all she would have seen would be more of herself, reflected in the mirror. In the dream she pulls back the bedsheets where the mirrored figure has put the flower. It is a knife, not a flower. In an appropriate upper-angled shot, she looks down on her reflection in the blade. When she takes the knife to kill herself and turns on her own seated, sleeping figure, the murderess has silver-ball eyes that reflect.

This mixture of confusion of identities, of reality and unreality, of real space and uncontrolled space, adds to the aspect of terror that the film communicates. Frequently, Maya's face has expressions of confusion, seeking, and trance. But it is a face of stark terror when, in a side close-up, she gropes with her mouth toward the figure she has just seen placing the rose on her bed. Later, when she is in the ritual game with her other two selves, the third to lift the key has suddenly a knife, not a key. In terror she puts her hand to block out the eyes of each self in turn. The terror also comes from the depth of presence that the viewer has in the film. If the viewer identifies the eye as a metaphor for the camera, then everything the camera sees is what the viewer sees.

"I try," Maya said, "to maintain the integrity of movement by making my camera a participant, a definite part of the film. In most motion pictures the camera only watches." Since the camera is your eye in *Meshes of the Afternoon,* you truly participate.

This is a film to use with classes in women's studies, art, psychology. Of all of Deren's films, *Meshes of the Afternoon* was most successful with my high school class in film. The students clearly read the filmic language and were mesmerized by the suspense. Some even told of having nightmares based on the film.

Meshes of the Afternoon (1943): 14 mins., b/w; rental $35; purchase $175. Filmmaker: Maya Deren. Distributor: Grove Press.

SUGGESTED FEMINIST READING
See suggested readings for *At Land.*

Mosori Monika

I didn't want to have children. One day the Lord called me . . . I left everything to become a missionary.   —Nun in film.

We treat each other like brothers or else we'll get sick.
—old Mosori woman.

Chick Strand's film presents a visual essay on the Mosori Indians of Venezuela that is both anthropologically valid and aesthetically appealing. Her main intention seems to be to present two views of the Mosori: one from the point of view of a missionary, whose order brought "civilization" and Christianity to the tribe twenty years earlier; the other from an old Mosori woman, whose long life includes years before the missionaries' arrival. While the nun and old woman often present conflicting attitudes, it is clear that the old woman sees no conflict in their sometimes compromising positions. She takes what is good from the missionaries' ways just as she does from the ancient ways of her people. To me her strength is an inner strength (not one assumed from an organized approach to life).

The natural benefits of the life of the Indians—the landscape, the ready foods, the respect and love for one another—are shown both in long tracking shots and in close-ups of the details of their lives. You see an old woman tying a hammock, a person pounding food, chunks of fish going into the mouth of a child. Civilization is also shown in extreme close-ups—the scrubbing of vegetables in the nun's kitchen, the wedding cake, a blood test. To me these images are edited to point out the validity of life before the missionaries came and to question the value in their presence. At one point a naked child is putting on a large leather shoe. In voiceover the nun says, "We civilized them. We taught them how to live like the human life, the life of men."

In a Catholic wedding the priest says, "Two sons of God, two brothers to take on the sacrament of marriage . . . may the women subject yourselves to your husbands." Later at the wedding party the nun, dressed in her white habit, passes behind the seated bride in her white gown. When I saw this shot, all the years of the oppressive structure of Catholicism for women snapped to my view. Yet I am sure that the nun in the film would look at it and still say, "That is right—that is the way it is—aren't we good to do all this for these people."

Mosori Monika deserves to be seen more than once and discussed more fully than it is here. It is rich both visually and conceptually. Use it freely with high-school-age students and older. It is excellent for women's studies, since you see and hear the Mosori women and the Catholic nun. It would also be good for anthropology studies (this film was done with the cooperation of the Anthropology Department of UCLA).

Mosori Monika (1971): 20 mins.; rental $24, purchase $275. Director: Chick Strand. Distributor: Contemporary Films/McGraw-Hill.

SUGGESTED FEMINIST READING
Leavitt, Ruby R. "Women in Other Cultures." *Woman in Sexist Society,* pp. 393-427. Edited by Vivian Gornick and Barbara K. Moran.
Mountain Wolf Woman. "Excerpts from her Autobiography." *Growing Up Female in America: Ten Lives,* pp. 263-283. Edited by Eve Merriam.

Nobody's Victim

Nobody's Victim is excellent. We particularly like the factual, direct manner in which the information is presented. Other films we have seen have presented some of the same material but in over-dramatic terms.
—Detroit Police.

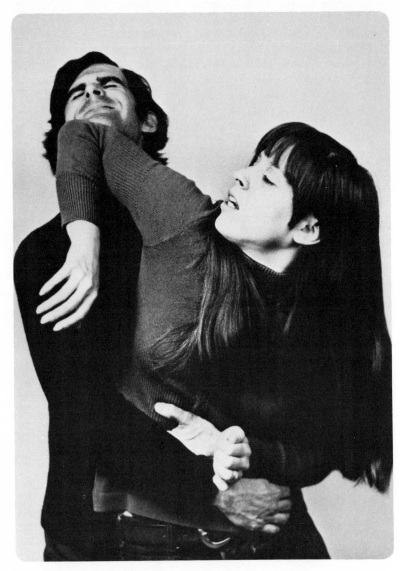

I have seen a couple of films about self-defense for women that were not only over-dramatic, but also condescending. This film can help people (not just women) prepare, both psychologically and physically, for the possibility of aggression at home, in the car, or on the street. Beverly Moss, the actress, narrates and a woman self-defense instructor demonstrates physical defense.

The approach is always positive. The films says, this is how to protect yourself; here is what you should avoid; this is how to be prepared. It warns: "Use physical self-defense techniques only if you have to protect yourself from bodily injury. These should only be employed as a last-minute resort." There are a few personal testimonies, but they are not gruesome. For instance, a woman who was raped while hitchhiking determinedly states: "I was angry at myself for not being able to do anything about it." That, I feel, summarizes the attitude of the film. There are personal dangers, but we can be cautious and prepared to defend ourselves.

This film is good to use for high school age groups and older (both men and women), and it is particularly well suited for library and community screenings. Self-defense summary sheets are available upon request.

Nobody's Victim (1972): 20 min., color; rental $20, purchase $230. Directors: Vaughn Obern, Alan Baker. Distributor: Ramsgate Films.

Park Film

Now when I do see a couple I still wish I were the girl, but I think of the film and I just forget about the whole thing. I don't get into the complicated and emotional thoughts that I usually get into when I see a couple. —student, age 15.

Have you ever watched a young couple enviously? Do you remember, particularly as a teen-age girl, waiting for a film to begin, sitting at a dance, or walking through the park with another girl and wanting so much to be a couple? Linda Feferman starts with that feeling in *Park Film*. As Linda and her girl friend are walking through Central Park, they see a young couple swing by hand in hand. Both look at the couple enviously. How do they deal with the feeling? Linda puts her hair under her hat, buttons her jacket, smokes like a boy, struts ahead of her friend, swings from a tree—until the whole joke ends laughingly as Linda's hair falls out of the hat.

The film is simple, yet it is touching, honest, and sensitive. We've all had the down feeling of not being paired off with a boy or man. Being a couple is the height of joy according to advertising in *Seventeen* magazine, *Cosmopolitan,* and so on. Because of this media image, seeing couples often lowers a girl's self-esteem. What a refreshing change to see the myth nudged (though not busted) and girls dealing with it!

Park Film was successful with my students and led to fruitful discussion of shared feelings. We examined why we, like the girls in the film, have these feelings.

Park Film (1969): 2 mins., b/w; rental $10. Director: Linda Feferman. Distributor: Linda Feferman.

SUGGESTED FEMINIST READING
DeCrow, Karen. *The Young Woman's Guide to Liberation.*

Egan, Andrea. *Why Am I So Miserable When These Are Supposed to Be the Best Years of My Life?*

Nunes, Maxine, and White, Deanna. *The Lace Ghetto.*

Phoebe

This film makes me realize what responsibility you have when you're a girl. I know now when I get ready to have sex, I will be mature enough to get some protection.

—Liz Newton, age 15.

As of 1968, one-fourth of twenty-year-old girls had had at least one baby while in their teens. Unfortunately, there is little (or nothing) in documentary or fiction films dealing with the problems faced by the young pregnant woman; her attitudes; and the way in which the conditions of her homelife, education, and religion determine what will happen to her next. Many of us got married when we were pregnant; many of us were the unwanted children of a teen-age pregnancy; and most of us were brought up to think of teen-age pregnancy as a mistake (sin) for which a girl deserved to suffer. *Phoebe,* a film from the National Film Board of Canada, deals with a summer day in the life of a teenager who is trying to tell her parents and boyfriend that she is pregnant.

The film opens with an out-of-focus close-up shot of Phoebe in bed. As the shot comes into focus, there is a slow pan of the objects in Phoebe's room—a Modigliani print, a candle, a copy of *The Catcher in the Rye,* some stuffed animals, a picture of a boy. By the time her mother nags her out of bed to the phone, you sense Phoebe's discomfort. You fully realize her condition as she vomits and then imagines herself as a mirrored image that is very pregnant.

Phoebe hitches a ride to the beach with her boyfriend. At the beach they go to an abandoned house to change, then to the water. In these sequences we see Phoebe's fantasies of the possible reactions of her parents, teachers, and Paul to the news, "I'm going to have a baby." Later at home, Phoebe runs to her room and nervously dials the phone. "Paul," she says, "what I've been trying to tell you all day is I'm going to have a baby." She hangs up before she can hear a response and goes to the window. Tears stream down her face.

Sequences that show what Phoebe is thinking are particularly well done. From a close-up or a zoom-to-close-up you are immediately given entrance into her imagination or memory. Differences in clothing, hair style, and piano sound all aid in distinguishing the real from the remembered or the imagined. Toward the end of the film, however, when she imagines that she is running away, the real and the imagined are only vaguely distinguished. She has on the clothes of that day and is imagined in the house that she is about to enter. When she enters the house, she will finally allow the imagined—telling Paul and her family that she is pregnant—to become part of the real.

Since Paul is a joking, mimicking kind of boy, he is in sharp contrast to the cold reality of the pregnancy that Phoebe faces. Sound is used very appropriately to characterize Paul. Early in the film you realize that the tinny, out-of-tune piano music you have been intermittently hearing comes from a piano that Paul plays in the abandoned house.

Of course the mother is screened as a nagging bitch. She yells at Phoebe because her breakfast is cold and criticizes her boyfriend. In Phoebe's imaginings the mother is shown as crying when she and her husband fight. And, as always, the father is characterized as the king of the roost. Again in Phoebe's imagination, the mother says, "What have you done? What will your father say? Phoebe, he'll kill you."

The film consistently presents Phoebe's feelings of guilt. She feels completely responsible for having "given in" and "gone all the way." In a quiet moment Paul asks, "What's wrong? Are you sick? Is it something I did?" She answers, "Oh, no, nothing to do with you."

The film makes it quite clear that the possibility of abortion is not really open for Phoebe. She always says she is "going to have a baby," never that she is pregnant. Yet in her imaginings she never thinks of herself with a child. She is concerned only with whether Paul will leave her, what her parents will say, and whether she will have to drop out of high school. In a brief memory sequence a friend tells Phoebe about her abortion. The filmmaker makes this scene seem forbidden; the whole tone is back-alleyish. It is the only time music other than the piano is used. Everyone is dancing and drinking. The friend speaks in whispers, with a foreign accent. After this memory Phoebe asks Paul if he is afraid of dying. "When you're young, you're not supposed to think about dying, just living. Why? Are you afraid of dying?" "No, not that," she answers. 109

Phoebe is a well-organized piece of short fiction. It certainly will provoke discussion, particularly if it is coupled with a film like *It Happens to Us* or *Lucy*. Whenever I have used it, I have asked the students (or participants) to discuss how Phoebe's situation is like and/or different from the situation in their neighborhood. One way or another the problem of the pregnant teen has entered our lives as teens, and certainly it is a concern of the feminist movement.

Phoebe (1967): 28 mins., b/w; rental $14, purchase $200. Director: George Kaczender. Distributor: Contemporary Films/McGraw-Hill.

SUGGESTED FEMINIST READING
DeCrow, Karen. *The Young Woman's Guide to Liberation.*
Pierce, Ruth I. *Single and Pregnant.*
Rains, Prudence Mors. *Becoming an Unwed Mother.*

George Kaczender

The men and women of my films are the victims of social compromise; the situation in which they find themselves usually involves an often ironic awareness of this malaise in their lives and what results from it.
—letter to Jeanne Betancourt, June 20, 1973.

Hungarian by birth (1933), Kaczender was educated in the Academy of Theater and Film in Budapest. He worked as assistant director in the Hungarian Film Studios until 1956. In 1957 he immigrated to Canada, where he began working for the National Film Board of Canada. By 1969, when he left the Film Board, he had edited eighty-five films and written/directed twelve. Between 1969 and 1971 he helped set up International Cinemedia Center Ltd. and Minotaur Film Productions Inc. George Kaczender is now making feature-length films with his own production company.

FILMOGRAPHY
U-Turn (1972). Feature length. George Kaczender Prod. Ltd.
Brown Wolf (1972), 28 mins. Learning Corporation of America.

The Story of a Peanut Butter Sandwich (1971), 13 mins. International Cinemedia Center Ltd.

Five short films (1970-1971). Produced for International Cinemedia.

The Edible Woman (1970). Feature length at script stage. Co-writer.

Anarchists in Love (1970). Feature length at script stage. Oscar Lowenstein Productions Ltd.

Mr. G. A. in X (1970). Feature length at script stage.

Newton (1970), color, 20 mins. Dramatized documentary. International Cinemedia Center Ltd.

Marxism (1969), color, 22 mins. Dramatized documentary. International Cinemedia Center Ltd.

Freud (1969), color, 27 mins. Dramatized documentary. International Cinemedia Center Ltd.

Don't Let the Angels Fall (1968), black and white, 100 mins. National Film Board feature film.

Sabre and Foil (1967), black and white, 8 mins. National Film Board.

Track a Shadow (1967), color, 20 mins. Dramatized. National Film Board.

Little White Crimes (1967), color, 20 mins. Dramatized. National Film Board.

The Game (1966), black and white, 28 mins. Dramatized. National Film Board.

The World of Three (1966), black and white, 28 mins. Dramatized. National Film Board.

You're No Good (1965), black and white, 28 mins. Dramatized. National Film Board.

* *Phoebe* (1964), black and white, 28 mins. Dramatized. National Film Board.

City Scene (1963), black and white, 28 mins. National Film Board.

Ballerina (1963), black and white, 28 mins. National Film Board.

Nahanni (1962), color, 20 mins. Co-author, editor. National Film Board.

*Reviewed in this book.

Ramparts of Clay

This film is a portrait of life in a North African village, but the theme of the struggle for human dignity and the desire to determine one's own way of life is universal. This universality, as well as the superbly accomplished techniques, should make Ramparts of Clay *an enduring classic, in the tradition of Robert Flaherty's films to which it is perhaps most closely related.* —Nadine Covert, *Film Library Quarterly,* Fall 1971.

"Praise be to God. Today she will be a woman." So sing the Algerian women as they prepare a young bride for her wedding night. She is draped with a white cloth and carried away by her husband. The bride is a victim of the traditional roles that enslave all her people to rigid customs and rituals, setting the political tone for their own victimization by colonial powers. But the story of *Ramparts of Clay* takes place after 1962 and the independence of Tunisia.

111

Jean-Louis Bertucelli filmed *Ramparts of Clay* on the basis of French sociologist Jean Duvignaud's five-year study (1961-1965) of a Tunisian village (as reported in his book, *Change at Shebika*, Pantheon Books, 1970). During Duvignaud's study of Shebika, Tunisia achieved independence from France. For the inhabitants of the village it meant little, since their Tunisian leaders were as oppressive as, if not more so than the French. When the men received half wages for their work in the salt-rock mountains, they went on strike. The government sent troops that surrounded the strikers. After a young woman, Rima, stole the rope from the only well, the soldiers left and the strikers won, at least temporarily.

When the Tunisian government refused to let Bertucelli film Duvignaud's report in Shebika, he went to a similar village in Algeria. There he reenacted the events in Shebika with the people of the Algerian village as the players. The only professionals were the Algerian foreman and Rima (played by Moroccan actress Leila Schenna). With the exception of the French cameraman, Andreas Winding, the crew was Algerian.

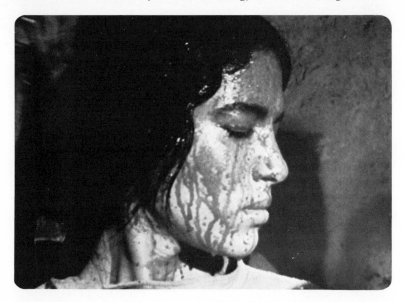

My concerns are with the ways in which the film depicts the women of the village and how Rima, growing in consciousness, struggles internally to free herself from the bonds of tradition, religion, and subjection. Bertucelli sums up the order of things in the villages of Tunisia and Algeria:

In order to film the women, I had to get in good with the men first. Then they ordered the women to let themselves be filmed and they didn't mind. —*Film Library Quarterly*, Fall 1971.

Rima, nineteen years old, orphaned at an early age, is virtually a slave in the home of the people who raised her. In striking close-ups you see her watching with envy and curiosity as mini-skirted, short-haired Tunisian social workers take the census of the village. She longs to read and write, crouching over newspapers that once wrapped groceries, trying to remember the words taught to her by her eight-year-old charge. Skepticism crosses her face as she watches a young woman prepared for marriage.

Even though the strike ended as a result of Rima's heroic and clever theft of the well rope, life goes on with boredom and frustration for her. One morning, after drawing the water up the well shaft, she lets the bucket drop back down and goes to sit motionless in a corner—her own strike against oppression. As she leaves the well she travels an eternity in time, her consciousness moving rapidly through the time and space of her limited experiences to an awareness and declaration of independence. The visuals show this by short shots of her face, some only a few frames long. These catch her quickly moving face in close-up, from several angles, with all the contrasts of light and shadow that characterize the village. The shots contrast her consciousness with the reality of her life in the village, with its limitations.

Finding her motionless, the women sprinkle her with chicken blood and try to pray away the evil that possesses her. Rima accepts this with seeming calm, but by now you know the struggles brewing within her, struggles described in the final scene of the film as a Berber chants:
Mother, O tender mother, My will is twisted like a grapevine. There is no doorway back to the past. The sun has fallen low behind the ramparts. I am free inside my loneliness.

In another scene Rima is shown on her sleeping mat, awake as the others sleep. Then she is seen running across the desert and away from the village. The camera follows, getting her at increasing distances, until finally she is indistinguishable on the terrain. The camera makes a sharp swing to the right, taking a close-up of a helicopter window. The sound track cuts abruptly from the Berber chant to the sharp clatter of helicopter wings. The credits appear superimposed over the close-up of the helicopter window.

It was meant to destroy the film a little . . . it puts the film in the present. Without that, one gets the impression that these people live in the Middle Ages, that they are very primitive. Whereas, they are not at all primitive.
　　　　　　　　　　　　　　—Bertucelli to *Film Library Quarterly*, Fall 1971.
Ramparts of Clay is a powerful, quiet film. The visuals are extraordinary in their calmness, capturing the quiet dignity of the people. Use it with high school aged groups and older as a valid document of the Algerian village. Modern history, anthropology, sociology, and religion classes would find it particularly valuable.

Ramparts of Clay (1971): 87 mins., color; rental $75, purchase (apply). Director: Jean-Louis Bertucelli. Distributor: Cinema 5.

SUGGESTED FEMINIST READING
de Beauvoir, Simone. *The Second Sex.*
Leavitt, Ruby R. "Women in Other Cultures." *Woman in Sexist Society*, pp. 393-427. Edited by Vivian Gornick and Barbara K. Moran.

Ritual in Transfigured Time

The form proper of film is, for me, accomplished only when the elements, whatever their original context, are related according to the special character of the instrument of film itself—the camera and the editing —so that the reality which emerges is a new one—one which only film can achieve and which could not be accomplished by the exercise of any other instrument.

—Maya Deren, *Anagram.*

The reality emerging in *Ritual in Transfigured Time* is an exploration of the "point of view from which the external world itself is but an element in the entire structure and scheme of metamorphosis. *Ritual* is about the nature and process of change." (From *Anagram.*)

Many things change in *Ritual*, mostly through action which is controlled in a time that is possible only in the worlds of cinema and dream. The story (if that is what it is) is of Rita Christiani, a widow, walking in her dream and assuming her other self, Maya. She goes to a party which is acted out as a ritual dance. Figures move in slow motion, then freeze. Movements are repeated. Everyone—while greeting and departing, dancing, talking, and gesturing—is very depersonalized. Christiani and Frank Westbrook are seeking out each other. When they meet, they touch hands in a dance movement and are immediately transported to a sculpture garden. There, as they dance in slow motion, she flies while he does two jumps like a rooster. Three women, (one of them Anais Nin) who are dancing together, come—one by one—to dance with him. After each dance he does his cock jump. As Rita flees from him, she turns to the camera with the face of Maya. Frank jumps and turns in a third-position pose. When he lands he is not on the ground, but in another part of the garden as a statue on a pedestal. As Rita discovers him there, he moves off the pedestal in several shots of freeze-frame release. Then he pursues Rita, leaping as she runs. In order to flee him she, now Maya, runs into the sea. We see Rita turning, dropping through the lower edge of the frame. Then, through the upper edge, a white form drops twice in close-up, each time falling, falling, until the full form has passed through the screen. Her widow's garb is white in negative. A close-up of her face ends the film as she lifts her veil and opens her eyes.

The magic of the camera, which explored space in *Meshes of the Afternoon* (page 102), here examines the qualities of time. Time as it influences change. Time is contracted, expanded, stopped. The changes, metamorphoses within these weird times, are controlled on a larger scale, the scale of the art form of film, one that can reflect the larger controls at work in a universe where there are worlds and domains of worlds in our own minds in which there is no time as we experience it daily. The camera is the form that can express these worlds to the point where the stock itself can be the medium of the metamorphosis in time. When Rita changes from widow to bride, her change, as we visually experience it, is effected by using the negative film stock.

It is a concept of method: a controlled manipulation of any or all elements into a form which will transform and transfigure them.

—Maya Deren, *Film Culture*, Winter 1965.

When Maya is disappearing, she doesn't disappear by fading away, as you would expect from the possibilities of the film form. She disappears by going in slow, slower, slowest motion.

The sexual-feminist aspects of *Ritual* are put forth by a woman who is not only honest in the representation of sexual connotations that emerge from the state of women's oppression, but positive in the conclusions that she reaches.

In trance, Rita is searching for a love. She is led to Maya Deren by Anaïs Nin, her Cerberus. Maya, vivacious and in control, is unwinding the yarn of her life. She has Rita roll it. As the yarns runs out, Maya disappears and Rita goes to the party. I take this to mean that Rita has taken strength from another woman, an example, a feminine hero. The party is an ordeal for Rita. She is constantly thwarted in her search for her love. Having found him, she is honestly disillusioned by his "cockiness" and interest in other women. Deservedly, he becomes a statue—lifeless. Down from his perch, he becomes a hunter pursuing his prey, Rita. She runs, twice turning into Maya. It is the strength from Maya which leads her to the sea, where she finds the only escape from his male domination: death. It is now that she becomes a bride, united (I would suspect) to Maya in death.

Use *Ritual in Transfigured Time* with college classes and adult groups. It is appropriate for groups in women's studies, aesthetics, art, and dance.

Ritual in Transfigured Time (1945-46). 15 mins., b/w, silent; rental $35, purchase $150. Director: Maya Deren. Distributor: Grove Press.

SUGGESTED FEMINIST READING
See suggested readings for *At Land*.

Salt of the Earth

Whose neck shall I stand on to feel superior? I don't want anything lower than me. I want to rise up and push everything with me as I go.
—Esperanza.

Herbert Biberman, one of the blacklisted Hollywood directors, served six months in jail for refusing to answer questions for the House Committee on Un-American Activities. Rather than direct in England or work under a pseudonym, like other blacklisted directors, he chose to make *Salt of the Earth* independently in the States. He had to work with open interference from the film industry, unions, and the corporate interests of major motion picture companies.

The story line, by Michael Wilson, is based on the experiences of the Chicanos of Mine-Mill Local 890, who successfully struck the Delaware Zinc Company for equal treatment with Anglo miners. The strike was notable because it was successful only when the men recognized the equal status of the women among them.

Biberman shot the footage on location, using the miners and the women for most of the roles. A few white professionals were necessary since the Mexicans had so few Anglo friends. The female lead role,

Esperanza, is played by Rosaura Revelutas. There were many problems on location: constant threats from the community, difficulties in coordinating shooting with the miners' work schedule, limited equipment, inexperienced technicians, and shortage of crew. Besides the difficulty of shooting on a six-week schedule, the company was deprived of Rosaura for the last week of shooting. Immigration authorities saw to it that her passport stamp was illegal on some minor technicality, so that they were able to deport her to her home in Mexico. By the time shooting was nearly completed, the threats of the Anglo community and the mine company has become so convincing that the crew had to leave by cover of night.

Yet Biberman's difficulties had barely begun. Not only was he limited by low budget from editing, taping the sound, synchronizing sound, and making prints; he was also constantly being thwarted by film industry unions from getting studios, skilled help, and processing. Much of the work was done in pieces, each sent to a different studio, so that there would be less chance of recognition. Finally completed, the film was boycotted from the theaters by the projectionists' union. Though it is rarely seen publicly in the U.S.A., *Salt of the Earth* has received world-wide recognition and many prizes.

A description of the strike might well begin with a look at the women and their involvement in the struggle. First with quiet purpose and then with proud realization of their strength, the women ask to form an auxiliary of the miners' union. Then they insist that plumbing become a strike demand. Soon they begin to serve coffee and food to picketers; they also type and mimeograph materials. Later, when a court injunction takes the men off the picket line, the women take over; and finally they go to jail.

Against this background the film presents the internal struggle of Esperanza and Ramón, one couple who are tradition-bound in a stereotyped husband/wife relationship. Through the strike, Esperanza gains a sense of purpose outside her home. Ramón's pride and his own feelings of self-worth suffer as he sees his wife's successful efforts in maintaining the strike, while he takes care of household matters. In one of the first sequences of the film, Ramón says to Esperanza, "Can't you think of anything except yourself." As the strike develops, she starts to think of herself as a person with responsibilities outside the limits of her home, a political being with effective power.

One of the women says, "These changes come with pain, not just for Ramón, but for other husbands too." Painful or not, the changes are there: Esperanza relates to herself, her family, and her community with new dignity and self-respect. Her rise to an equal footing with her husband is seen as an essential element in the Mexican-Americans' growing efforts against discrimination. There is no turning away, just as there wasn't for the workers once they decided to demand equality with the Anglos.

The simplicity and directness of the camerawork reinforces the honesty and authenticity of the Mexican struggle. Many front close-ups, without makeup, bring the people close to the viewer. By the end of the film they are friends, brothers and sisters to all people who have had

to struggle to find equality in marriage or community. Gentle super-
imposition helps make transitions. Frequently Esperanza narrates, re-
minding you of the authenticity of the story. The simple dialogue carries
all the tonal variations and speech patterns of the bilingual workers.
Mike Wilson has captured their terse, direct speech.

Use *Salt of the Earth* with high school age groups and older. As a
document of unionism in the fifties, the oppression of women within
minority groups, and the indomitable human spirit, it is particularly
useful for classes in women's studies, modern history, sociology, and
psychology.

Salt of the Earth (1954): 94 mins., b/w; rental $55. Director: Herbert
Biberman. Distributor: Macmillan/Audio Brandon Films.

SUGGESTED FEMINIST READING
Jones, "Mother" Mary. "Excerpts from her Autobiography." *Growing
Up Female in America: Ten Lives,* pp. 211-232. Edited by Eve
Merriam.
Longauex y Vásquez, Enriqueta. "The Mexican-American Woman."
Sisterhood Is Powerful, pp. 379-384. Also read Elizabeth Sutherland's
introduction to this article, pp. 376-379. Edited by Robin Morgan.

Herbert Biberman

*You can't find out about a country in its jails any more than you can
in its congresses. You don't find out about a country in its extremities
but in its center, in the ratio between its people's discovery of themselves and their acceptance of those who stifle their self-knowledge.*
—from *Salt of the Earth, The Story of a Film* (Beacon Press, 1965).

Born and reared in Pennsylvania, Herbert Biberman was graduated
from the University of Pennsylvania in 1921. After a few years in his
family's textile business, he went to Yale to study drama under George
Pierce Baker. Then he traveled to Europe. Soon after returning to New
118 York in 1928, he became top director in the Theater Guild. He was

founder of the Directors' Guild and the Hollywood Anti-Nazi League and was active in the Screenwriters' Guild.

In 1947 Herbert Biberman was called before the House Committee on Un-American Activities for refusing to answer the question, "Are you now, or have you ever been a member of the Communist Party?" He served six months of a twelve-month sentence. His comment on this period of his life; "Citizens in cultural pursuits, such as myself, had to choose in such a way that history will not label us as cowards or chumps." His wife, the actress Gale Sondergaard, was also blacklisted. Biberman died in 1971 at the age of seventy-one.

Sambizanga

Sambizanga presents the story of an Angolan worker and revolutionary, Domingos Xavier (played by Domingos Oliviera). Early in the film Domingos is arrested and tortured to extract from him information on the other secret forces in his area of Luanda. His wife Maria (Elisa Andrade) is the focus of the story as it shows her being shocked into becoming a political person by her husband's arrest. As a typical village wife and mother, Maria was not aware of her husband's political involvement. Child strapped to her back, she walks from town to town, prison to prison, searching for him. By the time she reaches the right place, she is too late to see him alive. The film ends with evidence of the growing numbers and strength of the resistence, encouraged and supported by this new martyr.

119

The simple plot, played by an amateur cast, is shot in a lyrical but unpretentious style. Sara Maldoror sensitively captures the strength and beauty of Maria by repeated close-ups as she trudges over many roads. That the Angolan struggle still goes on, underground, is witnessed by the fact that *Sambizanga* could not be filmed in Angola, but was shot in the Republic of Congo.

Like morality plays and many Third World message films, *Sambizanga* presents characters that are either all good or all bad, all right or all wrong.

I have seen *Sambizanga* only once and have not had the opportunity to screen it for an audience. It seems appropriate for high school and older. You might want to precede or follow the film with some political history of Angola.

Sambizanga. (1973): 101 mins., color; rental $110. Director: Sarah Maldoror. Distributor: New Yorker Films.

Schmeerguntz

Schmeerguntz is one long raucous belch in the face of the American Home. A society which hides its animal functions beneath a shiny public surface deserves to have such films as Schmeerguntz shown everywhere—in every PTA, every Rotary Club, every club in the land. For it is brash enough, brazen enough, and funny enough to purge the soul of every harried American married woman.
—Ernest Callenbach, Film Quarterly.

It is hard to think of yourself as a lovely pregnant lady when you have to put on your support stockings and can barely reach your swollen feet. It is hard to see yourself as the darling mother in the soap ads when you have to clean a dirty diaper. Yet the realities of flushing toilets, swollen bodies, and puking babies are rarely included in the barrage of images of womanhood and motherhood presented to women from early childhood.

With a vengeance *Schmeerguntz* corrects some of those omissions in visual collages of the more mundane aspects of womanhood. The images and sounds we commonly are pressed to associate with being a woman —televised beauty pageants, love-song lyrics, the smiling ladies of advertising—are contrasted with "unsightly" ones like a pregnant woman vomiting, flushing toilets, soiled diapers, and so on.

I saw *Schmeerguntz* only once but was delighted to see so many unmentionables thrown on the screen with blatant realism. Use the film freely with high school age classes and older. It is clever and fun in its technique and strong in its impact. Be sure to screen it more than once.

Schmeerguntz (1965-66): 15 mins., b/w; rental $15, purchase $130. Director: Gunvor Nelson. Distributor: Canyon Cinema.

SUGGESTED FEMINIST READING

Embree, Alice. "Media Images 1: Madison Avenue Brainwashing—The

Facts." *Sisterhood Is Powerful*, pp. 175-191. Edited by Robin Morgan.
Florika. "Media Images 2: Body Odor and Social Order." *Sisterhood Is Powerful*, pp. 191-197. Edited by Robin Morgan.

The Smiling Madame Beudet

I view Madelaine Beudet as a proto-feminist revolutionary; she attempts to overthrow the husband who is her oppressor.
                    —Joan Braderman, *Art Forum*, September 1972.

A loveless marriage, a woman trapped by financial dependence, an attempted murder—these are the narrative elements of *The Smiling Madame Beudet*. Despite such a conventional plot, this film has two saving and exciting features. First, the story is related with a feminist perspective. Second, it is a classic of the silent film, revealing the psychological state of the characters through purely cinematic devices. For example, visual techniques reveal Madame Beudet's struggle with fantasies of freedom. The handsome tennis player of a magazine page becomes live and carries her husband off; yet the husband remains calmly at his desk. When the maid asks for the night off, Madame suddenly sees the maid's handsome fiancé beside her.   121

As the film progresses, you sense Madame Beudet's mounting oppression from her coarse, bourgeois mate, who blissfully lives as master of the house. He exercises his authority so blatantly that when his wife refuses to go to the opera *Faust* with him, he locks her piano and takes the key so that she can't have her one private pleasure. When he crushes the head of a decorative doll, he looks guiltily at his friend and says, "So fragile, just like women."

Madame, never smiling, watches as her husband repeats a well-worn joke.

When something disturbs the husband, he puts an unloaded revolver to his head and pulls the trigger . . . . Need I say more about the attempted murder, except that it backfires. When Monsieur Beudet picks up the revolver (now loaded), he points it at his wife, saying, "I should shoot you." (She hadn't kept the household records accurately!) When the revolver goes off, the shocked Beudet is so oblivious of his wife's wrath that he thinks she loaded the revolver to kill herself. "You wanted to kill yourself. What would I do without you?" She stares at the camera with a stolid, unflinching expression. Her act of courage is unrewarded; she must go on. The closing shot is of this couple greeting a local priest as they walk through their small town.

Much of the imagery of the film is based on Madame Beudet's feelings of imprisonment by her surroundings and the regulated order of time. Clocks and calendars are always in evidence; Beudet is ever looking at his watch. Madame Beudet looks out the window only to see the courthouse and local jail. She approaches what seems to be a window, but it is a mirror reflecting her sorrowing face. As she wakes up to a new day, a long shot of her sitting up in bed is superimposed by an animated pendulum. Taking her head between her hands, she moves back and forth, keeping time with the seconds marked by the pendulum, forcing herself into the order. It is only in her imagination that things appear in slow or fast time. Her real life will not allow any deviation from the norm.

In *Women and Madness* (p. 235), Phyllis Chesler asks:

Why didn't our mothers and grandmothers and great grandmothers tell us what battle it was we lost, or never fought, so that we would understand how total was our defeat, and that religion and madness and frigidity were how we mourned it?

Why were our mothers so silent about rape and incest and prostitution and their own lack of pleasure?

Germaine Dulac was not silent. In *The Smiling Madame Beudet* she has shown us the typical plight of the bourgeois housewife of France in the twenties. Unfortunately, Madame Beudet's situation is not unlike that of many women today. Show this film—possibly more than once. It is certainly good as early as high school.

The Smiling Madame Beudet (1923): 35 mins., b/w, silent; rental $18.
Director: Germaine Dulac. Distributor: Museum of Modern Art.

SUGGESTED FEMINIST READING
Cornwell, Regina. "Maya Deren and Germaine Dulac: Activists of the Avant-Garde." *Film Library Quarterly* (vol. 5, no. 1), pp. 29-38.

Friedan, Betty. *The Feminine Mystique.*
Horney, Karen. *Feminine Psychology.*
Woolf, Virginia. *Mrs. Dalloway.*

Germaine Dulac

Photo courtesy of Charles Ford.

—with D. W. Griffith in a visit to the U.S. in 1921.

Germaine Dulac (1882-1942) was reared in Amiens, France, where she studied the arts. After her marriage to Albert Dulac in 1905, she started a career as a writer, working on two feminist journals, *La Fran-çaise* and later *La Fronde.* Soon after watching *Caligula* being shot, she formed her own film company, Delia Film. Dulac's first films were done within the framework of commercial film. By 1927, however, she found she was having too many hassles with producers and distributors and was making too many compromises with her film aesthetics. Consequently, at forty-five she became part of the second avant-garde in France and started making "pure" cinema.

For many years Dulac was involved in the film-club movement in France, which promoted good films from both France and abroad. Dulac, a foremost critic, also lectured frequently in special cinema theaters and clubs around Europe in order to promote film as an art form with its own aesthetics. Later Dulac, suffering from ill health, began working for France Actualities-Gaumont, a newsreel company. Little is known of the last twelve years of her life.

FILMOGRAPHY

Germaine Dulac's work includes nearly thirty films. However, only a few are available. For a complete filmography, see *Anthologie du Cinéma*, vol. 4, p. 47 (L'Avant-Scene, Paris).
The Seashell and the Clergyman (1928). Distributor: Museum of Modern Art.
* *The Smiling Madame Beudet* (1923). Distributor: Museum of Modern Art.

*Reviewed in this book.

Something Different

Both Eva and Vera are captives of quiet desperation while at the same time expressing a determination to shape their own separate destinies.
—Naome Gilburt, "To Be Our Own Muse: The Dialectics of Culture Heroine," *Women and Film*, (Fall 1972), p. 28.

Something Different describes the lives of two Czech women: Vera Uzelac, housewife and mother, and Eva Bosakova, gymnast. Both are under continuous pressure from their jobs. Eva, supervised by a demanding male trainer, is restricted by the rigorous physical demands of training for the Olympics. Vera, bound by family responsibilities, is restricted by the continual demands of caring for husband and child. During the course of the film, each faces a crisis. Eva must push her physical strength and conquer her fear to do a difficult exercise. Vera, having gone into an affair, must choose between husband and lover. Having faced their respective crises, each goes back to her daily life— Vera staying within the family, Eva going from winning an Olympic gold medal to training a young gymnast.

The brilliance of the film is in the way the camerawork and editing reflect the story. As the film develops, the two lives are intercut with increasing rapidity, emphasizing the similarities between the two women. At times one woman will drop out of the frame as the other rises; one will turn her back as the other completes this gesture by facing the camera. Their similarity is also stressed by showing the repetitive structure of their activities. Eva has her training program with its repeated exercises; Vera has the smaller, but also redundant, tasks of child rearing and house cleaning. Both are confined physically—Vera by the physical barriers of walls, halls, doors; Eva by the spaces of the studio. In watching the comparisons, I sensed that Chytilova respects Eva's role more than Vera's. Or at least finds it more appealing. The gestures of her training are grander than Vera's scrubbing vegetables or picking up children's toys; winning the Olympics is more positive than giving up a lover.

Watching Eva's exercises is really a visual treat. Chytilova does not confine her within the frame. She has her in the spaces beyond the screen, kicking into our vision, then out again, rising with jumps up into an empty frame, then out again. This is in marked contrast to the smaller movements of the housewife, which are diminished by the narrowing of the screen space by doors, walls, and furniture. Also, though Eva is pushed to the breaking point by exhaustion and fear, there is a surge of victory and the glory of the public arena at the Olympics. Vera has only the memory of her affair and the renunciation of that love in order to keep her marriage together. It is as if Filmmaker, Vera, and Viewer are asked to admit that indeed the demands and activities of housewife and mother are of their very nature more confining and frustrating than many public careers.

At the end we feel the two women have more to unite than divide them. If one has more to show for her moment of triumph than the other, they both ultimately take responsibility for the decision and their lives. —Molly Haskell, *Village Voice*, June 29, 1972.

Something Different is a good film for college-level classes and older. Since the lifestyles and demands that they make are so carefully exposed, it is particularly good for psychology and sociology classes. A must for women studies.

Something Different (1963): 80 mins., b/w; rental $50. Director: Vera Chytilova. Distributor: Impact Films.

SUGGESTED FEMINIST READING
de Beauvoir, Simone. *The Second Sex.*
Oakley, Ann. *Sex, Gender and Society.*

Sometimes I Wonder Who I Am

Making Sometimes I Wonder Who I Am *enabled me to explore a role I was not sure of, to clarify my thoughts on marriage and having a family. It made me realize it wasn't something I wanted.*
—Liane Brandon to Jo Ann Greene, December, 1972. **125**

Liane Brandon's film shows the aspects of wife-mother that brought her to reject that role. In black-and-white footage, a young woman is shown doing dishes, feeding her baby, sitting, then cleaning the kitchen again. Since there is no one there to talk with her, she talks to herself and us in a voiceover. Her thoughts all have a rainy-Monday tone to them:

He never had to choose between being a father and having a career . . . I think he thinks that caring for house and baby is women's work . . . It seems the jobs for women are less rewarding than being home . . . I get the feeling people think of me only as my husband's wife and my baby's mother . . . I'm really worried about what is going to happen to me in ten years.

All in all the film doesn't portray a glowing image of motherhood. But it is a realistic image of many women's feelings during the early years of child rearing. Since many attitudes toward the wife-mother role are imposed on our young women through *Bride* magazine and soap-commercial optimism, it is good for them to see another view. Other young mothers who are in the situation of questioning who they are will benefit from seeing that the feelings they may feel guilty or confused about are not unusual.

Sometimes I Wonder Who I Am does not present the role of wife-mother in all its complexities; nor does it give solutions for the many women who are involved in the dilemmas of the woman shown here. No film can or should either, for life is not a Doris Day movie which can happily solve the most intricate problems in 110 minutes. All that films on the wife-mother role can do is present some of the feelings, realities, and fantasies of the women who live it. It is good to have movies like this that define that role with a new consciousness and realism.

Use *Sometimes I Wonder Who I Am* with groups from high school age and older. It would work well in a grouping with *Janie's Janie, Schmeerguntz, Joyce at Thirty-four,* and *3 A.M. to 10 P.M.*

Sometimes I Wonder Who I Am (1970): 5 mins., b/w; rental $14, purchase $85. Director: Liane Brandon. Distributor: New Day Films.

SUGGESTED FEMINIST READING
Bernard, Jessie. *The Future of Marriage.*
de Beauvoir, Simone. *The Second Sex.*
Friedan, Betty. *The Feminine Mystique.*

String Bean

The old woman sort of grows on you after watching her. I mean you change your feelings about old people as you see String Bean.
—Rolanda Lewis, age 15.

In *String Bean* Edmond Séchan thoughtfully engages us in the life of an old seamstress. Her warmth, self-sufficiency, and care for living things are revealed as she sews purses, cooks her slight meals, dusts her room, walks to the Jardin de Tuileries, and nourishes a string bean. In her walk-up room, she nourishes a bean seed into a plant. To ensure its full growth she transplants it to the Luxembourg Gardens where she watches it grow and flower. When it is uprooted by the gardeners and thrown away, she picks off the beans that have matured and brings them home, where she plants the seeds. Her solitude is emphasized by the sound track. Since there is no one for her to talk with, there is no dialogue. The fullness of her days is brought out, both by the activity of her life and the continuous musical score.

The color stock is unusual. All the sequences inside her room and in her courtyard are in black and white while the shots in the garden are in color.

The role of the old woman is played by Dr. Marie Marc, a famous French Doctor, who is indeed very old.

Many of us have been conditioned to equate old and wrinkles with the ugly. This film helps to dispel that kind of conditioning. Marie Marc is exquisite with her long nose, hunched shoulders, large knobby hands, drab loose clothing, and dry hair. These physical qualities are the medium through which she communicates her gentility, strength, persistent care of life, and resilient will to begin again.

String Bean is deservedly becoming a classic of the short film, proving again how valuable it is that filmmaker and public respect and develop films of varied lengths.

By all means, plan to show *String Bean* more than once, organizing discussion and questions of self-reliance, old age and death around it.

For any age group.

String Bean (1964): 17 mins., color and b/w, rental $15; purchase $175. Director: Edmond Séchan. Distributor: Contemporary Films/McGraw-Hill.

Sweet Bananas

Sweet Bananas is Ariel Dougherty's first film. A documentary, it briefly explores the feelings of seven women toward themselves and one another. In the first section of the film, face-camera monologues of five of the women are intercut so that you get an idea of what each of them does and what she wants. One is in charge of a number of looms in a factory, but prefers working a manual loom by herself. Another is a go-go dancer who talks about napalm and the war in Vietnam. One makes puppets and describes the joy of working an object from raw material to product. And so on. Later, in ad-lib scenes, two of the women hitch up with the other three and together they get themselves invited to stay at a New York woman's New Jersey retreat. After a time they all leave.

The film is suspenseful, emotionally unsettling, and ultimately (like life) follows no specific direction. As characters, the women are interesting. Each tries to express her own identity through the film, even through the arbitrarily-set-up fiction scenes in the country. In commenting to me, Dougherty mentioned how these women, with no acting experience and very little previous contact with one another, developed new relationships and experienced personality frictions that show through in the loosely designed scenes of the film. Since this was a film without a script, at the same time that these tensions show through the ad-libbing, they gave direction to it.

I showed *Sweet Bananas* to my high school students, but feel that it requires a more mature audience, possibly college psychology or sociology classes. The film seems to be much more of a process than a product

—a process that continues after the film, as each of these women continues to live the life that she expressed on the film.

Sweet Bananas (1972): 30 mins., color; rental $30, purchase $300. Director: Ariel Dougherty. Distributor: Women Make Movies.

SUGGESTED FEMINIST READING
Davis, Elizabeth Gould. *The First Sex.*
Diner, Helen. *Mothers and Amazons.*
Oakley, Ann. *Sex, Gender and Society.*

Ariel Dougherty

Photo by Gwenn Thomas

Movies are for people to share their different fantasies with other people.
—response to questionnaire.

During her senior year at Sarah Lawrence College, Ariel Dougherty taught animation to fifth-graders in Bronxville. Over the next few years she held several jobs in teaching film. First she was a consultant from the New York State Council of the Arts to the film program at John Bowne High School in Queens. Then she taught film to Chinese immigrant children in Lower Manhattan. Later she taught adults at the Ninety-Second Street "Y" and a course (for teachers) in Super-8 at the Metropolitan Museum of Art.

In all of these situations, Ariel realized how few women participated in filmmaking. She noticed that those who did participate frequently dropped out because the men "took over," their parents punished them, not allowing them to attend; or the demands of child-rearing interfered. It was then, in 1972, that she and Sheila Paige proposed a community center that would be an environment designed to give women an opportunity to make movies. That center (Chelsea Picture Station—see *Women Make Movies*), is sponsored by the New York State Council of the Arts and local merchants.

FILMOGRAPHY
Sweet Bananas (1972), color, 30 mins.

Take Off

Striptease. In burlesque, an act in which an actress, usually at the end or as a part of a song number, removes her clothing before the audience, piece by piece—'strip-tease,' adj.—'strip-teaser,' n.
—*Webster's New Collegiate Dictionary.*

Take Off opens with a pen-and-ink close-up drawing of a seductive woman. As she smiles and moves forward, the drawing changes into a real woman, a striptease artist. A sensuous, classic striptease begins. The filmed striptease is a whole new number, as the camera selects what you will see in tight closeups, superimpositions, and dissolves. As the film makes its erotic way through the striptease, the dancer plays to the audience with her gestures and smiles. An intimate relationship is contrived between artist and audience by the large screen, dark background, flashing lights, and close-ups. Electronic music and pulsing lights sustain a mesmerizing effect, and, as the act works toward a climax, the pulsing light and music become faster. Having removed her G-string, the high point of the striptease, the dancer carries nudity further as she proceeds to remove her hair, ears, legs, bust, nose, head, arms. The artist maintains the same stage presence throughout, removing nose and breasts with the same unblushing playful sensuality that she expressed as she took off bra and G-string. The true climax occurs as her trunk floats off into the cosmos, the dark background now studded with stars.

Satiric, humorous, cinematically brilliant, *Take Off* is one of my favorite shorts. It can be coupled interestingly with several of the feature-length films reviewed in this book.

Take Off (1972): 10 mins., b/w; rental $15. Director: Gunvor Nelson. Distributor: Canyon Cinema.

SUGGESTED FEMINIST READING

Greer, Germaine. *The Female Eunuch.*

Thigh Lyne Lyre Triangular

This film is the shortest and least medically graphic of the birth films. In recording his third child's birth, Stan Brakhage wanted to show his own inner vision. He said that in more intense moments he sees with an outer vision that incorporates "closed-eye" views of flashes of color and light. He approximates that kind of vision in this film by hand painting over the developed film of his child's birth. Consequently, you don't see the physical aspects as clearly as you do in the other films. While understanding and appreciating Brakhage's explanation of the abstraction on his film, I personally find that I identify with those same abstractions as objectifications of the intense physical sensations of childbirth.

If you feel that your audience is conditioned to be repulsed by a more detailed film on birth, you might decide to use this film before or instead of one of the other childbirth films. Be sure to explain why the film has been painted.

Thigh Lyne Lyre Triangular (1961): 5 mins., color; rental $15, purchase $95. Director: Stan Brakhage. Distributor: Grove Press.

SUGGESTED FEMINIST READING
The Boston Women's Health Book Collective. *Our Bodies, Our Selves.*
Brakhage, Jane. "The Birth Film." *Film Culture Reader,* pp. 230-233.
Edited by P. Adams Sitney.

3 A.M. to 10 P.M.

There is very little emotion in this film between the husband and his wife. The child seems to be the only thing that they both pay any attention to and show any affection for. —student, age 14.

This terse Eastern European film follows the daily activities of a young woman whose work day begins at three in the morning and ends at ten at night. With quiet purpose and little joy she performs the daily routines of housework, her work in a textile factory, and the care of a small child. The simplicity of the film techniques correspond to the simplicity of her life. There are no fades, superimpositions, or fancy dolly shots, just the directness of close-ups on the details of her life—her hands at work, clocks, the tools of child care, housework, and her work at the looms.

The sounds are the sounds of her work—shuttling looms, factory whistles, the bustle of the market, and baby noises. She speaks to no one. She eats alone at the plant. She eats in silence with her husband at home.

131

Throughout the film, the strong form of this mother-wife worker fills the screen, her face smiling only in the caresses she gives her child. You never see her husband's face clearly, not even when he helps in the housework by holding a rug that she is beating. As she washes the floor, he takes a nap. Later he leaves on a bicycle. Is it to go to a second job or the pub?

The harshness of the family's life, without plumbing and electricity, is not overlooked; nor is it sentimentalized. It is simply and directly presented. The film doesn't say, "This woman's life is good," or "This woman's life is bad." It is a simple visual description.

The film closes with a close-up of the woman, lying down, staring straight up. Her eyes close slowly in exhaustion. As the camera zooms out from a medium shot of her home, the alarm clock rings, signaling a new day.

Here is a good biography of a working mother, demonstrating some of the demands of that role. Junior high school age and older.

3 A.M. to 10 P.M. (1967): 15 mins., b/w; rental $12.50, purchase $115. Producer: Zagreb Film. Distributor: Contemporary Films/McGraw-Hill.

SUGGESTED FEMINIST READING
Bernard, Jessie. *The Future of Marriage.*
Friedan, Betty. *The Feminine Mystique.*

Three Lives

I wanted to make a film and talk about what women's lives were really like because I was sick of watching movies with chicks, and dames, and broads in them.
Kate Millet, *Filmmakers Newsletter*, January 1972.

To make *Three Lives* Kate Millet formed a collective of an all-woman crew and three co-directors to present real women on film. They wanted to make their film without the hierarchical authority structure that is typical of the film industry. Their three subjects were women that they knew—Mallory Millet-Jones, Kate Millet's sister; Lillian Shreve, the sound-person's mother; and Robin Mide, one of the co-directors. For the three weeks of marathon shooting the crew and directors stayed together. Everyone got the same daily salary, and each now receives 5 percent of 50 percent of the net made by the film. (The other 50 percent goes into a foundation set up by Kate Millet for women filmmakers.) The seven hours of film that resulted were edited down to seventy minutes.

Technically *Three Lives* is not even interesting, but the way it was made is both interesting and politically important. All that you hear in the film is what the three women tell you, and all that you see is what the crew shows you of their environments.

First Mallory speaks. She is newly divorced from a "comfortable" marriage and is now on her own for the first time in her life. As she is experiencing many contradictions in herself, finding her own strengths and weaknesses, so she expresses them to the camera.

The most important thing about Mallory, from the point of view of the audience, is that she reached the epitome of what culture calls success for a woman: a husband, money, servants, possessions—and she was unhappy with it.
—Louva Irvine, *Filmmakers Newsletter*, January 1972.

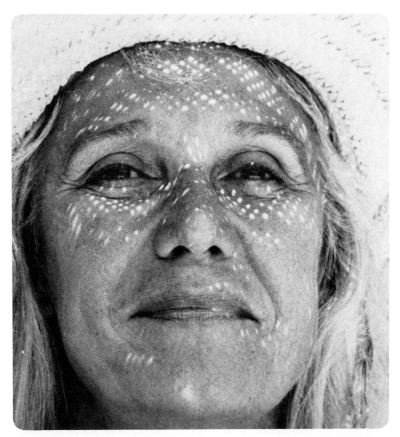

Lillian is older and seems less comfortable with the camera. A chemist, Lillian claims to be content in her marriage and talks rather superficially of her years as a wife and mother. Since so much of the film's power is based on comradeship and co-energy, I suspect that some of Lillian's shyness came from the difference in her age and experience. Moreover, she wasn't in on the entire three weeks of the shooting; both Mallory and Robin were.

Robin Mide, a lesbian ("I was a nice Jewish girl from Queens"), confronts the camera with a bold display of her imaginative lifestyle. She appears in a cage, in an auditorium surrounded by her few belongings, and among empty cable spools. Many jump cuts, interrupting half-completed stories, also indicate Robin's sense of constant moving, searching.

133

Three Lives is a good film to use in women's groups and in college classes, particularly psychology, family living, and sociology classes. *If you really want to get to people—think of how film dominates people's minds! It's so huge. It's a very powerful way to express oneself. I did not want to analyze anymore, but to express.*

—Kate Millet, *Filmmakers Newsletter,* January 1972.

Three Lives (1970): 70 mins., color or b/w; rental $75, purchase $750. Co-directors: Louva Irvine, Robin Mide, Susan Kleckner. Producer: Kate Millet. Distributor: Impact Films.

SUGGESTED FEMINIST READING
Bernard, Jessie. *The Future of Marriage.*
Bird, Caroline. *Born Female.*
de Beauvoir, Simone. *The Second Sex.*
DeCrow, Karen. *The Young Woman's Guide to Liberation.*
Firestone, Shulamith. *The Dialectic of Sex.*
Friedan, Betty. *The Feminine Mystique.*
Oakley, Ann. *Sex, Gender and Society.*

Unfolding

My films are always described by others as "a woman's viewpoint." I doubt this, but I have made ('breakthrough films,') taking the subject matter that is usually pornographic, sexuality, and made it beautiful, the way it really is. Maybe it took a woman to make films about feelings rather than things, but I think a man could do it and will do it.

—Constance Beeson, in response to questionnaire.

Unfolding is a very lyrical and erotic film. Young couples are seen first clothed, then nude, as they run, feel, and eventually have intercourse.

I have seen *Unfolding* only once and so my comments on it as film are necessarily scanty. I remember it as more gimmicky in terms of film technique than *Holding,* Beeson's film on two women making love. I suppose dramatic music, slow motion, birds in flight, romantic settings by the sea, and double exposure could act as softsell techniques for students who might otherwise be embarrassed at the screening. Beeson's explanation for some of these techniques:

For me a person in love reacts expansively; she wants to embrace the whole universe through the one she loves, and her emotions have to be free to take and give, to allow the full flow of energy to be her "media." To film a person in love, I think on changing levels of experiencing. That is why I so often use double exposure, because one's emotions are so complex, because the imagination dives and turns and reaches and falls and ebbs and flows.

—Constance Beeson, letter to Jeanne Betancourt, June, 1973.

Unfolding and films like it can help young people become more com-

fortable with their own sexuality.

Unfolding (1969): 16½ mins., b/w; rental $40, purchase $200. Director: Constance Beeson. Distributor: Radim Films.

SUGGESTED FEMINIST READING
The Boston Women's Health Book Collective. *Our Bodies, Our Selves.*

Constance Beeson

Photo by Joedy Nerini.

As a woman filmmaker I find that I live in a world wherein you have to find your own place, your center of balance, because women are exploited and treated as second class societally. You have to move into your own world, away from the clutch of society as much as possible, to build a positive directive for your life and realize some of the potential of your own creativity. —letter to Jeanne Betancourt, June 1973.

Constance Beeson did graduate study at the University of California, American University, and San Francisco Art Institute. It was at the last that she studied photography and filmmaking. In 1967 she made a sixteen-millimeter theater piece with stills in collaboration with Ronald Chase. She was so pleased with it that she started making sixteen-millimeter moving films.

Currently she is working in both film and video tape. She lives in Belvedere, California, with labor lawyer Duane Beeson and their three children.

FILMOGRAPHY
Women (in progress). "A satire on women, visuals are in episodes, and present visions of women that are known, including the vastness of the variety of the species. A rap of statements by women is part of the sound track."—C.B.

On Sir (in progress). Inner journey out of the ghetto.

The Letter (in progress). "This is the psychic journey of a woman who has been rejected in love. It is abstract, surreal, introspective, mel-   135 ancholy and deals with the subterranean barrage of mental and emotional torture that goes along with the regaining of balance."

—C.B.

High on Drag (in progress). Comedy: men in women's clothing.

The Doll (in progress). Inner journey; self identity.

Dead or Alive (in progress). ". . . first full feature. It is a Ballad, a ghost cowboy film based on the legend of Joaquin Murietta. I think it will be a new kind of cowboy movie, with erotic and primitive quests."

—C.B.

Watercress (1972). Alternative lifestyle and group caring.

Stamen (1972). Male erotic fantasy.

Ann: A Portrait (1971), 21 mins. Art-form documentary of Ann Halprin.

Holding (1971). Erotic; female fantasy.

The Now (1970), black and white. Reincarnation.

* *Unfolding* (1969). Erotic; tapping universal feelings.

Prelude to Medical Care (1968). Documentary.

Five (1967). Theatre piece with Ronald Chase.

Dione. Pregnant to childbirth fantasy.

The Moon Is My Balloon. Children's film fantasy.

For information on the distribution of the films above, contact Constance Beeson (see list of distributors).

*Reviewed in this book.

Veronica

Yes, yes! This film is very good. The thing I like best about it is that the people in the film seem very real and not afraid to give their opinion. It shows that people shouldn't be prejudiced. They should think the way Veronica thinks—MATURE. —Anita Wiltshire, age 15.

The form of personal documentary in film has been used frequently in recent years. Lightweight portable cameras and improved sound systems make it possible to document personal biographies more effectively and less conspicuously. Moreover, the personal documentary is particularly suitable for the exposition of *real* women in film—women who face problems, live, and think out solutions, rather than women who only cause crises, bewitch, and wane.

Veronica employs the personal documentary with sensitivity. The ease with which Veronica expresses her feelings in the voiceover and the naturalness with which she faces the camera show that the filmmaker's relationship with the subject was developed over a period of time.

A high school senior in New Haven, Connecticut, Veronica is confronted with the pressures of her black peer group in an integrated school. She is labeled an Uncle Tom when, as president of the student body, she tries to walk the gap between the various cliques in the school. It is clear that her concerns are more with her own feelings and development as she comes to see how superficial and transient peer group criteria are. In a combination of dialogue—with other students, teachers, and her closest friends—and voiceover first-person narration, you come to see Veronica in the variety of settings that shape her life.

The opening sequences are some of the best in the film. Before the title there is a tight close-up of Veronica as you hear a woman's voice say, "You've got to stop being so sensitive about what people think of you, Veronica. Just be Veronica, just be yourself." Then there are several separate close-up shots of Veronica in different settings. This sequence cuts to a parade scene with Veronica as queen riding in a car. In the next few minutes you see and hear the sights of the parade. The sound track, however, alternates between the sounds of the parade and a voiceover of Veronica explaining how she felt during the parade. All the fallacies of being queen are exposed: "I had to smile, but I didn't feel like it. Everything was so disorganized. Besides the fact that I was in the wrong car." She ascends the steps; her African wrap unsnaps. As it is being rearranged, she sees a go-go girl dancing on stage. She is embarrassed to be part of this whole scene and wonders when she will make her speech. Now that she doesn't look right, however, the parade organizers don't want her on the stage and she is literally carried off. The discord in her feelings is reflected in the tinny, off-pitch sound of the marching bands that accompany the parade.

Veronica's desire is always to communicate, to get across what she is feeling. As her voiceover states in a school sequence, "Being a leader of anything isn't as great as it looks!" What disturbs her most is that people group and exclude others on externals: "You have to stay with the group to survive." But she fights it: "Should I get into this group because all black kids are here, or should I go where I want to go?" She listens to her peers and to the Afro-American studies teacher, but finds in the end she must be her own woman. It is an increasingly self-reliant Veronica who says, "Miss Lang is very sure of herself, but sometimes I'm not so sure of her." And later, "I kept trying to explain to her, but she kept talking and interrupting . . . it's really hard to communicate with some people."

It is Veronica as an individual, dealing with her unique problems and circumstances, who creates the intimacy of this documentary. The fact that she is young, black, and female is neither the point nor the feeling of the film. The fact that she is Veronica, a unique human being, is conveyed to the viewers, particularly the young viewers, helping each to sense her/his own individuality.

In a summary scene toward the end of the film, against a folksong background, you see Veronica with friends on a carnival ride, with her mother at home, and with her boyfriend on the beach. It is interesting that Veronica's boyfriend is never heard and is seen only in the last sequence. This girl is not being defined by the men in her life.

The film closes with the graduation at her high school. Veronica starts her senior speech: "The beginning of reality. The time has come. It has seemed an eternity to get here." As the pompous, emotional music and clapping close out the film, you recall that it is not the beginning of reality for Veronica, but only a continuing.

A documentary of this type allows the viewer insights. At the same time that you are objectively watching a scene in which the subject is   137 participating, you hear her feelings in the voiceover. This intimacy isn't available even to the people present at the scene, and it is one of the contributions of documentary film.

Veronica has been a favorite with most of my classes. They are always impressed with her comfortable manner with the camera and find some of her problems a reflection of their own. Particularly good for junior high school and senior high school students.

Veronica (1969): 25 mins., color; rental (apply), purchase $300. Director: Pat Powell. Distributor: Jason Films.

SUGGESTED FEMINIST READING
Beal, Frances M. "Double Jeopardy: To Be Black and Female." *Sisterhood Is Powerful*, pp. 340-353. Edited by Robin Morgan.
Cade, Toni (ed.). *The Black Woman.*
DeCrow, Karen. *The Young Woman's Guide to Liberation.*
Hansberry, Lorraine. *To Be Young, Gifted and Black.*
Norton, Eleanor Holmes. "For Sadie and Maude." *Sisterhood Is Powerful*, pp. 353-359. Edited by Robin Morgan.

A Very Curious Girl

This is a fairy tale, a female pipe dream . . . but it is exhilarating, not numbing, triumphant, not defeated. In its own special way it is a celebration of courage, enterprise, and an impeccable sense of direction. Such celebration gives the film an immediacy for women . . .
—Gerry Sachs. "A Pair of Very Curious Girls,"
Aphra, vol. 3, No. 4 (Fall 1972).

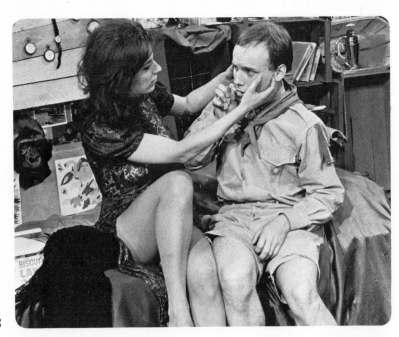

Of *A Very Curious Girl* Picasso said: "This is insolence raised to the status of high art." (Herman G. Weinberg, "Reflections on the Current Scene," *Take One*, Vol. 3, No. 2, p. 37.) Besides being insolent, this film is downright revengeful. There aren't too many stories in film that end with the woman having revenge on her oppressors, acquiring a goodly amount of money, and, surprisingly, surviving (women have had revenge before, but they usually repent or die).

Marie (Bernadette Lafont) and her mother are victims of the prejudice, pettiness, and hypocrisy of the residents in a small provincial town in France. When the mother dies, the townspeople exploit Marie sexually as well. Suddenly, however, the tables start to turn as Marie experiences a shift in her view of this small world. This change, or click in consciousness, begins when the townspeople refuse to bury her mother and grows when she sees a movie from a traveling projectionist.

Since the village men expect Marie's sexual favors, she starts to charge them. With the money she fixes up her shack in the woods; buys some clothes, makeup, and a tape recorder. She also has money to save since everyone from the postman to the mayor has become her customer. Soon she raises her prices, striking a serious blow to the tight village economy. In a scene that disturbs many men, she fights against a handyman who tries to rape her by kicking him repeatedly in the groin, reducing him to a helpless fool. (Some of the same men who cringe at this particular scene and call Kaplan "unfeeling" considered *A Clockwork Orange* "arty" and cooly watched women who hadn't harmed anyone being raped and mutilated.)

The great revenge for Marie, however, is psychological. One Sunday she takes her tape recorder (which has heard everyone's tawdry confessions) to the church. Using a ladder, she sets the recorder high on a ledge and walks off with her ladder. Meanwhile the respected members of the church and community listen to the mayor refer to his wife as a "frigid old hag," the priest try to bribe Marie out of busines, and so on. Marie? She makes a colorful free-standing sculpture out of the artifacts she has acquired, takes her full purse, sets fire to her house, and skips off, throwing her high-heeled shoes away. She may have scoffed at some of the props of her life of revenge, but she doesn't throw off her new confidence, self-possession, and wealth. Recognizing the need for revenge, she gives the villagers a chance to strike back by leaving the sculpture, which they tear to pieces.

The film is funny and gay; all the sorrow of her oppression, poverty, and her mother's death turn to happy victory. Bright colors of the countryside and Marie's decorated hut add to the spirit of farce. Close-ups of Marie's expressive face and examples of her growing confidence quickly involve the audience.

Use this film. It is particularly good for college screenings or with any group that likes a good story and would like to see a heroine who doesn't die.

Insolence is good for the skin. It's stronger than I am. Since the age of six I've been raising hell. They told me not to rock the boat but I can't help confronting taboos. Insolence is good for the skin. I like those who, 139

*having been humiliated and offended, revolt against their tormenters. I
don't hold with offering the other cheek.*
                    —interview with Nelly Kaplan in *Le Monde*, 1972.

A Very Curious Girl (1969): 107 mins., color; rental $125. Director:
Nelly Kaplan. Distributor: Universal Films.

SUGGESTED FEMINIST READING
Millett, Kate. *The Prostitution Papers.*
Strong, Ellen. "The Hooker." *Sisterhood Is Powerful*, pp. 289-297.
    Edited by Robin Morgan.

Nelly Kaplan

Photo courtesy of the French Film Office.

*The film industry has a prejudice against me because my films are not
too sweet. They allow women to make film about babies' problems and
then say they act like very bad people. They read my scripts trying to see
what is underneath and say I will never make a nice film.*
            —to Kay Harris, "An Interview with Nelly Kaplan,"
                    Women and Film, No. 2 (Fall 1972), p. 36.

Nelly Kaplan's family lived in Buenos Aires for three generations.
When she was a student of economic science at the University of
Buenos Aires, she raised money to leave South America by selling ar-
ticles on film to an Argentinian film magazine.

Alone in Paris, she did menial jobs and continued to write articles
about film for Argentinian publications. In 1954 Kaplan met Abel
Gance, who hired her to work with him on his films. She was an assistant for *La Tour de nesle*, an assistant for shooting and editing *Magirama* (a triple-screen program), then a collaborator for *Austerlitz*. She
also published two books, *Magirama: Le Manifesto d'un art nouveau*
and *Le Sunlight d'Austerlitz*.

Starting in 1961, she directed a series of short films on art which are
known around the world. Under the pseudonym Belen, she published a
140 collection of short stories, *Le Reservoir des sens*, which won great criti-

cal and public success. In 1967 she directed a one-hour color film, *Le Regard Picasso*, which won the Golden Lion at the Venice Film Festival. Kaplan's two feature films to date, *A Very Curious Girl* (*La Fiancée du pirate*) and *Papa The Little Boats*, were made in collaboration with Claud Makonski. Of her work Kaplan says,

Everything is an act of revenge. Let's face it, for men it's the same thing. All creators have to take revenge on something, if not . . . if they're happy like vegetables . . . they don't need to create.

—An Interview with Nelly Kaplan,
Women and Film, no. 2 (Fall 1972), p. 36.

FILMOGRAPHY

Papa les petits bateaux (1971). Feature length.
* La Fiancée du pirate (A Very Curious Girl) (1969). Feature length.
Le Regard Picasso (1967). Short film.
A La Source, la femme aimée (1961). Short film.
Abel Gance hier et demain (1961). Short film.
Les Annés 25 (1961). Short film.
Dessins et merveilles (1961). Short film.
Rodolphe Bresdin (1961). Short film.
Gustave Moreau (1961). Short film.

*Reviewed in this book.

Virginia Woolf—The Moment Whole

"A woman must have money and a room of her own if she is to write fiction." We could add to Virginia Woolf's requirements that a woman must also have a sense of independence and single-mindedness. This brief, unpretentious film of some of her feelings and ideas represents the independence and single-mindedness in Virginia Woolf.

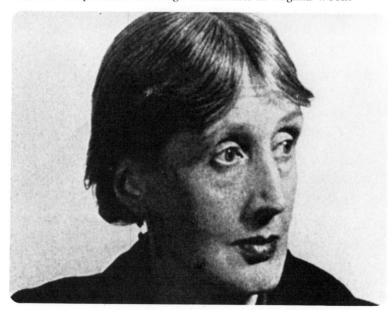

The texts, read by actress Marian Seldes, are from Woolf's *A Room of One's Own*. Camerawork (frequently reverting to still photos of Woolf) records Ms. Seldes in the settings of Woolf's own life. The striking resemblance between Marian Seldes and Virginia Woolf is strongly accented by a dissolve connecting Seldes's face and an old portrait photo of Virginia Woolf.

Short documentaries should not be expected to give a full history of a person, and fortunately this film doesn't have that ambition. It provides a glimpse of some of the feelings and thoughts of a great writer, whetting the appetite for more or bringing back fond memories. In its refreshing simplicity you will find this a good short for an English class. I wouldn't use it with high school students unless they had studied Woolf's works.

Virginia Woolf—The Moment Whole (1972): 10 mins., color; rental (apply), purchase $150. Director: Janet Sternberg. Distributor: ACI Films, Inc.

SUGGESTED FEMINIST READING
Bell, Quentin. *Virginia Woolf: A Biography*.
Woolf, Virginia. *Mrs. Dalloway*.
————. *Orlando*.
————. *A Room of One's Own*.
————. *The Waves*.
————. *A Writer's Diary*.

Wednesday's Child

Female children are quite literally starved for matrimony: not for marriage, but for physical nurturance and a legacy of power and humanity from adults of their own sex ("mothers").
                              —Phyllis Chesler, *Women and Madness*, p. 18.
You're my daughter and I know exactly what you want.
                              —Janice's mother in *Wednesday's Child*.

Janice, the acquiescent "good" girl of a middle-class London family, is constantly torn between trying to be what her mother wants her to be and following her own faltering inclinations toward independence. The strain of these conflicting personality developments results in schizophrenia, institutionalization, and muteness for Janice. At the end the film gives no hope that she will ever recover.

Wednesday's Child presents steps that Janice's parents take to get her help. At first she is placed in an "experimental ward" where a psychiatrist works with thirty patients through R.D. Laing's method of treatment, which includes no drugs, peer-group help, casual dress. The psychiatrist heading the experiment, Dr. Donaldson, works with Janice's parents, who resist admitting their part in Janice's illness and still hold on to the conviction that she must conform to their image of her if she is to be "normal." As Dr. Donaldson says, "You want her to stand on her own feet, but you want her to want what you want." The parents are uncomfortable with the casualness of the ward. When Donaldson's project is terminated, they find it easier to adjust to Janice's placement in a traditional behaviorist ward.

In the new ward Janice becomes a number. Her symptoms are treated with shock therapy and drugs. The doctors never suggest that the parents have any role to play except to wait until their little girl is "good" and normal again and everything can go its tidy way. Janice's boyfriend, confounded at the prison-like hospital and the change in Janice, takes her home with him. She is, after all, a voluntary patient. Her parents then demand that the state seize her and commit her to an institution. In the closing scene Janice is used as an example to a class of bored students. The professor-psychiatrist point out her muteness as the result of extreme schizophrenia. "Now . . . are there any questions?" he asks his students.

This film, while it seems propagandist in the contrast it demonstrates between the behaviorist and the Laing psychiatric approaches, is in many ways an interesting study. It first appeared in England in 1967 as a TV special, "In Two Minds," by David Mercer. The film version (known as *Family Life* in England) was directed by Kenneth Loach. The actors are unknown, and some of the footage was shot on location in hospitals with ex-schizophrenic patients in group-therapy sessions. Logical sequence provided the order for shooting scenes, giving the new actors a chance to build their characterizations.

Though the film is shot pleasantly and interestingly, it is visually discreet and allows the ideas to develop through dialogue and acting. As in many recent films, the actuality of subway, factory, and hospital is convincing and frightening, shot realistically. Brief scenes of family members together, single lines, facial expression are edited to show the ways in which Janice's schizophrenia is developing.

The repressive sexual attitudes of Janice's parents provide the context for one of her major conflicts. For example, Janice's mother doesn't want the word *abortion* used in her house, but she insists that Janice have one. "She cut out my baby," says Janice, "because it was bad. But I'm bad too . . . I'm always in trouble . . . and that's bad." Her mother is very disturbed when Janice is out late and insists that sex belongs in marriage, where, she says, it is "very beautiful." Yet, on their sex life, the father says of his wife; "She's done her duty."

If Janice were a boy there would be little complaint if she were out all night; she would be encouraged to study toward more meaningful employment; Most parents would consider it "normal" if she were having sexual relations outside of marriage. Yet, being a girl, she is even chastised when she goes for a walk with a fellow patient (male) at the state hospital. As the nun says, 'We don't want you to be taken advantage of, Janice."

The case against the parents is explicit, yet sympathetic. Her father shouts, "I'm a responsible man, a normal man. I've brought the family up in a normal way . . . Do you think we've spent a lifetime building a house like this to be spoken to like this? It's a lifetime's work when you have children."

I found it most successful to precede the screening of *Wednesday's Child* with open discussion of attitudes toward mental illness and some of its known causes. My students discussed difficulty in treatment and described why they thought people were ashamed of mental illness. Some spoke about their own experiences with psychiatrists and psychologists.

Even after several screenings I had difficulty understanding some of the sound track; the British accent is very heavy and the concept load is high. Therefore I would advise that you use it with mature high school students through adult. Certainly it is appropriate for college classes in psychology, sociology, and women's studies. Be sure to consider how the apparent causes of Janice's illness are related to her role as a woman.

This film brought me face to face with something that has been happening to me, where I am trying to be the girl my mother wants me to be, but yet I know that I am not made that way. I want to be carefree, a going out sort of person, while she wants me to be a humble, modest person. Although I please her by doing these things, there is something in me that hates it. So I have come to a decision. I am going to be the person that I want to be, even if it takes some pain. I have gone through a complete change since being in this class. —Paula Grant, age 17.

Wednesday's Child (1972): 108 mins., color; rental $125, purchase (apply). Director: Kenneth Loach. Distributor: Cinema Five.

SUGGESTED FEMINIST READING
Chesler, Phyllis. *Women and Madness.*
Horney, Karen. *Feminine Psychology.*
Milford, Nancy. *Zelda.*
Miller, Jean Baker (ed.). *Psychoanalysis and Women.*
Oakley, Ann. *Sex, Gender and Society.*
Plath, Sylvia. *The Bell Jar.*

What I Want

I want to know what I want. I want to know how to get it.

—from film.

There is delightful wit in the ten minutes of Sharon Hennessey's *What I Want.* A very clever piece of sustained film humor, it arouses the quiet smile of "I know just how you feel." It is touching in its perception, innovative in its technique, and appropriate in its execution.

The film opens with a close-up of the filmmaker looking at a paper. From it she reads a series of sentences that open with "I want." As she reads she never looks up. The things that she wants are so diverse that they encompass many things that we all want. As the list proceeds, the camera is moving out in slow zoom, until, by the end of the film, we see Susan in a medium shot with a reel of shelf paper (the list) at her feet. She continues to read, but there is no longer writing on the paper as she repeats over and over, "I want to know what I want. I want to know how to get it." Some of the things that she wants? "I want to fly without an airplane . . . I want to see more lady truck drivers on the road . . . I want to live at a high altitude . . . I want clarity of motives . . . I want every man I have ever known to get down on his knees and beg forgiveness."

It is enjoyable to see the randomness with which Hennessey goes from attainable things that she wants to totally impossible wishes. The film, in its simplicity, demonstrates that even though the human condition is constantly thwarted by inaccessible goals, it is easily comforted by those that are more available.

As a provocative, humorous piece, *What I Want* is good for high school age groups and older. It is an excellent short with *Goodbye in the Mirror, A Very Curious Girl,* or *Dream Life,* since each of these films shows young women coming to realize what it is they want and their efforts to get it.

145

What I Want (1972) 10 mins., color; rental $12. Filmmaker: Sharon Hennessey. Distributor: Sharon Hennessey.

SUGGESTED FEMINIST READING
Davis, Elizabeth Gould. *The First Sex.*
DeCrow, Karen. *The Young Woman's Guide to Liberation.*
Diner, Helen. *Mothers and Amazons.*
Nunes, Maxine, and White, Deanna. *The Lace Ghetto.*

Window Water Baby Moving

We both knew that I could be most there if I were creating a film as she was giving birth . . . I literally could not have watched that birth if I had not been working.

—Stan Brakhage

In *Window Water Baby Moving*, Stan Brakhage edits together film shot the day before his daughter was born and film of the actual birth. When Jane was in the early stages of labor, Stan filmed her taking a bath. The imagery of her large belly immersed in water, bright sunlight from the window, playful kisses between her and Stan contrasts sharply with later footage of Jane roaring in the sensations of advanced labor. The film emphasizes the contrast by intercutting from Jane's sunlit laughing face in the bath to her intensely labored expressions during the delivery. Later when the baby is born, the shots of the water-bound belly are intercut with shots of the newborn child. (This is the only birth film I have seen with detailed filming of the afterbirth.)

At the end of the film Jane takes the camera from Stan and you see a close-up of his ecstatic, wondering face. He is in awe of this woman who has taken a heavy sixteen-millimeter camera from him and is shooting film only minutes after delivering their child.

. . . I hear the doctor very excited saying "The head is born—anterior shoulder—posterior shoulder—" and then there is the baby held by her heels, and she's crying, and I'm saying, "Baby, Baby," over and over, and the doctor and nurse do this and that to the baby, while I take some pictures of Stan because he is so beautiful, and then they all have a drink, but I am quite drunk, and I eat a sandwich, and the baby is in the cradle and asleep, and then we were left alone and happiness everywhere.
—Jane Brakhage, "The Birth Film," *Film Culture Reader, p. 233.*

Window Water Baby Moving (1959): 17 mins., color; rental $35, purchase $225. Director: Stan Brakhage. Distributor: Grove Press.

SUGGESTED FEMINIST READING
See suggested readings for *Thigh Lyne Lyre Triangular.*

Women Make Movies

"Women Make Movies, Inc., a non-profit, educational organization, was formed in the Spring of 1972 to promote film and video productions

made by people who are unrepresented in public media and to present, in particular, new and alternative images of women to a broad national audience." —brochure from Chelsea Picture Station.

Once organized by Ariel Dougherty and Sheila Paige, Women Make Movies designed Chelsea Picture Station. This is a community film and video center which, through its productions, is developing unique entertainment and information within Chelsea, an ethnically diverse community on the lower east side of Manhattan. Although the center has a teen-age radio club and a parents' video workshop, it is the productions of Women Make Movies that interest me the most.

Fifteen women from diverse lifestyles, occupations, and ages have made sixteen-millimeter films that represent points of view completely fresh to commercial TV and movie audiences. These films are offered individually and in packages. Some of them amazed me, not only for the unusually good technical work for first films, but for the gutsy representation of a woman's problems and sensibilities as she struggles with her supposed roles in an urban environment. The films are almost frighteningly and embarrassingly personal (none of them had to pass under the rake of producers or audience demands). All of these women have a great deal to say and use their medium well.

The films listed below are those ready for distribution at the time of this writing. By the time you read these pages, many more will be available.

Just Looking

"An older woman's dull morning turns into an adventurous and unpredictable afternoon."

Photo by Susan Meiselas

At sixty-five, Suzanne Armstrong is the oldest filmmaker of the group. Her film is pleasant and positive, giving a sense of community feeling in Chelsea. She is shown filming *Just Looking,* assisted by Marie Celine Caufield, CND.

Just Looking (1973): 5 mins., b/w; rental $9, purchase $50. by Suzanne Armstrong.

Fear

"A secretary revolts against her conditioning and triumphs over her would-be rapist."

As the secretary in *Fear* is going to work, she faces the too-familiar hassles from construction workers. Once she is at work, her boss courteously tells her that she has been passed by for a promotion. All the anger of these experiences is taken out on a would-be rapist who corners her in the bathroom. You'll be cheering when you see her not only get his gun and shoot him in the leg, but chase him for blocks and finally push him to the ground. There is some fine editing: As she chases him, she sees all the other male-dominated situations of her morning.

Fear (1973): 6 mins., b/w; rental $10.50, purchase $60. By Jean Shaw.

Domestic Tranquility

"A woman is haunted by sacrifices she made in order to be a wife and mother."

Domestic Tranquility is poignantly haunting. The wife-mother, Rachel, was once a painter. When she takes out a book of Renoir prints at the playground, other mothers comment on how fat Renoir's models are. As Rachel continues to look at the pictures, she remembers catcalls of men on the street and her view of these pictures is interrupted. Later, at a club meeting in her home, the women talk in chipmunk speed until one of them mentions the painting on the wall. "It's called 'Domestic Tranquility,'" says Rachel. "A Dutch housewife painted it. She committed suicide." In the final scene one of the children shouts demands at Rachel who is working at a tragic expressionistic portrait, tears streaming down her face.

I have never seen a film so successfully portray the creative frustration of an artist turned housewife-mother. A fine film to show with *Joyce at Thirty-four.* Both explore—from the level of personal experience—some of the most difficult feelings an adult has to deal with when assuming the responsibility of parenthood.

Domestic Tranquility (1973): 8 mins., b/w; rental $14, purchase $80. By Harriet Kreigel.

It's a Miracle

"A Sister's work in a new community hinges upon her winning the affections of a teen-age boy."

It's a Miracle (1973): 7 mins., b/w; rental $12.50, purchase $70. By Marie Celine Caufield.

Paranoia Blues

"A young woman in the city precipitates a larger-than-life, tragicomic series of catastrophes."

Paranoia Blues (1973): 6 mins., b/w; rental $10.50, purchase $60. By Jane Warrenbrand.

For Better or Worse

"Before and After the Marriage, or How a Woman Pediatrician Changes Her Marriage into a Partnership."

For Better or Worse (1973): 7 mins., b/w; rental $12.50, purchase $70. By Judy Acuna.

Movie programs are currently available from Women Make Movies. These are groupings of the women's films on twenty-five minute (approximately) reels. The films are classified under themes (boys, women at work, men and husbands, etc.) They also provide discussion plans. For more information contact:
Women Make Movies, Inc., 257 West 19th Street, New York, New York 10001, (212) 929-6477

SUGGESTED FEMINIST READING
Check for books with similar themes when ordering specific films.

Women on the March

The mad, wicked folly of women's rights. —Queen Victoria

Nature has given woman so much power that the law has wisely given her little. —Samuel Johnson 149

At the time of this writing, *Women on the March* is the only film
I know about that deals at length with the woman's suffrage movement
in England and America. Though this film offers many disappointments,

the footage is of such value that you should screen it. Do not, however,
order Part II of this film. Since it deals with women—from after the vote
until the late fifties—in a manner that is downright boring and condescending, I will review only Part I.

Part I opens with the pompous music that characterized the March
of Time newsreels, then cuts to a medium shot of Queen Elizabeth II
opening the 1958 session of Parliament. At this session peeresses first

appeared (so the male narrator informs us). Next are two on-the-street interviews with men who register their opinion that "politics isn't for women." This introduction reinforces a feminist position that you really haven't "come a long way baby."

From this rather disappointing introduction, the film proceeds to show, in authentic documentary footage, the life of the well-bred Victorian lady with her limited occupational alternatives. Some of this footage is staged, but it is done so poorly that it is obvious and doesn't break the credibility of the documentary footage that follows, showing the harsh life of the factory worker and housewife. When the film goes back to shots of the leisure upperclass, it is clear why the movement began in the parlor and not in the workhouses. Poor women had neither time nor energy for organizing.

The development of the struggle for woman's suffrage is shown in both motion picture footage and still photos. Particularly impressive are the shots of the Panquirst family; women being arrested; and the description of the "cat and mouse" act (whereby those arrested would go on hunger strikes, resist force feedings, and be released—only to be rearrested as soon as they regained their health).

Lest you think that the violence and radical measures of women were taken seriously, there is a sequence from Ashley Miller's film, *Women—How They Got the Vote*, which ridicules the women and makes light of the movement. The compiled footage that I found most stirring was that of Emily Wyling Davis's suicide. A leader in the suffrage movement, she walked out in front of the king's horse and was trampled to death. Footage of her funeral is also shown.

For the remainder of the film you see women's contributions to the war effort; women building, pushing, and flying airplanes; haying; holding down a blimp; going off in troop trains; caring for the wounded. The narration at this point of the film becomes particularly condescending, "The women proved that they had the strength and courage to do *men's* work . . . and they *even* learned the mysteries of the new flying machine" (italic mine).

If having a male narrator for a film on the fight of women for suffrage disappoints you, wait until you see the closing credits. I didn't notice that one woman was involved in the research, organization, and editing of that material. A rather ironic conclusion to a film on how far women have come in attaining equal rights. Another weakness in this document is the heavy musical background, which distracts from the visual experience. At one point, music reminiscent of a graduation march is played, along with the narration, to back up the scene of scores of women marching in the streets of London. One of the great failures of many compilation films composed of passages from silent footage is that the narration is so obviously pasted on. This failure is evident in *Women on the March*, Part I.

This film is visually and intellectually a teaser. The history of women as they worked toward political equality is recorded in countless bits and pieces of documentary film stock, private and published writings, and tape recordings. Serious filmmakers should research and assemble it. But until they do, use Part I of *Women on the March* with high school age students through adults.

Women on the March (1958): 30 mins., b/w; rental $15, purchase $160. Producer: National Film Board of Canada. Distributor: Contemporary Films/McGraw-Hill.

SUGGESTED FEMINIST READING
Catt, Carrie Chapman, and Shuler, Nettie Rogers. *Woman Suffrage and Politics.*
Goldman, Emma. *Living My Life.*
————. *Red Emma Speaks: Selected Writings and Speeches of Emma Goldman.*
Millett, Kate. *Sexual Politics.*
Schneir, Miriam (ed.). *Feminism: The Essential Historical Writings.*
Stanton, Elizabeth Cady. "Excerpts from her Autobiography *Eighty Years and More." Growing Up Female in America: Ten Lives,* pp. 55-80. Edited by Eve Merriam.

Women Up in Arms

It's all halfway to something new.

—from the film.

Women Up in Arms, one of the first United Nations Television programs to deal with women's rights, shows the changes for women in Tunisia since law reform granted women some legal rights. Since there are no "women up in arms," in this film, the title is deceiving. What the film does show is a sixteen-year-old high school girl's daily life as she goes to school, visits in her parents' store, dances at a mixed party, and listens to rock and roll in her room.

Alistair Cooke narrates, announcing at the beginning that the life of Tunisian women has changed more in the past ten years than in the past ten thousand. The changes, however, are in the laws, not in the lives of the majority of the women. So even though the film's subject is living as freely as her American counterpart, she is in relief against thousands of women who still wear the veil, sit in the back of the mosque, and are the possessions of their fathers, brothers, or husbands. As Cooke puts it, the new laws of the past ten years are an effort in "abolishing a system of marriage that was incompatible with the dignity of women. Not many speak out against the new laws, but many act in the old ways."

This film is quiet and informative, but uninteresting cinematically. Like the other films I have seen from United Nations Television, it is aimed at a broadly based audience, presumably a sexist one that needs a soft-sell approach. The film ends with a slow zoom out on the subject as she walks through the square of her small city. Rock and roll music is in the background as her voiceover states, "I will have to tell my children that 'when I was a girl, a man could have more than one wife . . . her father would choose her husband . . . and that in my time things changed' . . . I will choose my own husband." Perhaps her daughter will be able to say, "I will choose if I will marry."

Women Up in Arms is suitable for junior high school age through adult. It is a good film to show with *Ramparts of Clay*, which, as a contrived documentary, actually shows the real lives of most Tunisian women.

Women Up in Arms (1966): 29 mins., b/w; rental $8, purchase $130. Producer: United Nations Television. Distributor: Contemporary Films/McGraw-Hill.

SUGGESTED FEMINIST READING
de Beauvoir, Simone. *The Second Sex*.
Leavitt, Ruby R. "Women in Other Cultures." *Women in Sexist Society*, pp. 393-427. Edited by Vivian Gornick and Barbara K. Moran.
Millett, Kate. *Sexual Politics*.

Women's Happy Time Commune

Humor is such a strong weapon, such a strong answer. Women have to make jokes about themselves, laugh about themselves, because they have nothing to lose. So far they are terribly serious. They have discovered solidarity. They can share a problem, and that's beautiful. But they should let themselves enjoy it. I've seen groups of American women, and I've found them fascinating, but also very frightening. They are too serious.

—Agnes Varda to Barbara Confino, *Saturday Review*, August 12, 1972, p. 35.

Sheila Paige's film enjoys itself. Set in a fictional 1850, *Women's Happy Time Commune* is the first all-woman Western. When the crew went for its four shooting days in Virginia, each of the actresses (all nonprofessionals) came with her own self-chosen role and attending props. Their choices? One decided to be a retired prostitute ("You know the old saying, 'You know a man loves you if he beats you hard enough?' It's not true."); a chicken feeder ("If Prince Charming would come along on his white chicken and take me to a dance hall, I'd leave the commune."); a dance-hall girl ("Oh, no, my cowboy's a woman!"); a cowgirl ("What difference does it make if I am a man or woman if you're attracted to me?"); and a robber queen who starts the commune ("They can live now their dreams . . . then they can go if they still want the penis.")

There was no script, and how the roles would intersect was left until the actual days of shooting. Then the women, operating with their preconceived notions of their Western role and the dynamics of inter-reacting personalities, created the film. The greatest strength and direction from within the cast came from Roberta Hodes, the robber queen. Roberta discovered that a Communist Manifesto had been published in the States in 1850. Taking that as a lead, she developed a character who tries to recruit women to a commune. ("I hate men, women, children, and animals—but I'm willing to settle for women.") Roberta's antics in getting her members and the fantasies each woman has of her own West direct the narrative. Ultimately Roberta has her commune, but the vision of that commune forty years later, as provided by the film, and thus the actresses, is not a very happy time.

While the film pokes fun at the stereotypes of the old West, it realistically faces the new myths—that women can set up Utopian alternative lifestyles; that people who share a common political outlook will automatically live well and happily together.

The drama operates on two levels: first, the actresses as the characters that they created; and secondly, their own personalities working with and against each other. And through it all comes some fine humor.

I would use this film with mature, sophisticated groups, particularly women's groups that are willing to take a good look at their own feelings and the diversity in the ways in which they react on one another.

Women's Happy Time Commune (1972): 50 mins., color; rental $50, purchase $500. Director: Sheila Paige. Distributor: Women Make Movies.

SUGGESTED FEMINIST READING
Brown, Dee. *The Gentle Tamers.*
Cooper, Arvazine Angeline. "From Her Unpublished Manuscript *Journey Across the Plains.*" *Growing Up Female in America; Ten Lives,* pp. 137-157. Edited by Eve Merriam.
Oakley, Ann. *Sex, Gender and Society.*

Sheila Paige

"My next movie will be an action picture with absolutely no talking."

After Sheila Paige was graduated from Radcliffe, she worked as a volunteer at Young Filmmakers' Workshop in Lower Manhattan. She was soon a salaried member of the staff and, over the next few years, she started the Super-8 program for younger children, later training others to take over her position. Then she initiated the video program for twelve- to fifteen-year-olds.

Paige's own films have always taken a feminist perspective—from her first four-minute film, *Testing, Testing, How Do You Do?* (documenting the 1969 Miss America pageant with its attending women's liberation demonstrations) through *The Trials of Alice Crimmins* to *The Women's Happy Time Commune.* The first two films document current situations that reflect women's position in American society, and the newest work puts women with a contemporary consciousness into an historic era (1850) in America. Sheila Paige co-founded Women Make Movies with Ariel Dougherty (see page 131).

FILMOGRAPHY
*The Women's Happy Time Commune (1972), color, 50 mins.
The Trials of Alice Crimmins (1971), black and white, 6 mins.
Testing, Testing, How Do You Do? (1969), color, 4 mins.

Woo Who? May Wilson

May Wilson is the heroine of a true story of liberation and a beacon not only to our growing up but to our growing old.
— Molly Haskell, *Village Voice.*

"Always be prepared to be alone. Always be prepared to fall back on your own inner resources . . ." (May Wilson, from the film). When May Wilson was in her early sixties, her husband told her that the plans for the rest of his life did not include her. She wasn't prepared for it, but she certainly found the inner resources to fall back upon. After living her adult life caring for her husband and children in a fashionable Connecticut suburb, she struck out on her own to live in the Chelsea Hotel in New York.

Through this film her friend, Amalie Rothschild presents a loving, comfortable portrait of May Wilson. One of May's seriously playful art forms is "four for a quarter" photos of herself pasted as the heads of different magazine pictures. The film opens with the animated effects of these self-effacing images ("Only a rich personality can allow herself the luxury of making herself ridiculous").

The rest of this portrait ("This will simply be a film. It won't be a life," states May Wilson) shows her greeting friends in her apartment, at a gallery, shopping in her neighborhood, entertaining her son and two young grandchildren, working on her junk sculpture. Intertwined in it all are voiceover first-person comments.

You don't come away from the film feeling that life is suddenly gay and carefree for May Wilson. She talks about the fleeting relationships that occur in New York as her young friends go off to study or work in other places. She frequently mentions her psychiatrist and that she wants to "accept myself as an artist; with freedom to do what I want without guilt" (the puritan ethics are still there). Her apartment is colorfully cluttered with her sculpture of found objects and bright clothing. She admits, "You must have fun all the time in this room," but adds her personal note, "all the pain doesn't show."

May Wilson is an encouraging model for any age group and is well represented in this film.

Woo Who? May Wilson (1971): 33 mins., color; rental $35 (plus $2 handling); purchase $375. Director: Amalie Rothschild. Distributor: New Day Films.

SUGGESTED FEMINIST READING
de Beauvoir, Simone. *The Coming of Age.*
Lessing, Doris. *The Summer Before the Dark.*

themes

Theme Index

ABORTION—Bed and Sofa/It Happens to Us/Crash/Women Who Have Had an Abortion (Are You Listening?)

BIOGRAPHIES—Angela Davis/Betty Tells Her Story/Cover Girl: New Face in Focus/Gertrude Stein/Judy Chicago/Madalyn/Three Lives/ Veronica/Virginia Woolf/Woo Who? May Wilson/Janie's Janie/Joyce at 34/Films About Women & Work

CHILDBIRTH—Childbirth/Joyce at 34/Thigh Lyne Lyre Triangular/ Kirsa Nicholina/Loving Couples/Window Water Baby Moving

COMMUNITY—I Am Somebody/Janie's Janie/L'Opéra Mouffe/Ramparts of Clay/Salt of the Earth/Mosori Monika/Just Looking (Women Make Movies)/Women's Happy Time Commune/Sambizanga/Woodlawn Sisterhood (Are You Listening?)

FEATURE FILMS—Black Girl/Cleo From 5 to 7/Dream Life/For Boys Only Is for Girls, Too/The Girls/Goodbye in the Mirror/Loving Couples/Maedchen in Uniform/Ramparts of Clay/Salt of the Earth/ Something Different/A Very Curious Girl/Wednesday's Child/Women's Happy Time Commune/Sambizanga

FRIENDSHIP—Women's Happy Time Commune/Veronica/Park Film/ Maedchen in Uniform/Dream Life

DISCRIMINATION—Angela Davis/Anything You Want to Be/Behind the Veil/Black Girl/Fear Women/For Boys Only/Growing Up Female/ I Am Somebody/Lavender/Madalyn/Ramparts of Clay/Salt of the Earth/Smiling Madame Beudet/A Very Curious Girl/Women on the March/Women Up in Arms/Sambizanga

GROWING UP—A to B/About Sex/Anything You Want to Be/The Cabinet/Crash/Dirty Books/Growing Up Female/Happy Birthday Nora/Park Film/Veronica/Wednesday's Child/For Boys Only Is for Girls, Too/How About You/Lucy/Phoebe/Maedchen in Uniform/ Women Up in Arms

HOMOSEXUALITY— About Sex/Lavender/Women's Happy Time Commune

MIDDLE AGE—Fear Women/Smiling Madame Beudet/3 Lives/Virginia Woolf/Madalyn

MARRIAGE—Bed and Sofa/Behind the Veil/Crocus/Joyce at 34/Loving Couples/Smiling Madame Beudet/Sometimes I Wonder Who I Am/ Salt of the Earth/Domestic Tranquility (Women Make Movies)/For Better or Worse (Women Make Movies)

OLD AGE—Woo Who? May Wilson/String Bean/Mosori Monika/ Just Looking (Women Make Movies)

WOMEN ON WELFARE—Janie's Janie/Welfare Mothers (Are You Listening?)/Would I Ever Like to Work (Films About Women & Work)

PARENT-CHILD RELATIONSHIPS—A to B/The Cabinet/Crocus/ Joyce at 34/Lucy/Phoebe/Wednesday's Child/3 A.M. to 10 P.M./Janie's Janie/Sometimes I Wonder Who I Am/Dirty Books/Films About Women & Work (see individual annotations)

PREGNANCY—About Sex/How About You/Bed and Sofa/Schmeer-guntz/Salt of the Earth/Joyce at 34/L'Opéra Mouffe/Lucy/Phoebe/ Menilmontant

PROSTITUTION—Game/Menilmontant/A Very Curious Girl

RAPE—Cycles/Fear (Women Make Movies)

RELIGION—Mosori Monika/Behind the Veil/Ramparts of Clay/ Women Up in Arms

SEX—About Sex/How About You/Unfolding

SELF-DEFENSE—Nobody's Victim/Paranoia Blues (Women Make Movies)/Fear (Women Make Movies)

SILENT FILMS—Menilmontant/Smiling Madame Beudet/Bed and Sofa/Ritual in Transfigured Time/At Land

TEEN YEARS—A to B/Anything You Want to Be/Lucy/Phoebe/Park Film/Veronica/Wednesday's Child/Women Up in Arms/How About You/About Sex/Black High School Girls (Are You Listening?)

TWENTIES & THIRTIES—Dream Life/Bed and Sofa/Black Girl/An-gela Davis/Betty Tells Her Story/The Cabinet/Cleo From 5 to 7/ Crocus/Crash/Dirty Books/The Girls/Goodbye in the Mirror/Happy Birthday Nora/Lavender/Joyce at 34/Judy Chicago/Ramparts of Clay/ Something Different/3 A.M. to 10 P.M./3 Lives/A Very Curious Girl/ What I Want/Domestic Tranquility (Women Make Movies)

WOMEN IN OTHER CULTURES—Behind the Veil (Arabia)/Black Girl (Senegal)/Fear Women (Ghana)/The Girls (Sweden)/Maedchen in Uniform (Germany)/Mosori Monika (Venezuela)/Ramparts of Clay (Tunisia)/Something Different (Czech)/3 A.M. to 10 P.M. (Czech)/ Women Up in Arms (Arabia)/Women on the March (England, France)/ Bed and Sofa (Soviet Union)/Menilmontant (France)/The Smiling Madame Beudet (France)/A Very Curious Girl (France)/Loving Couples (Sweden)/L'Opéra Mouffe (France)/Wednesday's Child (England)/ String Bean (France)/Phoebe (Canada)/Goodbye in the Mirror (Italy)/ For Boys Only Is for Girls, Too (Eastern Europe)/Films About Women & Work (Canada)/Dream Life (Canada)/Sambizanga (Angola)   161

CAREERS—Films About Women & Work (see individual annotations)/ Anything You Want to Be/Angela Davis (educator, revolutionary)/ Black Girl (maid)/Cleo From 5 to 7 (singer)/Cover Girl: New Face in Focus (model)/Dirty Books (writer)/Dream Life (film editor/film animator)/Fear Women (chief of tribe/businesswoman/Congresswoman)/ Game (prostitute)/Gertrude Stein (writer)/The Girls (actresses)/Goodbye in the Mirror (teachers of English)/I Am Somebody (hospital workers)/Joyce At 34 (filmmaker)/Judy Chicago (educator/artist)/Madalyn (organizer)/Something Different (gymnast)/Take Off (striptease)/3 A.M. to 10 P.M. (factory work)/A Very Curious Girl (prostitute)/Virginia Woolf (writer)/For Better or Worse (Women Make Movies) (pediatrician)/Woo Who? May Wilson (artist)/Domestic Tranquility (Women Make Movies) (artist)

WOMEN ON THEIR OWN—Ramparts of Clay/Something Different/ String Bean/Three Lives/A Very Curious Girl/Virginia Woolf/Woo Who? May Wilson/At Land/Janie's Janie/Happy Birthday Nora/ Goodbye in the Mirror/Dream Life/Dirty Books/Crash/Angela Davis/ Bed and Sofa

VIOLENCE—Fear (Women Make Movies)/Paranoia Blues (Women Make Movies)/Sambizanga/Salt of the Earth/Nobody's Victim/Menilmontant/I Am Somebody/Cycles

WOMEN 1900-1930—Gertrude Stein/Virginia Woolf/Women on the March/Maedchen in Uniform/Menilmontant/The Smiling Madame Beudet

BLACK WOMEN—Angela Davis/Black Girl/Fear Women/Game/ Growing Up Female/I Am Somebody/Veronica/Sambizanga/Woodlawn Sisterhood (Are You Listening?)

SPANISH WOMEN—Vasectomia (Are You Listening?)/Mujeres Colombianas (Are You Listening?)/Lucy/Salt of the Earth/Mosori Monika

162

programs

Double Features

The following "double feature" suggestions are a few of the interesting groupings of the films reviewed in *Women In Focus*. In some cases I have combined a fiction film with a documentary film. These pairings do not consider the shorter films (under fifteen minutes), which are listed as Shorts with Features on page You will be able to see the logic of these groupings once you have read the annotations. As you use films in your communities and schools, groupings will suggest themselves. In each case I have placed the films in the order in which I would present them.

Fiction Double Features

Menilmontant
Bed and Sofa

Ramparts of Clay
Salt of the Earth

Maedchen In Uniform
Woman's Happy Time Commune

Goodbye in the Mirror
Dream Life

Loving Couples
A Very Curious Girl

The Smiling Madame Beudet
Something Different

Cleo From Five to Seven
Dream Life

Sambizanga
Black Girl

Wednesday's Child
Maedchen In Uniform

Fiction/Documentary Documentary/Documentary

A to B
Veronica

Janie's Janie
Welfare Mothers (Are You Listening Series)

Phoebe or Lucy
It Happens to Us

Phoebe
Lucy

It Happens to Us
Women Who Have Had an Abortion (Are You Listening? Series)

Women Up In Arms
Ramparts of Clay

Cover Girl: New Face in Focus
Angela Davis: Portrait of a Revolutionary

Janie's Janie
Joyce at 34

How About You?
Lucy

Women on the March
I Am Somebody

Virginia Woolf: The Moment
Whole
Joyce at 34

Behind the Veil
Ramparts of Clay

I Am Somebody
Woodlawn Sisterhood (Are You Listening? Series)

Game
A Very Curious Girl

Shorts With Features

The following coupling of a short with a feature is offered for both classroom and festival use. Films seen in sequence inform one another. When a short and feature are mindlessly adjoined, the effect can be somewhere between disconcerting and ridiculous. Most theaters ignore all the potential of showing an appropriate short with a feature-length film. These couplings give you a chance to pair shorts and features interestingly and provocatively.

Take Off or Cycles
A Very Curious Girl

Domestic Tranquility (See Women Make Movies)
The Girls

Three AM to Ten PM
Salt of the Earth

Sometimes I Wonder Who I Am
Something Different

The Cabinet
Wednesday's Child

What I Want
Goodbye in the Mirror or
The Girls

Schmeerguntz or Park Film
Dream Life

Anything You Want to Be
Maedchen in Uniform

Schmeerguntz
Bed and Sofa

Take Off
Cleo From 5 to 7

Sometimes I Wonder Who I Am
Loving Couples

bibliography

Annotated Bibliography

By Madeline Warren, whose book on the women screenwriters, *The Women Who Wrote the Movies,* will be a 1975 Bobbs-Merrill title.

BOOKS (key: hc = hardcover/pb = paperback)

Abbott, Sidney, and Love, Barbara. *Sappho Was a Right-on Woman.* New York: Stein and Day, 1972 (pb $1.95). This is not an account of lesbian sexual practices, but a study of recent lesbian history and the lesbian experience: the relationship of lesbianism to feminism and the contributions of lesbians to the women's movement; the growth of the gay activists movement in New York City; and the "purge" of lesbians from New York-N.O.W. The lesbian experience is described without romanticizing its problems: "coming out," gay bars, role-playing, lesbians' relations to their families and co-workers.

Bell, Quentin. *Virginia Woolf: A Biography.* New York: Harcourt Brace Jovanovich, Inc., 1972 (hc $12.50). A long, moving and very readable biography of the English writer by her nephew. Bell discusses his aunt's childhood and education during the waning of the Victorian era; the youthful sexual experiences which may have caused her adult sexual problems; relations with family members; marriage; her writing; her periodic mental illnesses and the reasons for her suicide. The history of the "Bloomsbury Group," a circle of literary and artistic friends, is especially fascinating.

Bernard, Jessie. *The Future of Marriage.* New York: Bantam Books, 1972 (pb $1.95). It is commonly supposed that more women than men desire marriage—but sociologist Bernard reveals that marriage is statistically more advantageous to *husbands* than to wives! Includes an historical survey of marriage; examines the psychological strains intrinsic to traditional marriages which result in acute depression among wives; and suggests alternatives to traditional marital roles which would improve marriage for both partners.

Bird, Caroline. *Born Female.* New York: Pocket Books, 1968 (pb $1.25). A highly readable study of the unequal treatment of the sexes in education, business, and law, with particular emphasis on the forms of economic discrimination (lower pay for equal work, "protective" restrictions on types or hours of work, salary ceilings) which keep women down. Also details the skirmishes which have taken place in the battle for equal rights . . . and suggests legal reforms necessary for women to achieve full equality.

The Boston Women's Health Book Collective. *Our Bodies, Our Selves.* New York: Simon and Schuster, 1971 (pb $2.95). A group of women cooperatively researched and wrote this "course" on women's health, and it is probably the most clearly written and sympathetic book on the subject. Topics include anatomy and physiology; sexuality; venereal disease; birth control; abortion; pregnancy and childbirth; and the relation between "Women, Medicine and Capitalism." Each chapter is supported by interviews with women and illustrated with explicit diagrams. This book can and should be read by women of high school age and older; useful for sex education classes.

Brown, Dee, *The Gentle Tamers*. Lincoln, Nebraska: University of Nebraska Press, 1972 (pb $1.95). A man wrote this history of women who settled the old West, and sometimes his sexism is detectable. Still, this is a fascinating collection of anecdotes about courageous and little-known women, including the first woman justice of the peace, frontier schoolteachers, prostitutes, and entertainers. The hardships endured by all in their daily lives are remarkable.

Cade, Toni (ed.). *The Black Woman*. New York: Signet Books, 1970 (pb 95¢. Stories, poems, and essays by black women writers on many aspects of their lives: politics, racism in education, child-raising in the ghetto, reflections on being black and female, and other concerns. Among the writers are Nikki Giovanni, Paule Marshall, and Joyce Green.

Catt, Carrie Chapman, and Shuler, Nettie Rogers. *Woman Suffrage and Politics*. Seattle: University of Washington Press, 1923 (pb $3.95). An inside look at the American suffrage movement, written by two participants. They offer a detailed story of nationwide events leading to the passage of the 19th Amendment and the reasons why the United States lagged behind many other nations in ratifying women's right to vote.

Chesler, Phyllis. *Women and Madness*. Garden City, New York: Doubleday and Co., Inc., 1972 (hb $8.95). A psychology professor examines the double standard of mental health, under which women are punished for exhibiting "masculine" traits and rewarded for accepting "feminine" roles. The interview subjects are all women who have sought help through therapy or mental institutions. Chapters discuss asylums, clinicians, lesbians, Third World women, feminists, "The Female Career as a Psychiatric Patient," and "Female Psychology: Past, Present and Future."

Davis, Elizabeth Gould. *The First Sex*. Baltimore: Penguin Books, 1971 (pb $1.45). An historical and sociological account of woman's role in world civilization. Archaeological findings and ancient myths are cited to support the author's contention that woman's contribution to civilization has surpassed that of man. Davis ties the denigration of women to the advent of Christianity and charts the subsequent decline of women through the following centuries to our own "aquarian age."

de Beauvoir, Simone. *The Coming of Age*. New York: Warner Paperback Library, 1972 (pb $2.25). De Beauvoir's theme is the degradation of the aged, and in this encyclopedic work she examines the causes and effects of aging; different treatments of the elderly in various societies throughout history; and images of the elderly in world literature. Vignettes of historical figures, from the Spanish artist Goya to the statesman Winston Churchill, illuminate some personal confrontations with old age.

de Beauvoir, Simone. *The Second Sex*. Translated and edited by H. M. Parshley. New York: Bantam Books, 1952 (pb $1.25). One of the best books on womanhood, covering virtually every aspect: biology; the evolution of women's role through history; mythology about women; women's life today, from childhood through old age; homosexuality; prostitution. In a chapter entitled "Liberation," the author asserts that the psychic tensions of home and family have inhibited women from realizing their creative potential.

DeCrow, Karen. *The Young Woman's Guide to Liberation*. New York: Pegasus Books, 1971 (pb $2.95). This book may not answer all of a young woman's questions about planning her life, but it will open her eyes to the ways in which her life is controlled before it is too late. The author examines the forces which shape young lives: family, school, business, religion, etc. Examples are drawn from feminist writings, the media, statistics, and the author's personal experience. A good book for discussion and consciousness-raising; for high school age and older.

Diner, Helen. *Mothers and Amazons*. Introduction by Brigitte Berger. New York: Anchor Books, 1965 (pb $2.50). Intended to supply a cultural history for women who have learned almost exclusively about patriarchal societies, this book examines matriarchal civilizations around the world, and contends that most primitive societies were dominated by women. Practices such as circumcision, male "childbirth," and totemism are explained, and matriarchal gods are studied.

Doely, Sarah Bentley (ed.). *Women's Liberation and the Church*. New York: Association Press, 1970 (pb $2.95). A collection of articles on women's demands for greater participation in Christian churches. Included are "A Christian Perspective on Feminism," "Women in the Seminary," "Women in the Ministry," "The Sisters Join the Movement," others.

Edwards, Lee R., Heath, Mary, and Baskin, Lisa (eds.). *Woman: An Issue*. Boston: Little, Brown and Co., 1972, pb $3.75). Originally published as a special issue of the prestigious *Massachusetts Review*, this collection includes feminist writings on a wide spectrum of subjects: fiction, poetry, literary analysis, interviews, and articles on women in history and politics; also, reproductions of paintings and photographs by women artists. Articles of particular interest are Angela Davis's "Reflections on the Black Woman's Role in the Community of Slaves" and Cynthia Griffin Wolff's "A Mirror for Men: Stereotypes of Women in Literature." Other writers include Bella Abzug and Anais Nin.

Egan, Andrea. *Why Am I So Miserable When These Are Supposed to Be the Best Years of My Life?* (tentative title). New York: Pyramid Publications, tentative publication date June, 1974. The first feminist teen-age advice book encourages girls to think of their individual identities as women. Chapters discuss sex, birth control, pregnancy, family and social relationships, the legal rights of minors, typical problems in school, others.

Ellmann, Mary. *Thinking About Women.* New York: Harcourt Brace Jovanovich, Inc., 1968 (pb $2.65). A humorous but incisive examination of misogynous stereotypes in literature: women's supposed passivity, instability, piety; portraits of "the shrew" and "the witch," others. A useful book for courses in literature, good for discussion; for high school and beyond.

Epstein, Cynthia Fuchs. *Woman's Place.* Berkeley, Cal.: University of California Press, 1970 (pb $2.45). A sociological study of "options and limits in professional careers" for women, identifying the social factors which keep women from realizing their professional potential. The author concentrates on the fields of law, medicine, science, engineering, and university teaching, but her findings illuminate problems common to all women workers. This book is especially valuable for women planning to enter skilled professions, because it pinpoints the careers in which sex-roles are most flexible.

Firestone, Shulamith. *The Dialectic of Sex.* New York: Bantam Books, 1970 (pb $1.25). This "case for feminist revolution" attacks Freud's analysis of female children, examines the exploitation of women in the civil rights and peace movements, and claims the cultural emphasis on "romantic love" presupposes female subservience. Firestone suggests cultural alternatives which would break down traditional sex roles, end the present structure of the nuclear family, and promote larger households and new approaches to child-rearing.

Frankfort, Ellen. *Vaginal Politics.* New York: Quadrangle Books, Inc., 1972 (hc $6.95) (pb $1.95) Bantam Books. Frankfort, who writes the "Health Forum" column in the *Village Voice,* attempts to de-mystify the medical profession, which often intimidates women patients. Among the medical questions covered are the training of doctors, menstrual extraction, breast surgery, male contraceptives, the drug industry, and feminist therapy. Although parts of this book are medically controversial, women will find the "checklist" for gynecological examinations especially helpful.

Friedan, Betty. *The Feminine Mystique.* New York: A Dell Book, 1963 (pb $1.25). The book that gave impetus to the contemporary women's movement is still one of the most relevant texts on the problems of married women. Friedan reveals how the image of the "happy," self-sacrificing housewife was foisted upon women after World War II, and particularly emphasizes the role of the women's magazines in convincing women to surrender to the new stereotype despite their increasing independence, education, and business experience. The unhappiness of the many women who submitted to this brainwashing 171 and their difficulties in recognizing the reason for their discontent comprise a moving and horrifying story of too-recent history.

Goldman, Emma. *Living My Life*. Two volumes. New York: Dover Publications, Inc., 1931 (pb $3.50 each vol.). A long but lively autobiography, brimming with stories of Goldman's many adventures, sketches of her friends and fellow radicals, and assertions of her forthright views on a variety of subjects. The author was a female suffragist, anarchist, labor agitator, and World War I pacifist who was eventually deported to Russia, the country of her birth. She escaped and continued to travel but never returned to the U.S.

Goldman, Emma. *Red Emma Speaks: Selected Writings and Speeches of Emma Goldman*. Edited by Alix Kates Shulman. New York: Vintage Books, 1972 (pb $2.45). Topics include anarchism, socialism, "The Tragedy of Woman's Emancipation," jealousy, political violence, Russia, many others.

Gornick, Vivian, and Moran, Barbara K. (eds.). *Woman in Sexist Society*. New York: A Signet Book, 1971 (pb $1.95). An anthology of current feminist writings on the general topic of "power and powerlessness," by 31 women scholars and activists. Articles span psychology, sociology, sexuality; marriage, prostitution; the image of women in advertising, textbooks, and American fiction; lesbianism; the woman executive; women writers and artists; and more. Writers include Kate Millett, Lucy Komisar, Elaine Showalter, Sidney Abbott and Barbara Love, and Shulamith Firestone. A useful anthology for many fields of study.

Goulianos, Joan (ed.). *by a Woman writt*. Indianapolis: Bobbs-Merrill Co., Inc., 1973 (hc $14.95). An anthology of journals, letters, and creative writing from women of six centuries, offering glimpses of women's lives in many times and places, all of high literary calibre. Writers include Margery Kempe, Aphra Behn, Mary Wollstonecraft, Mary Shelley, Harriet Martineau, Kate Chopin, Anais Nin, Dilys Laing, Margaret Walker, Sylvia Ashton-Warner, Muriel Rukeyser, others.

Greer, Germaine. *The Female Eunuch*. New York: Bantam Books, 1970 (pb $1.95). Although Greer cites the historic treatment of women, her primary focus in this feminist examination of male-female culture is contemporary life. Intended as a consciousness-raising book, but written with wit and humor and divided into short, readable sections on such topics as: "Body" (how men regard different parts of the female anatomy), "Soul" (how women are socialized into accepting the prevailing stereotype), "Love" (including a criticism of romantic "women's novels"), "Hate" (uncovering misogyny), and "Revolution" (past and present). Greer punctuates her arguments with vividly recognizable images. This is a good book for provoking discussion, and could easily be used with high school or other groups who might object to overtly "revolutionary" texts.

Gutcheon, Beth Richardson. *Abortion: A Woman's Guide.* With a foreword by Alan F. Guttmacher, M.D. New York: Abelard-Schuman, Ltd., 1973 (pb $2.95). This Planned Parenthood book offers an extensive guide to methods of abortion and contraception. Easily readable. Recommended for women of all ages facing abortions, as it will help allay their fears with clear explanations of the procedure.

Hansberry, Lorraine. *To Be Young, Gifted and Black.* With an introduction by James Baldwin; adapted by Robert Nemiroff. New York: A Signet Book, 1969 (pb $1.25). Prize-winning autobiographical play by the late writer, consisting of many short pieces (dramatic readings, poetry, letters, diary excerpts) on the subject of growing up gifted, black, and female in America.

Haskell, Molly. *From Reverence to Rape: The Treatment of Women in the Movies.* New York: Holt, Rinehart and Winston, Inc., 1974 (hc $6.95). *Village Voice* film critic analyzes the image of women in American films from 1920 to the present. She devotes particular attention to the films of Hitchcock, Hawks, Ford, Lubitsch, and Sternberg, and includes a chapter on the "woman's film." Haskell believes the depiction of women has become more negative with the collapse of the Hollywood studio system and the growing inclination of directors to make semi-autobiographic (read misogynous) films. She also discusses the image of women in the modern European "art" film.

Herschberger, Ruth. *Adam's Rib.* New York: Har/Row Books, 1948 (pb 95¢). Beginning with an illuminating satirical attack on the biased formulation of conclusions in laboratory experiments on primate sex differences, this book proceeds to shatter a number of myths about women in a style which is both serious and witty. Topics include societal and biological sex differences; witchcraft; menstruation; the education of women for sexual frigidity; fallacies about miscarriage. Occasionally the writing seems dated, but many of the observations are still valid.

Horney, Karen, M.D. *Feminine Psychology.* Edited and with an introduction by Harold Kelman, M.D. New York: W. W. Norton and Co., Inc., 1967 (pb $2.95). Dr. Horney questions Freud's theories on women's psycho-sexual development (including "penis envy") and offers her own clearly explained theories. The collected essays include "The Flight from Womanhood," "The Distrust Between the Sexes," "Premenstrual Tension," "The Problem of Female Masochism," others. Although the vocabulary may be too difficult for high school students, women with no previous knowledge of psychological theories will find this book comprehensible and highly rewarding.

Johnston, Jill. *Lesbian Nation.* New York: Simon and Schuster, 1973 (hc $7.95). Johnston believes a feminist revolution is impossible until all women are lesbians. Drawing upon her *Village Voice* columns, she tells of her own evolution as a political and homosexual activist. 173

Chapters include "Lesbian Feminism" and "Amazons and Arch-edykes." Those not familiar with her writing will find her style some-what difficult at first.

Lerner, Gerda (ed.). *Black Women in White America*. New York: Vin-tage Books, 1972 (pb $3.95). This extensive history includes essays, newspaper articles, diaries, and other documents on the lives of black American women from the early 19th Century to the present. Topics include "Slavery," "The Struggle for Education," "A Woman's Lot," "Making a Living," "In Government Service and Political Life," "The Monster Prejudice," "Race Pride," "Black Women Speak of Woman-hood." Fascinating documents include court transcripts and inter-views. Among the many writers are Mahalia Jackson, Pauli Murray, Shirley Chisholm, and Fannie Lou Hamer. One of the best anthologies available on black women; well suited for high school use.

Lessing, Doris. *The Golden Notebook*. New York: Ballantine Books, 1962 (pb $1.25). This novel about a middle-aged woman searching for freedom is set in London during the Cold War period. Divorced, with a young child, Anna attempts to work out a new lifestyle with a divorced female friend; and through writing, affairs, and a job. Part of her search involves a descent into madness. Not easy reading, but rewarding and thought-provoking. Many women identify with Anna's struggle.

Lessing, Doris. *The Summer Before the Dark*. New York: Alfred A. Knopf, Inc., 1973 (hc $6.95). A 45-year-old woman, who is no longer needed by her husband and children, spends a summer working as an interpreter, traveling, and having affairs. She becomes severely ill, loses her looks, and becase of these external changes finds she must reassess her life. Among her resolutions is a rejection of the feminine stereotype.

Merriam, Eve (ed. and introd.). *Growing Up Female in America: Ten Lives*. New York: Dell Publishing Co., 1971 (pb $1.50). Ten fascinat-ing autobiographical accounts of the experience of growing up female in America, from the 18th Century through the 20th. The text is drawn from diaries, previously unpublished journals, and letters. The ten lives are: an 18th Century schoolgirl; Elizabeth Cady Stanton, founder of the women's suffrage movement; Maria Mitchell, an as-tronomer who became the first woman member of the American Academy of Arts and Science; the wife of a Confederate officer; a pioneer across the plains; Dr. Anna Howard Shaw, a 19th Century minister and doctor; a freed slave; "Mother" Mary Jones, a turn-of-the-century labor organizer; a modern Jewish working woman; and a Winnebago Indian. Also includes an "Attic" of miscellaneous short pieces. High school students will enjoy this.

Milford, Nancy. *Zelda*. New York: Avon Books, 1970 (pb $1.50). A biography of the wife of F. Scott Fitzgerald, especially valuable for its account of Zelda's schizophrenia. Milford follows Zelda's path through one mental asylum after another, speculates on the reasons for her illness, and covers her later life. This is an absorbing and tragic story in itself, but also an unfortunate example of the way creative women may be treated by psychiatrists—and by their husbands.

Miller, Isabel. *Patience and Sarah*. Greenwich, Conn.: A Fawcett Crest Book, 1969 (pb 95¢). This is one of the few lesbian novels which ends happily—a charming story of two young women in an early 19th Century New England farm community. Eventually they fulfill their dream of leaving the community and buying their own farm.

Miller, Jean Baker, M.D. (ed.). *Psychoanalysis and Women*. Baltimore: Penguin Books, 1973 (pb $2.95). Sixteen eminent psychologists revise Freud's theories about women. Articles include: Karen Horney, "The Flight from Womanhood"; Alfred Adler, "Sex"; Mary Jane Sherfey, "On the Nature of Female Sexuality"; Judy Marmor, "Changing Patterns of Femininity: Psychoanalytic Implications"; Robert Seidenberg, "Is Anatomy Destiny?"; Lester A. Gelb, "Masculinity—Femininity: A Study in Imposed Inequality."

Millett, Kate. *The Prostitution Papers*. New York: Avon Books, 1971 (pb $1.25). This book is divided into four parts: an essay by Millett on the relevance of the women's movement for prostitutes; two interviews with former prostitutes on their beginnings in prostitution and what the life was like; and an account by Liz Schneider, a feminist, of her first-hand observations in courts and detention centers which deal with prostitutes.

Millett, Kate. *Sexual Politics*. New York: Avon Books, 1969 (pb $2.95). Millett discusses the sexual revolution from 1830 through 1930 and the reaction against it; for example, Freudian psychology. She examines the image of women in four writers: D. H. Lawrence, Henry Miller, Norman Mailer, and Jean Genet; and writes on patriarchy in the "Theory of Sexual Politics."

The Milwaukee County Welfare Rights Association. *Welfare Mothers Speak Out*. With an introduction by Dr. George A. Wiley. New York: W. W. Norton and Co., Inc., 1972 (hc $5.95). Welfare mothers write about welfare rights, the war on poverty, welfare fraud, "Spanish-Speaking People and the Welfare System," "Guaranteed Adequate Income Now," other topics.

Moberg, Verne. *A Child's Right to Equal Reading*. Washington, D.C.: National Education Association, no date (pb 25¢). This litle pamphlet consists of "exercises" for examining sexual stereotypes in children's books and suggests ways to use favorite "stereotyped" books in new ways; for example, creating a de-stereotyped Cinderella. Very useful for teachers and parents.

Morgan, Elaine. *The Descent of Woman*. New York: Bantam Books, 1972 (pb $1.75). In response to male-centered theories of evolution, 175

Morgan examines the females of other species and discusses woman's contribution to civilization. Chapters include: "The Man-Made Myth," "Aggression," "Orgasm," "Love," "Speech," "Man the Hunter," "Primate Politics," "What Women Want."

Morgan, Robin (ed.). *Sisterhood Is Powerful*. New York: Vintage Books, 1970 (pb $2.45). An Anthology of more than 70 writings on women's liberation; good for consciousness-raising and discussion. Includes personal testimonies of professional women (medicine, publishing, television, the military, and journalism); writings on welfare, the Catholic Church, law, the aging woman, media "brainwashing," prostitution, lesbianism, black liberation, high school women, housework; also poetry, historical documents. Among the many writers are: Lucinda Cisler, Kate Millett, Eleanor Holmes Norton; Florynce Kennedy, Marge Piercy.

Nin, Anais. *The Diary of Anais Nin*. Vols. I-IV. Edited and with a preface by Gunther Stuhlmann. Vol. I: New York: The Swallow Press and Harcourt, Brace and World, Inc., 1966 (pb $2.85). Vols. II-IV; New York: Harcourt Brace Jovanovich, Inc., 1967, 1969, 1971 (pb $2.85, $2.45, $2.45). The personal record of Nin's struggles and pleasures as a woman and an artist. She believes that if she delves deeply into herself, universal truths will be revealed; and in fact many readers of this beautifully written diary feel she has perfectly articulated their own problems. Vol. I (1931-34) deals with Nin's life in France, including the publication of her first book. Vol II. (1934-39) describes the conflict between her psychoanalysis and her writing. In vol. III she moves to New York permanently and establishes her own printing press. Vol. IV. (1944-47) covers her critical breakthrough as a writer, and friendships with Edmund Wilson and Maya Deren.

Nunes, Maxine, and White, Deanna. *The Lace Ghetto*. Toronto: New Press, 1972 (pb $3.95). A collection of interviews, commentaries, pictures, advertisements, comics, letters, and book excerpts arranged in chapters according to topic: motherhood, women's rights, fashion, sexuality, etc. One of the best features is a children's discussion of masculine and feminine roles. An excellent book for consciousness-raising and discussion with young groups.

Oakley, Ann. *Sex, Gender and Society*. New York: Harper Colophon Books, 1972 (pb $2.95). Oakley's theme is gender "roles"—cultural, as opposed to biological sex differences—and how they limit an individual's free choice. She discusses the effect of sex hormones on physical and mental illnesses; the relation between sex and personality, intellect, and social role; and refers to anthropological studies of tribal cultures in which men and women are equally strong.

Pierce, Ruth I. *Single and Pregnant*. Boston: Beacon Press 1971 (pb $1.95). This book provides a good overview of the services available to the single and pregnant girl and discusses each of the alternatives: abortion, maternity homes, independent living arrangements and adoption; there is also a chapter on "concerns of girls who keep their babies." Other chapters discuss venereal disease, counseling and therapy, and delivery. The author writes in a warm personal style and the vocabulary is simple enough for teen-age readers.

Plath, Sylvia. *The Bell Jar.* New York: Bantam Books, 1971 (pb $1.50). An autobiographical novel by the late poet, about six tortured months in her twentieth year. A month as "college guest editor" on a New York fashion magazine keeps her too busy to recognize her growing desperation, but the freedom of a summer with nothing to do forces her to confront her problems. A near-successful suicide attempt is followed by an odyssey through mental institutions and gradual recovery. Many readers identify with her struggle to contend with society's expectations of her as a woman (marry, have children, settle down) and her own dreams of an independent, productive life. Students in the upper high school grades could probably handle this book.

Rains, Prudence Mors. *Becoming an Unwed Mother.* Chicago: Aldine-Atherton, 1971 (hc $6.95). Written by a sociology professor, this is a sociological account of middle-class white girls in a psychiatrically oriented maternity home and lower-class black teens in a day school for unwed mothers. Girls from both groups are interviewed extensively and describe the services each institution provides, week by week in their pregnancies, and also how they feel individually about their situation. The author believes that both social agencies encourage the girls to think of themselves as "good girls who made a mistake"—and thus fail to protect the girls against future mistakes. The book is intended for social workers, psychologists, community and public health workers, and students and teachers of sociology. However, it could also be used by high school teachers in discussing such social agencies with girls who have been or are about to become teenaged mothers.

Rosen, Marjorie. *Popcorn Venus: Women, Movies and the American Dream.* New York: Coward, McCann and Geoghegan, 1973 (hc $9.95). The image of women in American films from 1900 to the present is examined within the context of a cultural history of the times and of women. The author discusses the influence of women on movies, and vice-versa; also, the recent influence of European "art" films on American films. Among the women directors included are Dorothy Arzner, Lois Weber, Frances Marion, Elaine May, and screenwriter Anita Loos.

Schneir, Miriam (ed.). *Feminism: The Essential Historical Writings.* With an introduction and commentaries by Miriam Schneir. New York: Vintage Books, 1972 (pb $2.45). A collection of more than forty essays, memoirs, letters, and fictional pieces spanning 150 years of feminist writings on such pertinent issues as: the control of women's bodies, the economic dependence of women, the search for self, marriage. Some of the material is otherwise unavailable. Writers in-   177 clude Mary Wollstonecraft, Elizabeth Cady Stanton, George Sand, Sojourner Truth, Susan B. Anthony, Margaret Sanger, Virginia Woolf, John Stuart Mill.

Schulder, Diane, and Kennedy, Florynce (eds.). *Abortion Rap.* New York: McGraw-Hill, 1971 (pb $3.95). A collection of personal testimonies heard in the 1970 challenge to the constitutionality of New York State abortion laws. Among the transcripts are the speeches of women who underwent illegal abortions, a rabbi, a doctor, and a psychiatrist. Also included are speeches against abortion.

Shulman, Alix Kates. *Memoirs of an Ex-Prom Queen.* New York: Bantam Books, 1969, (pb $1.75). This novel about a beautiful "all American girl" is sometimes wryly humorous, sometimes bitter, but always involving and so honestly written that it can't fail to ignite sparks of recognition in the reader. Told partly in flashback, the heroine moves through life chafing at the constraint of her roles in a man's world: prom queen, philosophy student, office worker, wife, mother, divorcee, wife again. She establishes an enduring friendship with another woman and ultimately seeks to redefine her life. Although much of the novel is concerned with adult roles, the theme of the implications of physical beauty in a woman's life should make the story accessible to teen-agers.

Sitney, P. Adams (ed.). *Film Culture Reader.* New York: Praeger Publishers, 1970 (pb $4.95). This collection of articles from *Film Culture,* a magazine devoted to the independent American filmmaker, includes a few articles of interest to anyone ordering films by Maya Deren or Stan Brakhage. Writings about Maya Deren include "To Maya Deren" by Rudolf Arnheim (pp. 84-86), and "Poetry and the Film: A Symposium," (pp. 171-186), a transcript of a discussion in which Maya Deren participated. In "The Birth Film" (pp. 230-233) Stan Brakhage's wife, Jane, describes the joy of giving birth to her first child at home and how her husband (and at one point, she herself) filmed the event.

Smith, Sharon. *Women Make Films.* New York: Hopkinson and Blake, tentative publication date Winter 1974. A compendium of information about women in major fields of filmmaking, from 1896 to the present. Includes interviews with Shirley Clark, Juliana Wang, Barbara Loden, Faith Hubley.

Stein, Gertrude. *Selected Writings of Gertrude Stein.* Edited and with an introduction by Carl Van Vechten. New York: Vintage Books, 1933 (pb $2.95). This large anthology provides a representative sampling of much of Stein's work. Includes *The Autobiography of Alice B. Toklas;* passages from *The Making of Americans;* poems, plays; literary portraits of Picasso, Matisse, and Cezanne; "Melanctha," the story of a young black woman from *Three Lives; Tender Buttons;* the lyric drama *Four Saints in Three Acts;* others.

Stein, Gertrude. *The World Is Round*. With illustrations by Clement Hurd. New York: Camelot Books, 1939 (pb 95¢). The story of a little girl named Rose, her friends, and her trip up a mountain (accompanied only by her favorite blue chair) is intended for children and is delightful to read aloud. It also serves as an introduction for older readers to Stein's rather formidable style.

Weirdiger, Paula. *Every Month of Our Lives* (tentative title). New York: G. P. Dutton, tentative publication date Fall 1974 (hc, price?). This book is intended to cover virtually every aspect of mentsruation, from puberty through menopause. The orientation is feminist, and chapters include: the psychological effects of menstruation, myths and folk customs about puberty and menstruation; bleeding problems; the effects of contraception on menstruation. Written for an adult audience, but could be used with teen-agers.

Wilson, Ellen. *They Named Me Gertrude Stein*. New York: Farrar, Strauss, Giroux, 1973 (hc $5.50). A biography about the great writer, intended for "young readers" but could be used through high school. Stein's fascinating life is traced from her girlhood in California, her education at Radcliffe and medical school, through her long and exciting expatriate years in Europe, and her death shortly after World War II. Includes pictures and photographs.

Woolf, Virginia. *Mrs. Dalloway*. New York: Harcourt, Brace and World, Inc., 1925 (pb $1.65). An exquisitely written novel about the inner thoughts of a middle-aged Englishwoman on one important day in her life. He interior monologue reveals incidents of her rather cold marriage, memories of loving friends, and her feeling that she is excited by women and has never been quite capable of fully communicating with men. Intermittently contrasted with her thoughts are the dialogues and thoughts of other characters.

Woolf, Virginia. *Orlando: A Biography*. New York: A Signet Classic, 1928 (pb 95¢). A rollicking and satirical novel about a man who becomes a woman and lives 350 years. Along the way he/she has many adventures and learns about the differences between the sexes through personal experience. Woolf makes many humorous and valid points about society's expectations of women and historical customs (such as cumbersome clothing styles) which perpetually keep women "in their place." This is probably the most easily readable of Woolf's novels.

Woolf, Virginia. *A Room of One's Own*. New York: Harcourt, Brace and World, Inc., 1929 (pb $1.65). This long essay is a witty and angry attack on the education and position of women in England through several centuries. Although the intellectual liberation of women had begun at the time of her writing, Woolf believed women writers need a fixed income and a "room of one's own" to produce female Shakespeares. Her argument is still valid today.

Woolf, Virginia. *The Waves.* Together in one volume with *Jacob's Room.* New York: Harcourt Brace Jovanovich, Inc., 1931 (pb $2.45). An impressionistic, psychological novel in which six characters reveal themselves in monologues at different stages of their lives: childhood, youth, and middle age.

Woolf, Virginia. *A Writer's Diary.* New York: Harcourt Brace Jovanovich, Inc., 1953 (pb $2.95). Extracts from Virginia Woolf's diary, 1918 to 1941 (the year of her death), provide a fascinating, though discreet, record of her mature life. She deftly sketches her illustrious friends, such as Lytton Strachey and Maynard Keynes; contemplates contemporary problems; and reflects at length on the process of writing and her struggles with each of her books.

PERIODICALS

Film Library Quarterly. Vol. 5, No. 1 (Winter 1971-72). This special issue on "Women in Film" includes reviews of films by and about women; an interview with Madeline Anderson, director of *I Am Somebody* (pp. 39-41); commentary by professional women on their experiences working in film; "Maya Deren and Germaine Dulac: Activists of the Avant-Garde," an article by Regina Cornwell (pp. 29-38); others. For back orders of this issue, available at $1.50 each, write: Film Library Information Council, Box 348, Radio City Station, New York, N.Y. 10019.

Notes from the Third Year. The third in an annual collection of radical feminist writings includes articles on early feminists, women's experience, theoretical articles on feminism, women writers; also, "Men and Violence" (pp. 39-43), a transcript of a taped consciousness-raising session, and "Rape: An Act of Terror" (by Pamela Kearon and Barbara Mehrhof; pp. 79-81), on the political implications of rape. For back orders of this issue ($1.50) or information on the availability of *Notes from the First Year* and *Notes from the Second Year,* write: *Notes,* P.O. Box AA, Old Chelsea Station, New York, N.Y. 10011.

Take One. Vol. 3, No. 2. "Women and Film," a special issue, includes statements by women filmmakers on their working experiences; an interview with Shirley Clarke; filmographies of Canadian women directors; reviews of women's films; other excellent articles. For back orders (75¢ per copy) write: Take One, Box 1778, Station B, Montreal 110, Canada.

The Velvet Light Trap. No. 6 (Fall 1972). This issue on "Sexual Politics and Film" includes articles on Alice Blaché (owner of an American film studio from 1910 to 1914, and the most powerful woman in the history of the American film industry); women directors; images of working women in films of the 1930's; feminist criticisms of Hollywood films; others. For back orders (75¢ per copy) write: The Velvet Light Trap, Old Hope Schoolhouse, Cottage Grove, Wisconsin 53527.

Women and Film. Vol. 1, Nos. 1-4. No. 1 contains articles on women in the movies; the image of women in film; the film *Bed and Sofa*; women in the films of Howard Hawks; film reviews, others. No. 2 includes a review of the First International Festival of Women's Films in New York City; an interview with Nelly Kaplan, others. Nos. 3 and 4, in a double issue ($1.50), include articles on early suffrage films and international women directors; an interview with screenwriter Christiane Rochefort; and feminist reviews of *Klute, The Girls, Heat, The Green Wall.*

CATALOGUES

The Women's Film Co-op. *1972 catalogue.* The Co-op distributes several feminist films (including *Windy Day, The Woman's Film, Sometimes I Wonder Who I Am*) and publishes a catalogue describing short and feature films by and/or about women (including Cukor's *Adam's Rib,* Sternberg's *Blonde Venus,* Antonioni's *Red Desert,* the documentary *Radcliffe Blues,* many others). Distributors are listed for non-Co-op films. To order the catalogue, write: The Women's Film Co-op, 200 Main St., Northampton, Mass. 01060. They request a donation to cover printing and mailing costs.

Women's History Research Center, Inc. *Films by and/or about Women.* A catalogue of hundreds of films, filmmakers, and distributors, including descriptions of films, rental information, and filmographies of women directors. Films are grouped in categories: animated, anthropological, birth and birth control, child care, careers, biographies, Third World, etc. Other feminist catalogues are also available. For information or to order copies of *Films by and/or about Women* ($3 per copy to individuals; $5 per copy to institutions, groups, and organizations) write: Women's History Research Center, Inc., 2325 Oak St., Berkeley, Cal. 94708.

distributors

Distributors

ACI Films, Inc.
35 West 45th Street
New York, New York 10036
212/582-1918
  Virginia Woolf:
    The Moment Whole

Constance Beeson
99 West Shore Road
Belvedere, California 94920

  Unfolding

Canyon Cinema
Room 220
Industrial Center Building
Sausalito, California 94965
415/332-1514
  Crocus
  Kirsa Nicholina
  Schmeerguntz
  Take Off

Carousel Films
1501 Broadway
New York, New York 10036
212/LA4-4126
  The Cabinet

Cinema 5
595 Madison Avenue
New York, New York 10002
212/752-3200
  Ramparts of Clay
  Wednesday's Child

Contemporary Films/
  McGraw-Hill
Princeton Road
Hightstown, New Jersey 08520
Rental Libraries:
Hightstown, N.J.—609/448-1700
Evanston, Illinois—312/869-5010
San Francisco, Cal.—415/362-3115
  Cleo From Five to Seven
  Fear Woman
  Gertrude Stein: When This
    You See, Remember Me
  I Am Somebody
  Mosori Monika
  Phoebe
  3 A.M. to 10 P.M.
  Women on the March
  Women Up in Arms

Nell Cox
150 West 87th Street
New York, New York 10024
212/765-0653
  A to B

Creative Film Society
7237 Canby Avenue
Reseda, California 91335
213/786-8277
  Cycles

Judith Dancoff
1681 South Comstock Avenue
Los Angeles, California 90024
  Judy Chicago and the
    California Girls

Bob Elkins
11309 Q Ranch Road
Austin, Texas 78759
  Madalyn

Faroun Films Ltée
136 Est, Rue St-Paul
Montreal 127, Quebec, Canada
514/866-8831
  Dream Life

Linda Feferman
42 Grove Street
New York, New York 10014
212/691-4623
Dirty Books
Happy Birthday Nora
Park Film

Grove Press Film Division
53 East 11th Street
New York, New York 10003
212/677-2400
At Land
Childbirth
Crash
L'Opéra Mouffe
Meshes of the Afternoon
Ritual in Transfigured Time
Thigh Lyne Lyre Triangular
Window Water Baby Moving

Sharon Hennessey
654 A. Natoma Street
San Francisco, California 94103
What I Want

Impact Films
144 Bleecker Street
New York, New York 10012
Behind the Veil
Goodbye in the Mirror
Something Different
Three Lives

Jason Films
2621 Palisade Avenue
Riverdale, New York 10463
Veronica

Linda Jassim
2219 3rd Street, #1
Santa Monica, California 90405
213/392-5422
Cycles

Macmillan Audio Brandon Films
34 MacQueston Parkway So.
Mount Vernon, New York 10550
914/664-5051
Offices in San Francisco, Los
Angeles, Dallas, and La Grange,
Illinois
Bed and Sofa
Loving Couples
Salt of the Earth

Martha Stuart Communications
66 Bank Street
New York, New York 10014
212/255-2718
Are You Listening?

The Museum of Modern Art
Department of Film Circulating
Programs
11 West 53rd Street
New York, New York 10019
212/245-8900
The Smiling Madame Beudet

National Film Board of Canada
Suite 819
680 Fifth Avenue
New York, New York 10019
212/586-2400
Films About Women and Work

New Day Films
P.O. Box 315
Franklin Lakes, New Jersey 07417
201/891-8240
Anything You Want to Be
Betty Tells Her Story
Growing Up Female:
  As Six Becomes One
It Happens to Us
Joyce at Thirty-Four
Sometimes I Wonder Who I Am
Woo Who? May Wilson

New Line Cinema
121 University Place
New York, New York 10002
212/674-7460
  Cover Girl: New Face in Focus
  The Girls

New Yorker Films
2409 Broadway
New York, New York 10024
212/247-6110
  Angela Davis: Portrait of
  a Revolutionary
  Sambizanga

Odeon Films, Inc.
22 West 48th Street
New York, New York 10036
212/869-8475
  Janie's Janie

Perennial Education, Inc.
1825 Willow Road
P.O. Box 236
Northfield, Illinois 60093
312/446-4153
  Lavender

Pictura Films
43 West 16th Street
New York, New York 10011
212/691-1730
  Lucy

Radim Films, Inc.
17 West 60th Street
New York, New York 10023
212/279-6653
  Game
  Maedchen in Uniform
  Unfolding

Ramsgate Films
704 Santa Monica Boulevard
Santa Monica, California 90401
213/394-8819
  Nobody's Victim

Texture Films
1600 Broadway
New York, New York 10019
212/586-6960
  About Sex
  How About You?

Time-Life Films
43 West 16th Street
New York, New York 10011
212/691-2930
  A to B

Universal Films
445 Park Avenue
New York, New York 10022
212/759-7500
college use—ext. 505
general use—ext. 224
  Menilmontant
  A Very Curious Girl

Women Make Movies, Inc.
257 West 19th Street
New York, New York 10001
212/929-6477
Distribution:
43 West 16th Street, Suite 803
New York, New York 10011
212/691-1730
  Sweet Bananas
  Just Looking
  Fear
  Domestic Tranquility
  It's a Miracle
  Paranoia Blues
  For Better or Worse
  Women's Happy Time
    Commune

Xerox Films
Attn: Geri Mead
1200 Highridge Road
Stamford, Connecticut 06905
203/329-0951
  For Boys Only Is for Girls, Too